A LINCOLNSHIRE AU(

I have spent a lifetime working as an auct
south Lincolnshire.

As the title indicates this book is a story. It is mainly an account of experiences in my youth 50 years ago when the profession, agriculture and the property market were very different. I have taken some liberties by recounting some incidents as happening to me, when they were actually experienced by friends and colleagues.

The characters that appear either resemble people I have met or are imaginary.

The Grantham firm for which I worked is still going strong, so I have changed its title. The village names are all fictional, with the honourable exception of Corby Glen, as its annual Sheep Fair is unique.

My grateful thanks are due to my wife Mary for her patience, love and support, and to my friend Joe Flauto from the University of Evansville, Indiana for two fine drawings. Terry Shelbourne has kindly given me permission to print his two cartoons, and the Rutland County Council allowed me to photograph agricultural machinery from their excellent Museum collection in Oakham, and use three prints.

The Thelwell drawing on the front cover is reproduced by permission of Punch Ltd. and I am indebted to Sue Blunt who drew my attention to this and later painstakingly corrected my proofs. I am also grateful to Mike Wade for technical help with my computer.

Any opinions in the book - and any errors - are mine alone.

Published by R.A.Brownlow
Original drawings by Joe Flauto
ISBN 978-0-9551752-2-0
Printed by BJ's, Stamford, Lincs. PE9 1XP
Copyright R.A.Brownlow December 2014

£7

CHAPTERS

1. 'What am I bid'.
2. In the beginning
3. A Dead Sheep
4. Cake Breakers, Root Cutters and Sack Lifters
5. A Ring on High Ground
6. No Hearing, No Eyesight and No Parents
7. Listen to those Budgies
8. An Expensive Pram
9. Send the Meat on Later
10. Here's a Grand Pig
11. The Innermost Mystery of the Profession
12. Forty Loads of Manure
13. I've never seen a Better Crop
14. Possessing many Original Features
15. A Torch, a Ladder and a Damp Meter
16. A Stuffed Owl and a Magic Lantern
17. Sold to you Mr Couples
18. He's with the Lord
19. The family Bible and the Scrapbook
20. A Stooge and a Public House
21. A Family Feud and Coarse Cricket
22. Corby Fair

Chapter 1

'What am I bid'

There was a warm welcome from behind the bar as I walked into the Fox and Hounds Inn, Little Scroop -

'Now Robert, are you batting or bowling tonight?'

'Neither landlord, I'm auctioning!'

We laughed.

'You know I hate being called "landlord",' said Mike 'I'm an innkeeper'.

I did know. We played cricket for the same team, and I loved to wind him up.

'As you can see,' he continued 'I've set the bar out as you asked. There's a table at the far end with three chairs behind it – one's obviously for you, but who's going to sit on the others?'

'One's for the solicitor, and the other's for a colleague from the office, who'll make a note of the bids – assuming there are any.'

'You're selling Dairy Cottage tonight aren't you?'

'Yes, that's right. This is my first auction sale – I'm a bit nervous.'

'Well, I don't think you need worry about there being no bidders. I hear quite a bit from behind the bar, and the locals all say that a farmer up the road is going to buy it. There've been several strangers in as well during the last three weeks who've been to have a look – not that I eavesdrop on customers' conversations of course!'

'Mike – why ever would I think that!'

We used the Fox and Hounds Inn whenever we had a property in the area to sell by auction, because Mike Badger always made us welcome. Some landlords didn't want the bother of an auction, and hated to have their evening routine disturbed, however quiet the pub might be, but Mike knew we brought him extra customers and was pleased to see us. Many landlords charged us for using their pub, but last time we'd used the Fox and Hounds I asked Mike after the sale how much we owed him.

'Nothing,' he said, 'I'd like you to come every night.'

It had been two months since I received a telephone call from Ron Bellman, a solicitor in Grantham.

'I'm acting for the executors of the late Edith Scott who died on July 2nd. She lived at Dairy Cottage, Little Scroop and they've decided to sell it: I've recommended your firm.'

'Thanks very much, Ron.'

'She had two sons George and Ted who are the executors and beneficiaries

3

of her Will; you'll find that they're very different people. Will you contact George and make an appointment to look round the property with them. There are a few bits of furniture they'll probably want you to deal with as well. I'll send a letter to confirm everything.'

I made an appointment for a few days later, and saw the brothers standing by the cottage gate as I got out of the car. They certainly looked very different. As we shook hands and introduced ourselves I discovered that George was the stocky one with the florid face, whereas Ted was short, thin and looked harassed.

George spoke immediately.

'Well lad, what's it worth?'

'Let's have a good look round and then we can discuss the sale.'

Mrs Scott had lived at Dairy Cottage for many years – in fact both sons had been brought up there. It was the sort of house that many people dream about, shabby and old fashioned inside, but built of stone, with small-paned windows overlooking a grass paddock and a little stone barn. The garden had been neglected since her death, but a few hydrangeas and peonies were still evident above the tangled grass beside the path leading to the front door. Last year's runner bean sticks and a dilapidated garden shed stood sadly in the overgrown vegetable area.

They had already unlocked the front door and I walked into the tiny entrance hall, then the parlour, living room and scullery before climbing the stairs to the three bedrooms. I took the measurements of each room and noted down any 'selling features' such as beamed ceilings or original iron fireplaces. George and Ted showed me the few items of furniture they didn't want and I listed these. They could be collected later. The brothers stayed close behind as I walked outside to look at the privy, washhouse, coal store, barn and paddock.

I realised by this time that the sale of this cottage would create a lot of interest. Little Scroop was a small, attractive village with a shop and a pub, and Dairy Cottage was built of stone which made it more valuable than a brick property, had its own paddock, and needed 'doing up'. It would appeal to buyers who were looking for an opportunity to convert a run-down property into their dream cottage, as well as to developers who would improve it and sell at a profit.

This meant that Dairy Cottage wasn't easy to value, and I remembered the advice of Reg Weatherill, senior partner of the firm:-

'If you're asked to sell a house in a good position, with "roses round the door" and a few acres of land, and you don't know what the hell its worth, get all the people who want to buy into one room, and let them fight it out. Sell it by auction!'

After our tour the three of us sat down in the kitchen and the two brothers looked at me expectantly. Since I was inexperienced and the property was so attractive, I didn't feel confident in my ability to value it, so I tried to 'play for time' until I could get advice from colleagues back at the office.

'The sale of this cottage will create a lot of interest' I said. 'I think we should sell it by auction and fix a reserve price after we know how many people have viewed, and how many possible buyers we're likely to have.'

George would have none of this.

'We know what a reserve price is,' he said, 'we want to know what it's worth.'

I swallowed hard. 'I think we should fix a reserve price of £5000,' I said, trying to sound confident. To my relief the brothers nodded – the figure was obviously higher than they expected.

'We'll leave it to you,' said Ted.

'Have I set out enough chairs,' said Mike, and I looked around the bar of the Fox and Hounds. 'I reckon there are about thirty, and of course more people can sit on the benches by the windows.'

'Yes, that's fine Mike. I just hope we get enough people to fill the room. I really am nervous.'

I walked around putting copies of our sale brochure on the chairs, and it was well before 6 o'clock when I went to sit behind the table at the end of the bar on this September evening in 1962. I thought back over all that had happened since that meeting at Dairy Cottage. Had I done everything that should have been done? Our 'Weatherill and White – For Sale by Auction' boards had been put up in the garden several weeks ago. The sale brochures had been typed, and copies run off on the office duplicator: the firm had just started to take coloured photographs of properties they had for sale, and a view of the front elevation looked well on the first page. The brochures had been circulated to everyone who had shown interest in buying country cottages, and full details were displayed in the window of our Grantham office. The auction had been advertised in all the local newspapers: national coverage was far too expensive.

Interested buyers always ask for a guide price before viewing a property being sold by auction because they don't want to waste their time if it's likely to make more than they can afford. We had told everyone that a price of 'over £5000' was anticipated and nobody seemed deterred. Yes, everything had been done, and more than 30 people had viewed Dairy Cottage But I was worried – very worried!

A week ago Ted asked me if we were likely to have a good sale. I told him there was a lot of interest.

'Shall we get it sold?' he asked.

'I'm sure we will,' I said.

'What do you think it might fetch?'

5

Stupidly – oh so stupidly, I replied, 'Well, with all the enquiries we've had, and all the people that have viewed, we might get as high as £8000.'

The brothers had obviously conferred and two days later George came into the office and asked to see me.

'Ted says that you think that Dairy Cottage could sell for £8000.'

'Well, yes I did say that but…'

There was no stopping him.

'It's plain daft to have a reserve price of £5000 if you think it could make as much as that. That's where the reserve should be, so we've decided to increase it to £8000.'

I tried to explain that a reserve price is not a 'dream figure' that might possibly be reached, but a 'safety valve' to ensure that a property is not sold well below its value. However, it seemed that George had spoken to his equally forceful wife and received his orders, to which Ted had meekly agreed.

He listened to what I had to say, but it made no difference, 'We've made our decision – not a penny less,' he said.

The reserve price had been massively increased. Why, oh why hadn't I thought, before opening my mouth.

'Good evening Robert.'

Ron Bellman had arrived to sit beside me at the table. He had already prepared the sale contract which would be signed by the purchaser. At an auction sale the buyer signs the contract in the room, pays a 10% deposit, and is then legally committed to the purchase, which is completed by paying the balance of the price within a set time, usually four weeks. This is a big advantage to a vendor, who doesn't have to suffer the endless delays for surveys, mortgage valuations and legal enquiries that so bedevil sales by private treaty.

On my other side sat Stan Rowan, a clerk from the office, whose job was to record every bid made during the sale. This is important in case the proceedings are challenged afterwards or, as is more likely, in case the auctioneer gets carried away and forgets where he's got to!

I sat nervously between them looking at every newcomer that came in through the door. How would my first auction sale go? I hoped that all these people were possible buyers, but some of Mrs Scott's neighbours had obviously dropped by just to see how much her cottage would make. A few others had come for an early drink on this hot evening, as the pub was open a bit sooner than usual. I looked at the clock on the wall, realising that I normally did this to see how much time there was before closing time, but tonight I was waiting for 6 o'clock.

The time arrived, and when I got to my feet the talking stopped as everyone looked at me. I had often seen this happen when I was the clerk sitting by the auctioneer, but it felt very different when I was the focal point. When Reg Weatherill was auctioning he looked confident and seemed to dominate the room: I must try to do the same. It would have helped me a lot if I could have forgotten for a few minutes that increased reserve price stipulated by the Scott brothers, who sat together at the back of the room.

'Good evening, ladies and gentlemen,' I began, 'my name is Robert Brownlow from the firm of Weatherill and White. It is just after the time advertised for the sale' (a phrase that Reg always used) 'and it is my pleasure this evening to offer for sale the property known as Dairy Cottage, just down the road in Little Scroop. Sitting on my left is Mr Ron Bellman of Napier and Hardcastle, the solicitors acting for the vendors. The sale contract has been available for inspection at their offices and at ours for the last 14 days, and I assume that everyone interested in the property has looked at it, but if there are any questions regarding legal matters please ask Mr Bellman now.'

I have heard experienced auctioneers say that when they look around the room they can usually tell who is going to ask a question. I was not experienced, but I had been anxiously watching a pale-faced youth near the bar. He was sitting on top of the back of his chair with his feet on the seat, and I was expecting him to fall backwards at any minute. He raised his hand.

'Yes,' I said.

'I'm not married,' he announced.

We all waited.

'But I'm thinking of getting engaged.'

There was a longer pause.

'How can we help you?' asked Ron Bellman, wondering if he was about to start a new career in marriage guidance.

'Do I need to be married before I can buy a house?'

'Your marital position need not constrain you,' said Ron.

I don't think the youth understood this, but he obviously felt reassured, because he relaxed and leant backwards. There was a sharp intake of breath from those around him as the front legs of the chair left the ground, but mercifully the people on each side saved him from crashing to the floor.

I continued 'Since you are obviously satisfied with the terms of the sale contract, are there any questions with regard to the property itself?'

'Is there any rot in the woodwork?'

The question came from a red-faced man with a moustache and tweed suit sitting near the front of the room, who looked around and smirked, expecting general admiration for his discerning question.

'If there is any rot in the timber sir, it will be included in the sale.'

My answer wasn't entirely flippant. Under the doctrine of 'caveat emptor', or 'let the buyer beware', which prevailed at the time, it was a purchaser's responsibility to find out if a property had any faults, and not the vendor's duty to disclose them. The response had the desired effect of discomforting the red-faced man, and the company chuckled – hopefully they would be in a good mood for the auction. I pressed on.

'I do not intend to weary you with a long description of the property, as those that are interested will have already made their inspection (another Reg Weatherill phrase). I would just like to say that over the years there has been no better investment than property. There are very few chances to buy a cottage with the charm and potential of this one. Many people have bitterly regretted that they did not bid high enough to buy the property of their dreams at auction. I urge you not to be one of them. I will now ask for your bids for Dairy Cottage, Little Scroop.'

'Start me at £8000.'

There was no response.

'£7000 then.'

Still nothing.

'Well it doesn't matter where we start: it's where we finish that counts. Let's get started at £4000.'

A woman sitting near the front raised her hand. She looked tense and was obviously not used to auctions: experienced buyers like developers, or agents acting for clients, always stand at the back of the room so that they can see who's bidding.

'£4000 I'm bid'

A man wearing a flat cap and sitting in the middle of the room nodded his head.

'£4250,' I said, and then

'£4500,' as the woman bid again.

These two fought it out until he bid £6250, and the woman shook her head sorrowfully. She had reached her limit.

This was a decent price for the cottage, but well below the high reserve price brought about by my foolishness. Then Francis Potts joined the action. He owned a farm about a mile away: could this be the 'farmer up the road' that the locals expected to buy? I knew that his daughter was 'stepping out' with a neighbouring farmer's son. Dairy Cottage would make a good home for them.

'£6500,' he said.

The man in the flat cap bid again. The bidding had reached £6750.

Francis bid a second time and there was another nod in reply.

'At £7250 then, and still cheap for this property,' I said, 'they're not building cottages like this any more.'

Francis shook his head but his wife dug him hard in the ribs

'Go on then,' he said.

£7500,' I announced with relief. I had nearly reached the reserve price – but not quite.

The other bidder shook his head.

'Just one more bid for you, sir,' I said but to no avail. He got up from his seat and marched out of the room: he too had reached his limit and couldn't bear to be there a moment longer. No one else moved or spoke – they all stared at me.

I knew what I had to do. I couldn't sell Dairy Cottage below the £8000 stipulated by my clients, and the highest bid was £7500. No one else was bidding and so I had to put one in myself. I remembered Reg Weatherill telling me – 'If you ever have to bid yourself, do it quickly so the company thinks it's genuine, and take the "bid" from the back corner of the room. You'll be surprised how well a wall light or a flower arrangement can bid, when you're in a mess.'

I was certainly in a mess, and since the décor of the Fox and Hounds didn't stretch to flower arrangements, I took my 'bid' from a wall light.

'£7750 I'm bid: may I say £8000 from you sir,' I declared, looking at Francis Potts. I was hoping for another dig in the ribs from his wife, but she didn't move and he shook his head decisively.

I was now in a deeper mess. The highest bid was my own and unless another one was forthcoming I would have no alternative but to withdraw the cottage from sale. I stressed again the merits of property as an investment, but nothing came, and I realised that proceedings must be brought to a close.

'I will ask you three times if the bidding is completed.'

This is a standard auctioneer's ploy to heighten the tension before the hammer falls. It gives time for a last-minute change of mind, or a tearful appeal from an underbidder's spouse.

'At £7750 for the first time, at £7750 for the second time...' I was about to declare that Dairy Cottage was withdrawn from sale when a voice rang out from the back of the room...

'You can sell it at that price,' shouted George Scott.

I was furious. George had ignored my advice and insisted on a ridiculously high reserve price, and now at my first auction sale he was telling me in front of a roomful of people to sell the property when I had no bidder. Ron Bellman, a veteran of many auctions, was no help. He knew what had happened and could only control his mirth by blowing his nose vigorously into his handkerchief.

I gathered together the last shreds of my authority and, ignoring George, announced to the company, 'Ladies and gentlemen, I regret that Dairy Cottage is withdrawn from sale and is now available to be purchased privately. Thank you for coming this evening and I will be pleased to talk to anyone who wishes to make an offer for the property.'

George Scott stormed up the room, leant on the table and thrust his red face within inches of mine.

'What the hell are you playing at! I told you to sell at £7750.'

Having regained some composure I explained what had happened and told him that this was entirely due to his insistence on the high reserve. He was far from pleased, particularly when I told him that after the bad publicity which would undoubtedly follow this abortive auction, we would be lucky to get such a high price again.

'I shall speak to our solicitor,' he said.

Ron Bellman spoke quietly. 'Your solicitor is here,' he said. 'I know everything that's happened and my advice to you Mr Scott is not to be so greedy.'

George swore loudly and left the bar in a temper, followed by his brother. Ron then turned to me 'That's your first lesson as an auctioneer Robert. Always tell a client the lowest amount he can expect, but never give him high hopes.'

Chapter 2

In the Beginning

I stayed for a quiet pint to drown my sorrows after the disastrous auction, and Ron Bellman kindly kept me company. He was older than me, having navigated Lancaster bombers during the War, but after joining the Grantham Round Table I got to know him well, and he and his wife became close friends.

'That was unfortunate,' he said, 'I've heard of vendors pulling that trick, but I've never seen it done by a client of mine.'

'Yes – gossip travels fast and this sale will soon be a talking point in all the pubs and cattle markets round here: it makes me think I should have stayed put and been a chemist.'

'What do you mean?'

'My grandfather had a chemist's shop in Melton Mowbray and my father followed him, but I broke away and became the first auctioneer in the family.'

'That's a big change – why on earth did you choose auctioneering?'

'Well I'm wondering why at the moment, but my father had two friends who were auctioneers and estate agents in Melton Mowbray, and sold livestock every week in the town's cattle market, one of the largest in the East Midlands. I went to watch them in my school holidays, and was fascinated: I stood by the sheep and pig pens, watching the auction and was often told to move on by the buyers. When I started to sell in Grantham market I realised what a "pain" I was.'

'It must have been a hard decision, to leave the family business.'

When Ron said that, I thought back to my happy boyhood in Melton and my grandfather for whom I had great fondness and admiration. His parents were tenant farmers in north Lincolnshire, but he studied to be a pharmacist and served his apprenticeship in Nottingham. The hours were long and I remember him saying how unfair he thought it was that he had to be at the shop as the clock chimed the first stroke of 7 o'clock in the morning, but couldn't go until it sounded the last stroke of 9 o'clock in the evening.

In 1897, after he had finished his apprenticeship and was working for another chemist, he noticed that a retail pharmacy business was advertised for sale in Melton Mowbray. He told us he travelled to the town by train that evening to look at the shop, and was shocked when a man in the same compartment announced that he had made an appointment to buy this very business the next morning. According to grandfather, he went to see the owner that night and bought the business before his fellow passenger had the chance.

Melton (as everyone knew it) was a fascinating place at that time: it was not only a thriving market town, but had a worldwide reputation as a 'Mecca' for fox hunting. Grandfather used to tell me that during the season the town was taken over by hunting people, with over a thousand horses stabled there. They brought a good deal of trade to the shopkeepers and he remembered learning to grind up the husks of cochineal beetles to make the red dye for hunting coats. There were almost no packaged remedies then, and he had to make most of his tablets and medicines from the basic ingredients.

At this time hunting people bought or rented large houses in the town or nearby villages, where they would live for the hunting season and entertain their friends. The butlers ran these houses and had a position of power, which they exploited to the full.

Grandfather told me it was essential for shopkeepers to 'know their place'. His brother-in-law Will Esham kept a grocer's shop, and had a telephone call one morning from a butler who ran a hunting lodge in a village about eight miles away.

'Esham, will you deliver a jar of raspberry jam to the house this afternoon. I would have bought some butter from you but I see that Pearks are selling it a penny a pound cheaper. Fetch three pounds from them and deliver that as well.'

Pearks was a national chain of grocers' shops that had opened a branch recently in the town. Will was expected not only to deliver a single jar of jam to a house eight miles away, but go to a competitor, buy three pounds of their butter and take that as well. He had to do it, or the butler would have had him blacklisted by all the hunting households.

Fox hunting people expected this level of service but they didn't reciprocate when it came to paying their bills. Gambling debts were settled promptly 'as a matter of honour', but tradesmens' accounts were paid reluctantly – and late.

Making medicines and dye for hunting coats were not the only skills that grandfather had to learn. He was a Methodist, and when he came to Melton, church and chapel people did not mix. If a member of the Church of England was walking in the town and saw a Methodist coming towards him, one of them would cross to the other side of the street. The Melton Methodist circuit was large, with chapels in many of the outlying villages, and it was necessary to have a rota of laymen to help out the minister. Grandfather became one of these local preachers soon after coming to the town. He had no car, indeed very few existed at that time, so he went on his bicycle to take services in the village chapels. This was noted by the circuit stewards. He was summoned to meet them, and told firmly that it was not seemly for local preachers to travel in this way: he must go by pony and trap – much more dignified.

I realised that while I had been lost in my thoughts Ron and Mike had been talking about their early careers, and that Mike had brought another pint apiece, which he said was 'on the house' after the evening's unfortunate proceedings.

Ron said, 'I started as the office boy at Napier and Hardcastle, but the senior partner must have seen some good qualities in me before I went off to the War. When I came back…'

'With a DFC,' I interrupted, although Ron never mentioned the award, and didn't refer to it on the firm's notepaper.

'…he was very good to me, and let me take my law exams by postal course. It was hard work though – slogging through course notes every evening after a days work at the office. Did you go to College to get your qualifications, Robert?'

'My family didn't really agree with university education,' I replied 'they felt that after leaving school it was time to learn your job. They thought that study for its own sake at a university was an expensive luxury, and likely to produce an educated fool! When I was fifteen my father pressed me to decide what career I would follow, and since my elder brother was getting qualified to take over the family shop that wasn't an option. I wondered whether to become an auctioneer or a solicitor, but the influence of my father's friends proved decisive.

'Father made enquiries and discovered that I had to pass three examinations to become an Associate of the Chartered Auctioneers and Estate Agents Institute. After that I would need to be articled to an approved firm to learn the job.'

'What brought you to Weatherill and White?'

'One of father's friends said that it was a good firm, and Reg Weatherill was "as straight as a gun barrel": I wish he'd told us he could be just as explosive! Anyway we decided that I would study full time for a year at the College of Estate Management in London so that I could take the first two exams together, and do the rest by postal course – so I know how difficult that is.'

'Professional exams aren't easy,' said Ron. 'You know Jack Blackley in the Round Table.'

'Yes.'

'Well, he's the careers master at the Grammar School, and tells the boys that university degree courses are designed to be passed, to ensure their tutors have high success rates, but professional examinations are designed to be failed, to limit the number of entrants.'

'Does the Law Society do the same as the Auctioneers Institute and hold its entrance exams in a great big hall in London?' I asked.

'Yes, that's right.'

'I found them very stressful. We had an exam on a different subject every morning and afternoon for five days.'

'Yes, ours were much the same,' said Ron. 'I remember a group of anxious candidates waiting outside the hall, before every exam, for the doors to open. I couldn't deal with that.'

'Neither could I. They used to guess what questions would be asked in the next exam. If the subject was Law of Property, one earnest candidate would tell the others "my lecturer says we're bound to have a question on Section 146 of the Law of Property Act 1925, so I've concentrated on that". Another would ask the person next to him "what length of notice do you need to give to terminate the lease of a shop under the Landlord and Tenant Act 1954". I often didn't know what they were talking about, so I would walk around in the street outside, and would'nt go in until the doors had opened.'

'That was wise,' said Ron. 'It was the invigilators that gave me the creeps: I suppose part of their job was to watch out for any cheating, like referring to hidden textbooks. They seemed to be a special breed, usually bald men with horn-rimmed glasses, who glided up and down between the desks, stopping now and then to look at a candidate's work over his shoulder.'

'Since I've been in Lincolnshire,' I said, 'I've joined the Junior Auctioneers Association and met a lot of chaps in a similar situation to me, and a right bunch of characters they are: they'll be having a good laugh when they hear about tonight's auction. We have a programme of meetings with excellent speakers, but the main reason we go is to have a night out: I realise I was very lucky to get my first exams out of the way before I came to the county. Most of the lads study by postal course, and go up to London together each year for the examinations. Unfortunately these become liquid social outings so most of them fail, and the trip becomes an annual excursion.'

'I like a good night out,' said Ron, 'but that's downright stupid.'

'It certainly is, but fortunately the local attitude to exams has altered completely now, although there's still a great fund of stories told about the "old days". One of these is about some candidates from the county who were down in London for the exams, and after a convivial evening they were sitting round a table in the Regent Palace Hotel, when they realised that the group was smaller than it should be: one of them had lost his way after leaving the previous hostelry. They ordered drinks and were listening to the resident orchestra, when the music faltered as raised voices could be heard from the foyer. Their friend had found them and made a spectacular entrance, shouting "Tally Ho Lincolnshire" while launching his tweed cap towards them like a boomerang. Unfortunately however it did not return to him, but struck a waiter on the neck. The manager was following closely, and took time off from apologising to other guests to suggest that a rapid move to another establishment would be a good idea. A remark from one of the group, that a city slicker like him wouldn't last five minutes in a Lincolnshire cattle market, only accelerated matters!'

'Did you take any practical exams, Ron?'

Mike joined the conversation from behind the bar, 'I certainly did. I had to take an innkeeper's course before the brewery would let me take the pub.'

Ron said, 'I suppose the Law Society could have a mock courtroom where candidates would practise defending a pickpocket, or a bar where we could rehearse answering questions at a pub auction – but they don't. Did you have to stage a mock property auction?'

'No. I didn't do that – and it's probably just as well because I should have failed on tonight's performance, – but I did sit two practical forestry exams.'

'Is that where you get the strength for your cricketing prowess – felling trees?'

'He's not that good,' said Mike.

'No, I didn't fell any trees, but both exams were very strange. The first time there were about twenty of us, and we were told to report to a railway station near Burnham Beeches, and then taken by bus to a wood, where we met the examiner. He took us to a spinney where we had to identify some trees, and comment on diseases in others. We were then taken to a clearing in another wood, told to stand in a circle, and each given an object with a numbered label attached. When he blew his whistle we had to pass this to the person on our left, and receive another from the right. The whistle had blown twice before I realised that we were not supposed to just identify the object, but answer the question written on the label.

'I particularly remember the last question. The object was a small beech twig with the buds missing, and we were asked "What did this?" I wrote down "Eaten by a squirrel", before the whistle blew and our papers were collected.

'After the exam we had a cup of tea with the examiner and asked him about the answers to various questions. I asked about the missing buds and he said, "A hare ate them". I asked how he knew and he told us that he had stood behind a tree and watched it. The twig could have come from the top of a high tree, as far as we knew, and the question didn't seem to me to be a useful attempt to assess a candidate's knowledge of forestry.'

'I think it's a good job I didn't have a practical exam,' said Ron, 'I might have successfully defended that pickpocket and then find he'd nicked my wallet on the way out of court. But you still had another forestry exam to take: was that as strange?'

'Well, yes, in a different way. This time we met the examiner outside an estate office in the grounds of a stately home, north of London, where a bus was waiting for us. The head woodman was with us and sat behind me, sharing his seat with a charming candidate who started to talk to him. He established that the woodman's wife and family were "very well thank you", and that he had worked on the estate for 23 years – straight from school in fact. He had a staff of three under him, the estate had an area of 12,000 acres and – yes we were driving through lovely countryside.

' "Where are we going now," asked the candidate, and apparently High Wood was our first stop. "Had he seen it planted?" – well yes, it was the first one to be planted after he started work on the estate – and didn't time fly! His new friend supposed that conifers would have been planted at that time – and learnt that he was correct – High Wood was a mixture of Japanese larch and Norway spruce, which in the woodman's opinion would soon need thinning. "Mind you, perhaps I shouldn't be telling you this."

'We arrived at the wood and the examiner gave out the question paper. We were asked to identify the trees, estimate their age and comment on future management! I noticed that when we moved on to the next wood, the woodman sat at the front of the bus, and the examiner took his place beside the friendly candidate.'

Mike asked if we wanted another drink, but we'd both had enough.

'I'm enjoying these exam stories,' said Ron, 'have you got any more before we go?'

'Well I can't vouch for this one, but an auctioneer friend did tell me about a practical forestry exam that took place some years ago. It was the last exam of the week and the candidates were told to report to a landed estate south of London. After a tour around various woods and spinneys they were taken to a shed in the woodyard, and given two hours to answer a test paper. Facilities were very basic. There was no toilet, but half of an old metal oil drum had been placed behind a screen in the corner, to be used if really necessary. Fortunately, there were no female candidates.

'One youth had suffered a particularly bad week, having realised after only a brief look at several exam papers that he couldn't answer the questions and so walked out. He stood no chance of passing the overall examination, but was obliged to attend this final test so he could satisfy his employers that his leave of absence was justified. He had somehow learned about the toilet arrangements, and decided that although he wasn't going to pass, his presence would be remembered!

'After half an hour a candidate went to the drum, and the sound of his stream hitting the metal echoed round the shed, to general amusement. A few minutes later our friend stood up and made his way behind the screen, having previously secreted two rubber hot water bottles beneath his jacket, both full of water and with tubes attached. He took the stopper out of the first one and squeezed it hard, discharging the contents at full velocity through the tube into the drum. This took quite a long time and was very noisy: the candidates chuckled, marvelling at his capacity. When the process was repeated with the second bottle the chuckles became loud laughter, culminating in prolonged applause as he emerged from behind the screen and bowed low, before making a premature, but triumphal exit.'

Chapter 3

A Dead Sheep

After the convivial evening with Ron Bellman at the Fox and Hounds, I drove back to my lodgings in Grantham, thinking all the way about the disastrous auction. Reg Weatherill, senior partner of Weatherill and White, had insisted when I came to the firm as an articled pupil, that I must live in the town during the week, although my parents' home was only fifteen miles away in Melton Mowbray. My advertisement for lodgings in the local paper had been answered by Mrs Barker of 7 Britannia Terrace, and she looked after me so well that I was still living there seven years later, although I did go home at weekends. The house was within easy walking distance of the office, I had my own bed-sitting room, and every weekday she cooked breakfast and an evening meal for me.

I slept very little that night, turning over and over in my mind the complete mess I'd made of my first property auction. I knew that Reg Weatherill would have plenty to say when I got to the office, and I wasn't looking forward to it!

The firm's offices were at Oak House, a stone-built Georgian property, standing near the centre of Grantham just off the High Street. It had been a doctor's house and surgery for many years, before Reg's grandfather bought it around 1900. It was a handsome building, listed as being of architectural importance but previous Weatherills, preferring profit to aesthetics, had marred its appearance by adding an ugly 'lavatory brick' extension to provide a property saleroom and more offices.

The mahogany front door opened into a general office, which was dominated by a long counter spanning the full width of the room. This had been bought some years ago from a local bank that was modernising its premises. They thought it was old fashioned, but the partners of Weatherill and White felt that it had that air of faded elegance, needed to enhance their standing as land agents. Behind the counter was a partition, only two metres high, screening the rest of the office from public view, and in this area stood a table carrying a small switchboard manned by Ella, who was both telephone operator and receptionist. Beside her, sat George, whose job was to help her, deliver letters around the town, run errands and be a general dogsbody.

A door from the back of this office led to Stan Rowan's room: he was responsible for the clerical side of the cattle market and furniture salerooms, setting out farm dispersal sales and collecting weekly rents around the town. Reg and his two sons – the three partners of the firm – had their offices on the upper floor, which was consistent with the division they maintained between themselves and their staff. It was the 'upstairs/downstairs' situation of a country

17

house, transferred to offices in Grantham.

'Mr Weatherill wants to see you,' said Ella.

I knew that this directive came from Reg. If one of his two sons needed me, Ella would have said, 'Mr Arthur' or Mr Oliver'.

I left the general office by the side door, passing the room at the bottom of the stairs occupied by the chief clerk George Stainforth, a gaunt cadaverous man, whose forbidding appearance concealed a kindly nature. His role was to keep the firm's books, take cash and cheques to the bank, keep the holiday rotas and maintain stationery stocks. The office staff worked every Saturday morning until 1pm, and I often needed to leave earlier than this if I had a hockey or cricket match, so I 'played the field' by asking Reg, Arthur, Oliver and George in turn if I could leave an hour early. The other three wanted to know why, but George always nodded his assent with a knowing smile.

As I climbed the gradual staircase to the first floor I knew that the next few minutes were not going to be pleasant. Reg's office had outer and inner doors to ensure that he was not disturbed by noise from the remainder of the building. I knocked on the first one which was covered in green baize secured by brass studs, opened it, and then the inner one to find the senior partner of the firm sitting behind his imposing desk. He was a small man, nearly seventy years old, with black hair brushed sleekly back over his head. He reminded me of portraits I had seen of Napoleon, and I doubt if he would have dismissed the comparison. He was proud that he had no grey hairs and often mentioned it, but we in the office quietly suspected that he plucked them out at night! He had served with distinction in the First World War, and although short he had a commanding presence – and a temper to match. He continued to work at his papers while I stood and waited. Then he looked up.

'What happened last night?'

I gave him the full story.

'How long have you been here?'

'Seven years,' I replied, realising that he knew this perfectly well.

'For God's sake, you should have learnt in seven years that people are motivated by greed. You must know by now that when you're advising clients you can appeal to reason, and you can refer to morality, but avarice will always win. What happened last night has done the firm no good – made us a laughing stock in fact – and it mustn't happen again.'

'No, Mr Weatherill.'

'Robert, you must learn from this.'

I agreed. I had got off very lightly: it seemed that I had caught him and his temper on a good day. Only last week he had found a drover smoking in the cattle market against regulations, snatched the cigarette out of his mouth, stamped on it, and then sacked him.

'I've got an urgent job for you. Granville Hart has just been on the 'phone.

The Electricity Board has been replacing poles through his farm and done some damage. He wants someone there straight away.'

I was pleased that Reg still had enough confidence in me to give me another job, but this particular one was not the best news. Granville Hart farmed over a thousand acres to the west of Grantham, having started in the 1930s with a rented smallholding. He only survived in those difficult times by trapping rabbits and selling them for meat in the market, but over the years he worked hard, gradually buying and renting larger areas of land. He was however more feared in the area than admired, and was generally thought to have the worst temper of any farmer in the district, which was saying something, bearing his brother in mind.

The two brothers lived in the same village, and hated each other with a passion: their antipathy was beyond all reason. One brother would dial the other's number on the telephone and then leave the handpiece lying on the table so that the recipient was unable to use his instrument for the entire day. If a delivery lorry turned up at the wrong brother's farm by mistake, the driver would be told that he should be at a property many miles away, instead of directed to the other end of the village. Ron Bellman said that people in that village must know what it felt like to live in Chicago during the years of prohibition.

A few weeks ago Granville had featured in the local newspaper when a report was printed about a case in the local magistrates' court.

His solicitor stated, when opening the case for the defence: 'My client was moving sheep along a quiet road near his farm, and was following in a pick-up truck, while his two dogs kept them together. A lorry drove up behind and the driver sounded his horn several times, impatient at being delayed, and then waved his arm out of the window to indicate that the sheep should be taken off the road. Mr Hart took no notice of this provocative behaviour at first, but when the horn sounded more frequently and the driver began to shout, he felt he must show his disapproval, and got out of his truck.'

The remainder of the story was given in evidence by the driver.

'I climbed down from my cab as he got out of his truck, but when I saw him pick up a fence post from the back and walk towards me, I changed my mind and ran back to my seat. I had only just closed the door when he brought the post down heavily, just missing me but breaking my wing mirror and side window.'

Granville's solicitor made an eloquent plea in mitigation stressing his client's successful career, the provocation he had suffered, his thousand acres, and prominence in the agricultural community. The magistrates were not impressed and fined him £25 with a warning as to his future conduct. They were even less impressed when he asked for time to pay!

When I arrived at the farm Granville was waiting in the yard and asked me to come into the house. Mrs Hart poured out two cups of tea before disappearing upstairs, leaving the teapot and milk on the table. I then had to listen to a lecture on the shortcomings of the Electricity Board and how they were making it impossible to farm his land, and he was only halfway through this saga when he realised that our cups were empty.

'Have some more tea, lad?'

'Well, yes thank you.'

'Mother!' shouted Granville at the top of his voice, ignoring the full pot in front of him.

His long-suffering wife came down the stairs and into the kitchen, picked up the pot without a word, poured out two more cups of tea and disappeared again.

After enjoying this second cup we left the house and set off in his truck to the fields where the Electricity Board had been working: it had rained heavily for several days and their vehicles had made deep ruts in the first two grass fields. I made notes about the work that was necessary to rectify this damage, and estimated the area that had been affected, so I could calculate the compensation due for loss of grazing. We looked at the areas around the new poles that would need reseeding, and assessed the damage caused by heavy machinery to hedges, fences and gates.

As we drove into the third pasture, where the ruts were even worse, Granville suddenly exclaimed, 'Look at that!'

There in the centre of the field was a dead ewe, lying on its back in one of the ruts.

'Just look at that,' he repeated 'the poor creature fell into that rut and got cast – couldn't move, and that was the end of her.'

I had learnt that 'getting cast' means an animal has fallen onto its back in a rut, or between trees, and become trapped, so it cannot regain its feet. If it is not found quickly it will die.

'I shouldn't get too close,' added Granville. 'Dead sheep soon go rotten.'

I was only too pleased to agree, and kept well away from the carcass as I made more notes on which to base my claim. I was not surprised when he told me that the unfortunate animal had been by far the finest ewe in his flock. I had long since learnt that any dead animal that is the subject of a claim, was never a runt or weakling, but always exemplary in every way. Accidents only ever happen to the finest animals! We continued on our tour before Granville took me back to the farmyard, and I returned to the office with his diatribe against the Board still ringing in my ears.

Some days later I met the valuer acting for the Electricity Board, and the site foreman who had overseen the work, to agree the compensation due to my client. I gave them my calculations of the cost of the work necessary to level out the ruts in the grassland, my assessment of reseeding costs and the amount of compensation due for loss of grazing. These were all agreed with little difficulty. The assessment of the damage caused by their vehicles to hedges, fences and gates was more contentious because they thought they were in poor condition beforehand, but eventually agreement was reached, and I moved on.

'Then there's the sheep that got cast in a rut made by your vehicle, and died. It was a young Suffolk ewe that had only had one crop of lambs, and I suggest £40 is a fair figure.'

There was an immediate change in the attitude of the Board's representatives.

'We're not happy about this. Shall we tell you what we think happened.'

'I'm listening.'

'Well we think that your client found a sheep that had died somewhere else on the farm, brought the carcass to this field and turned it upside down in one of the ruts we had made, so he could claim compensation.'

I was outraged.

'How dare you suggest that my client would stoop to such conduct. I'm not in the habit of making false claims, and unless you have proof to the contrary that ewe died where I saw it – in one of your ruts.'

The Electricity Board men looked at one another. My outburst had shaken them, and they couldn't prove their assertion. Compensation for the dead ewe was settled at a figure close to £40, and we also agreed the amount of my fee, which they had to pay. I told Granville how much compensation I had agreed on his behalf; he thought it should have been much higher, but supposed he had no alternative but to accept. I regarded this as high praise, as he was unlikely to agree that any settlement was enough. I received a cheque from the Board after a few days, sent Granville the figure due to him after deducting my fee, and thought that was the end of the matter.

However a couple of weeks later I was enjoying a beer with Ron Bellman in the George Hotel, when we were joined by Jack Barry, a local builder.

'I was talking about you the other day,' he said.

'Why was that?'

'I was with Granville Hart. He's persuaded the landlord of one of his farms to install a new corn drier, and we're laying the concrete base. He said that you'd done a good job for him when you agreed that compensation claim with the Electricity Board, but he was still chuckling about the dead ewe.'

'You don't mean...'

'Yes,' said Jack 'he found the dead body at the other end of the farm and moved it. He said that only someone who looks as honest as you would have got away with the claim. He didn't want you to look at the body too closely, so he told you that dead sheep soon go rotten, and apparently you couldn't have moved away any quicker if it had been an unexploded bomb!'

'The old devil!'

'He's a very rich man,' continued Jack 'but he loves to outwit officials by breaking every regulation he comes across, and enjoys even more boasting about it afterwards. Did he tell you about the time he was fined by Her Majesty's Customs and Excise?'

'No.'

'Apparently some years ago he drove his truck into the cattle market and while he was watching his sheep being sold, Customs and Excise officials 'dipped' the tanks of several vehicles including his.'

I knew that fuel tax was levied at a concessionary rate on diesel used in tractors and other vehicles for agricultural purposes. Farmers are prohibited from using this fuel in their cars and trucks on public roads, and the agricultural diesel is coloured red to distinguish it from normal commercial fuel. Ministry officials make random checks to find out if the concessionary fuel is being used illegally, by 'dipping' – taking samples from fuel tanks of vehicles parked in public places

'Granville had of course ignored the regulations, and was using red diesel in his truck while using it on the public road. Customs and Excise discovered this, took him to court, and he was fined. He was furious that he had been outwitted by mere officials and vowed it would never happen again. He told the mechanic at his local garage to make a special fuel tank for him, with a division in the middle. The back part would be supplied through the outside filler cap in the normal way, but wouldn't be connected to the engine so it would contain a never-changing supply of taxed commercial diesel. The engine would be fed from the front half of the tank, which he would fill with "red" diesel from inside the truck. He said that the officials could "dip" the back part as often as they liked: they wouldn't catch him out again.'

'The cost of the new tank must have been much more than the few pounds he saved on the fuel,' I said.

'He just had to outmanoeuvre the civil servants,' said Jack 'it was a matter of principle.'

'But,' he continued 'if you stand up to him, he'll respect you. The job we had to do on his farm took about ten days. On the second day he saw my men brewing a cup of tea in the middle of the morning as they were entitled to do, and made sarcastic comments about idle b....s who drank tea all day instead of working. Before leaving the site that evening my chaps put the kettle and teapot in our site hut in the farmyard. When they arrived next morning they found them both squashed flat – probably by a heavy hammer. They were livid and when I visited the site later that morning, told me what they thought in no uncertain terms. We all knew Granville had done it, and when I saw him later that day I told him how furious we were. He said there'd been a lot of gypsies about recently – they must have done it – and let's hope it didn't happen again.'

'I said I knew a bit about gypsies, and I hoped that they didn't come again, because I could tell him exactly what they would do next. He asked what that was, and I pointed to a big tank full of diesel mounted on a wooden stand in the corner of the farmyard. I told him that if our teapot and kettle were crushed again, the gypsies would certainly come back the following night and put a chisel through the bottom of that tank. Granville got the message, nodded, smiled and walked away.'

Chapter 4

Cake Breakers, Root Cutters and Sack Lifters

For the first three of my seven years with Weatherill and White I had been an articled pupil – the professional equivalent of an apprentice. I was paid nothing during this time, in fact my father had to pay £100 a year to the firm so that I could get this practical experience, and I thought then he was being 'ripped off'. I certainly provided them with cheap – very cheap labour, but the partners did take me out with them occasionally as part of my education.

In view of his age and eminence in the profession Reg dealt only with the largest clients – professional work for the big fenland farmers and management of the best agricultural estates. He had served on a national committee of experts whose recommendations formed the basis of the Agricultural Holdings Act 1948. This revolutionary statute granted tenant farmers security of tenure for life, provided they complied with the terms of their Tenancy Agreement.

The existence of articled pupils was 'below his radar', and he rarely took me out. I was not a confident person and always felt that I had 'crawled under the door' when I went into his office, but he once took me to a village in Rutland to see an elderly, titled lady he was advising. When I was introduced she said:

'Are you related to the chemist in Melton Mowbray?'

'Yes, he's my father.'

She then turned to Reg, and said 'My word, you're lucky to have him.'

It may have been my imagination but I always felt he looked at me more favourably after that.

On the other rare occasions when I went out with him, the trip was usually eventful because he drove a large Jaguar car and his eyesight was poor. Despite this he always noticed attractive girls walking by, and was ready with a pithy comment, particularly if one was scantily dressed:

'Christ! Don't you see some sights when you're out without your gun.'

If he was driving in his usual stately manner and overtaken by a small car with a straining engine, and saw the driver looking back and smirking, he would wave a languid arm and say:

'That's right, go home and tell your missus you've passed a Jag!'

Arthur and Oliver took me out occasionally to their agricultural clients, gave me a notebook and told me what to write down. A day with Arthur was always rewarding because he had an air of quiet authority, partly due to his rapid rise to the rank of major in the War. Oliver was more like his father, and an outing with him could be turbulent. He dealt with many of the farm dispersal sales that we held each spring, and I sometimes went with him to see a farmer who was retiring – or one that had fallen on hard times and was going out of business. When a highly regarded farmer retired after a lucrative career, his sale was always well attended and good prices realised for his equipment and livestock. If an unfortunate farmer was in financial trouble, and really needed the support of his neighbours, they usually did little to help, and bought the lots at bargain prices.

With very little experience of farming I had a lot to learn about the wide range of agricultural machinery and equipment. When I went to a farm with Oliver, he would discuss the sale arrangements with the farmer, and leave me to list the machinery that was to be sold. He would check this afterwards, and at the beginning I was often wrong, but despite his irascible nature he was quite patient with me.

'No, Robert that's not a trailer it's a farm cart – you can tell by the big wooden wheels: a trailer is much lower to the ground and is used for carrying hay, sheaves of corn and the like. A moffre – (the Lincolnshire abbreviation of "hermaphrodite") – is a cross between the two. Carts and moffres were designed to be pulled by horses but have been adapted for tractors.'

Farm Wagon

And then – 'Yes, you've got that right – a flat roll is a larger version of a garden roller, but the other one is a Cambridge roll – it's made up of individual rings with protruding ridges.'

25

But his patience soon wore thin.

'For heavens sake, can't you tell the difference between harrows and drags. Harrows are sets of vertical tines that are towed along the ground by a tractor: a drag is mounted behind the tractor and only lowered when it's working. They're both used on arable fields to break the soil down to a level surface. A chain harrow is like a blanket of spiked chains and is used to improve grassland.'

'What do you mean, "you don't know what it is". It's a combine drill! Corn drills sow seed grain through tubes that extend below the soil, but a combine drill like that one sows grain and fertiliser at the same time.'

I could recognise a binder from the times when I helped my uncle with the harvest on his smallholding. I remember it being towed behind a tractor, cutting the standing corn, tying it into sheaves and throwing them onto the ground. We had to lift each one, and lean them against one another in groups of six or eight, to make stooks: it was hard work, particularly if barley was being cut and full of thistles.

Excitement grew as the binder continued on its way round the field, and the remaining area of standing corn became smaller and smaller. Rabbits that had taken refuge in the crop ran from this terrible machine towards the centre of the field, but as the area of standing corn diminished, they had to make a dash for freedom across the cleared ground. Farm workers with shotguns ensured that few were successful, and rabbit pies were plentiful at harvest time.

The sheaves were carted by trailer to be stacked in the farmyard and await the arrival of the threshing machine in the autumn. This fearsome wooden device – a whirlwind of revolving belts powered by a steam engine, separated the grain from the straw.

The combined harvester or 'combine' had now swept through the agricultural industry and revolutionised farming. On one of my earliest trips with Oliver he showed me my first. It was an amazing advance for agriculture, cutting the standing corn and separating the grain from the straw, which is thrown out of the back. The grain then went into an internal tank before being poured into a waiting trailer. The binder and threshing machine became obsolete in just a few years on all but the smallest farms, but they're seen occasionally at sales as a reminder of a bygone age.

I got another painful lesson from him about barn machinery.

'Will you never learn Robert! That's not a root cutter or a cake breaker, it's a chaff cutter. A root cutter slices up mangolds so they can be fed more easily to livestock, and a chaff cutter breaks up straw for the same reason. Some bought cattle feed comes in big slabs, or "cakes", and a cake breaker crushes them into small pieces.

'You've got that wrong as well! A sack barrow is just a frame with a pair of wheels at the bottom: that's a sack lifter. It's similar but has winding gear that can lift a full sack off the ground. For goodness sake get it right next time!'

There was a lot to learn about livestock too, but I got to know more every week at the cattle market. When I visited farms I found out that cattle were kept in yards during the winter, and these yards were enclosed by open fronted shelters, and by rows of small 'loose boxes' – like brick stables – which housed the younger stock.

My articled days were now long behind me and it was part of my job to organise farm dispersal sales – a task that I enjoyed very much. Oliver called me into his office one afternoon.

'As you know I do the annual stocktaking valuation for William Hall of Lodge Farm, Little Glen, but he's retiring and wants us to hold his farm dispersal sale. It's a sad day for us because we've done his work for a long time, and the landlord is merging this farm with another, which means one less client for Weatherill and White. I'd like you to deal with this, so make an appointment to see him as soon as possible. He wants us to sell his sheep and cattle as well as the implements.'

The sizes of farms had been regulated for generations by a farmer's ability to harvest his crops using horses and the basic equipment available. A farm was categorised by the number of horses needed to work it.

'Yon's a twelve-horse farm,' people would say.

The coming of the tractor, and then the combine, had dramatically increased the area that a farmer could harvest, and for this and other reasons the size of farms was growing rapidly: smaller ones – like Lodge Farm were being amalgamated with others. A farm dispersal sale was good business and welcome publicity for us, but so often meant a lost client and long-term shrinkage in our business.

I made an appointment to see William Hall, but before going I asked Stan Rowan what dates we had available for the sale.

'Ah yes, William Hall of Little Glen – he lives at Lodge Farm doesn't he,' said Stan 'that means it's a long way out of the village. Nearly every village has a Lodge Farm, and the locals used to say that because they were so isolated, some of the people living there got up to all sorts of deviant behaviour. Every farmer has a car nowadays but they're still lonely places to live. It's all right for the men, they can go down to the village pub in the evening, but I feel sorry for the women – they're marooned.'

William's farm followed the usual pattern, being a mile from Little Glen and approached down a long, stony track off the narrow lane leading to Shenton. The farmhouse dated from the late nineteenth century and was built of local limestone with a blue slated roof, typical of the area, but giving the property a 'cold' appearance, so different to the houses built of golden ironstone in nearby Leicestershire. The adjoining farm buildings were also built of limestone, but had roofs of interlocking red pantiles, giving them more warmth and character than the house.

There was certainly no sign of deviant practices as I drove up to the neatly painted farmhouse and immaculate buildings. I parked by William's Land Rover, and admired his wife's Triumph Herald as I walked towards the kitchen door, before I heard the noise of machinery working in the nearby outhouse. There was William standing by a lathe.

'What are you making?' I asked.

'I'm not getting on very well,' said William 'but it's meant to be a table lamp for the missus. I shall need a hobby when I'm retired.'

'Well, that's why I'm here.'

'Yes, let's go into the house and talk about it.'

It was a joy to walk into the farmhouse kitchen, with its large pine table, iron cooking range, and cured hams hanging from the beams, but I had little time to look round as we got straight down to business.

'There's only one place where we can hold the sale,' said William 'and that's in the grass field next to the stackyard. It's big enough and close to the farm buildings.'

'What about car parking?' I asked.

The long drive to Lodge Farm meant that parking on the public road was not practicable. Our farming customers would certainly not walk that far, and the drive would soon get clogged up with parked vehicles.

'That can be in the paddock on the other side of the farm buildings.'

'That's fine,' I said, 'we can sell the sheep from pens in the sale field, and build a "ring" with straw bales in the farmyard where the cattle will be sold.'

'Then there's the most important thing,' said William. 'I know the local publican well, and I'll ask him to get a special licence for sale day. He can set up a bar in the barn.'

We then went out into the yard and walked around the implement sheds, listing the machinery and equipment.

'Have you got the log books ready for the combine and tractors?' I asked.

'Yes, they're in the farmhouse.'

It was essential to note down the year of manufacture for the advertisements, and William would need to have the log books ready on sale day to hand over to the buyers. I also took details of the barn machinery and livestock equipment such as sheep netting, stakes and troughs. We needed to advertise these because only a few buyers would come to the sale for the big machinery, but many would be interested in the cheaper lots. I also listed the livestock to be sold.

He had a wide range of implements and equipment, and I had a lot of entries in my notebook when I got back to the office. My next job was to prepare the sale particulars – our name for the brochure. I had learnt long ago that this MUST be done in the traditional way. At Weatherill and White initiative was frowned upon, and change was downright dangerous! I wrote out a draft which was typed in the office and sent to the printers at the end of the street, for them to produce a foolscap sized card, folded to provide four pages of copy. The front page of the particulars for William's sale read:

Under instructions from William Hall
(who is retiring from farming)

LODGE FARM
LITTLE GLEN
(Grantham 7 miles, Melton Mowbray 8 miles)

SALE OF LIVE AND DEAD
FARMING STOCK

35 BEAST
220 SHEEP
IMPLEMENTS FOR 360 ACRES

TO BE HELD ON 25th MARCH 1963
At 11 am
(Licensed Bar Applied For)

When I first came to the firm this traditional format seemed ludicrous to me, but Ken Greening put me right. He was the only other qualified member of staff, and taught me a lot.

'Why on earth do we say "LIVE and DEAD" Farming Stock?' I asked. ' "Live" I can understand – but "Dead"! It looks as though we're going to sell rows of carcasses.'

'I know it does,' said Ken 'but that's the phrase we always use. The word "dead" was used by earlier partners of the firm to distinguish the inanimate lots in the sale –like implements and machinery – from the livestock.'

'You've got to realise,' he continued, 'that a Lincolnshire auctioneer is bound by traditions quite as rigid as those that regulate the order of service in the Church of England. Have you read the book "Portrait of Elmbury" by John Moore?'

'No'

'You must – he's a great author'. He opened a drawer in his desk and pulled out a well-thumbed volume, 'I'll read you a few sentences about his time working in an auctioneer's office:

' "The adjectives never vary. But perhaps after all it is not for lack of epithets that the auctioneer always uses the same one: there is a convention in the matter, as strict as that which bound great Homer himself. The Residence must be desirable; just as the dawn was always rosy-fingered".'

Stan Rowan had worked at many farm sales and when I was checking my draft sale particulars with him, he said:

'It's very unusual to see any horses in a farm sale now, and of course William doesn't have any, but they always used to be "kings of the farm". Twenty years ago they would have been the most important animals in the sale, and it was traditional for them to be "shown". The whole company would move out of the farmyard into the village street where these magnificent animals would be waiting, with their manes plaited and beribboned, and their flowing tails trimmed. A farmhand would take the bridle of each one and show it off by running down the street with it, between lines of watching farmers. It was a wonderful sight.'

Towards the end of my articled period we held a dispersal sale for a client who kept three Shire horses as a hobby: these were included in his sale and we revived the old custom in the village street. These tremendous horses stand up to two metres high, weighing well over a ton, and have an amazing capacity for hard work, including pulling brewery wagons. It's sobering to remember that when our knights went into battle in the Middle Ages they were not mounted on racehorses, but on awesome animals like these.

As William had said, it was crucial to encourage a good attendance at the sale by stating in our advertisements that there would be a bar. A Justice's licence had to be obtained, which took a few days, and we had to be careful because magistrates were inclined to refuse an application if we announced that there would be a bar at the sale, before they'd sanctioned it. The phrase shown on the particulars seemed to satisfy them, and gave the necessary information to thirsty farmers.

The next three pages on our printed card listed the machinery, equipment and details of the sheep and cattle to be sold. We gave the numbers and breed of the ewes and rams, together with the ages of the steers and heifers (steers are castrated male cattle, while heifers are young female animals that haven't yet borne a calf). The particulars were then circulated to neighbouring farmers, machinery and livestock dealers, and to the many farmers who just loved coming to sales. Advertisements were placed in local newspapers giving details of the cattle, sheep and principal machinery.

It was time to start the real work.

Chapter 5

A Ring on High Ground

Two days before the auction Stan Rowan, Bill and I went to Lodge Farm to 'set the sale out', which involves taking the equipment out of the yards and buildings into the sale field and arranging it in rows.

Arthur had employed Bill as Cattle Market foreman only three months beforehand. He had been his batman during the War, and walked with a limp after a bad injury at the battle of Monte Cassino. He lived in the north of England and had fallen on hard times, but Arthur heard about this through his Regimental Association, made contact and offered him the job, which he was delighted to take. He worked hard at his new post, and when I first met him I knew from his infectious smile that we would get on well. He and Alf were based at the cattle market, where they were responsible for general maintenance and for washing out after the livestock had been sold – not easy work.

'Where's Alf?' I asked.

'He's back at the market,' said Bill, 'there's a few gates need repairing.'

Alf was very different to Bill – there was no infectious smile – he was morose, sallow-faced, smoked constantly and had a permanent dewdrop on the end of his nose. The two men also did the manual work for our furniture sales – moving heavy lots, setting out the china and glass on tables, taking the outside lots into the yard and supervising viewing. Farm sales meant a trip into the countryside, and were a pleasant change for them.

This was Bill's first farm dispersal sale and he couldn't understand the phrase 'Live and Dead Farming Stock' either, so I explained it to him on the way, and continued

'It's not only the sale particulars that must be done in the traditional way. Weatherill and White take great pride in the way their sales are set out, so the organisation has to be spot on. The rows of machinery and equipment have to be twenty yards apart, and each lot at least ten yards from the next.'

We arrived at the farm to find Robin, one of William's men, waiting for us.

'I'm afraid I can't stop with you,' he said, 'but the gaffer wants me to clean a ditch out at the far end of the farm: he says you can use this tractor and trailer.'

'That's fine,' I said, 'there must be a lot of last-minute jobs to do before he leaves. Stan or I will drive the tractor.'

William was telling his men to do as much maintenance work as possible at the moment to minimise the dilapidation payment that would be assessed at his tenantright valuation: he would rather pay Robin to do this, than help us.

'I'll go and peg out the rows,' said Stan. He had to put wooden stakes at twenty-yard intervals at each end of the field, to indicate where the rows of machinery and equipment should be.

'Right Bill, you come with me,' I said.

I remembered where William stored his surplus fence posts, sheep netting and stakes. There were a lot of these in the barn, and we loaded them onto the trailer to take out to the sale field.

'The next tradition you have to learn Bill is that the first lot in a farm sale is always a heap of scrap iron. Farmers are not tidy people and when an implement breaks down or becomes obsolete it's usually abandoned in the stackyard, in a hedge bottom or where it was last used. We're going to be spending a long time hauling broken implements, old iron posts, cracked pig troughs and the like out of the buildings to make a great big heap. It'll fetch little or nothing when it's sold and makes no economic sense, but it's what we have to do.

'After that will come the obsolete implements, so we'll leave ten spaces for them. The next lots will be these rolls of sheep netting, and the wooden stakes that hold them upright. There aren't many hedges nowadays that are dense enough to keep sheep in a field without netting. We have to put the same number of stakes in successive lots, and leave spaces for the netting that is still being used in the fields: we shall have to fetch that on the morning of the sale.'

Stan joined us and we carried on emptying the farm buildings of wooden sheep troughs, galvanised pig feeders and ladders. Then came the barn equipment – the root cutter, cake breaker chaff cutter and sack lifter. William had kept poultry at one time and there were a number of small huts, or 'arks', in the stackyard, which we dragged into the field. We had soon set out two full rows, including a massive mound of scrap iron at the start.

'This is hard work,' I said to Bill, 'but we must get the tumbrels out of the cattle yard today.'

In Lincolnshire a tumbrel isn't a cart for taking aristocrats to the guillotine – much as I'd like to drive one with some in it – but a wooden feeding platform used in a cattle yard. They're very simple, but ingenious, because each one has four tall legs at the corners, so that in the autumn when the cattle are brought into the yard, the platform is at the height of their heads. During the winter the floor level of the yard rises as dung from the cattle mixes with their bedding straw, but the feeding platform can still be used, although now the animals have to lower their heads to use it.

Stan said, 'There's a fork lift on the front of the tractor that you can use for that job; I'll take the trailer off the back. If Bill stays and helps you I'll go and look for the best position to set up the sheep pens in the sale field.'

I drove the tractor into the cattle yard where the manure had accumulated to a depth of over a metre, and lowered the fork lift beneath the first tumbrel so

I could hoist it out, but soon realised I had overlooked something! The tumbrels were there to provide corn and hay to William's livestock, but cattle were not the only animals that benefitted. As the first one was lifted out of the manure, dozens of rats that had been living underneath fled in all directions. Bill quickly lost his infectious smile, and let out a torrent of abuse that must have been useful in the Italian campaign! After taking this first tumbrel into the field, we took the precaution of tying binder twine around our trouser legs before returning to the yard, but most of the remaining rats must have realised it was moving day, as fewer and fewer emerged when we tackled the other five.

After the last one had been taken to the field Stan came back, with the suspicion of a smirk on his face.

'You old b.....', I said, 'you knew what was going to happen in that yard.'

'There's nothing like learning lessons for yourself,' he said. 'Mind you, if William had been about with his terrier, I wouldn't have missed it.'

'Thanks a bunch,' I said. Even with a terrier I wouldn't be keen to do that job again! Still perhaps one day I would be able to pass it on to someone else, as keen, innocent and foolish as me.

It seemed that Stan was not the only one who wanted to avoid unpleasant work, because when he and I arrived the next morning – the day before the sale – Robin was waiting, and told us that this time he could stay. We had hired a lorry for Bill and Alf to bring a load of sheep hurdles from the cattle market, and they would soon be here.

Robin and Stan took the tractor to pick up the first of the mounted drags from the farm buildings, while I walked into the field to show them where it should go. As they set off to fetch the next one I saw the lorry coming into the yard piled high with sheep hurdles. These are low wooden gates, about two metres long – known in Lincolnshire as 'trays' – with two iron rings at one end so they can be fastened together to form pens. The driver was able to get the vehicle into the field, and I showed the men where the sheep would be sold, so the trays were unloaded there, and a row set up against the hedge secured by wooden stakes. The rest were fastened together into square pens about two metres away from the hedge, leaving an alleyway along which the sheep could be driven. On the other side of the pens we made semi-circular enclosures of wire netting in which the lambs would be put, beside their mothers.

Meanwhile the heavy and medium drags were in place and two sets of harrows were being brought out on the trailer. The chain harrows and seed harrows came next, followed by the hay turner, manure spreader, flat and Cambridge rolls, ploughs and combine drill. The baler, combine harvester and remaining tractors were in the sheds having a good wash down; they would be left under cover until the morning of the sale.

Setting up the pens for William's 220 sheep was hard work, so I helped Bill and Alf finish this before we had our sandwiches and left the field.

'The next job is to build the sale ring for the cattle,' I said as we walked into the stackyard, 'and this is where it will go. We shall need plenty of straw bales, so will you ask Robin to take the tractor and trailer to the stack over there, get a good load and bring them here'

'I can see why you're building it there,' said Bill.

'Why's that?'

'It's the highest part of the yard'.

'You catch on far too quickly! Yes that's right – we want the buyers, who'll be outside the straw bales, to look up at the cattle. They might even think they're bigger than they are! We're lucky that the centre of the yard is the highest part, because the cattle will be held in the loose boxes around here and it will be easy to drive them into the ring.'

The trailer was loaded and brought over to the middle of the yard. We started to build the ring with layers of straw bales, leaving several gaps for the cattle to be brought in from the buildings for sale.

'Is William about?' I asked Robin.

'He's in the house,' he said, 'he should have finished his after-lunch snooze by now.'

I went over to find him – and he had finished his nap.

'We need to decide how we're going to lot the beast' I said, so we walked around the yards to have a good look at them. They were all being sold as stores, since they needed more feeding before they could be sold as fat cattle.'

'Those five red Hereford cross steers can be sold as the first lot,' said William. 'They're the strongest cattle I've got: I bought them as one bunch when they were about six months old.'

'Yes they're grand cattle and should start off the sale well.'

'Then I thought those three Aberdeen Angus cross heifers would go well as one lot. They're only about a month younger than the Herefords'.

William had obviously given a lot of thought to this, and I agreed with all his suggestions. When the cattle ring was built the men joined us, and we isolated the first five steers inside their yard, before driving them over to a loose box near the ring where they would spend the night. The process was repeated with the remaining lots, including the calves, although sometimes two groups had to occupy the same building. The work was soon done and the cattle were all in position for tomorrow's sale.

'What about the most important man?' I asked.

'I've cleared the barn for him,' said William, 'and he'll be here early tomorrow morning to set up his bar. He had no trouble getting his special licence by the way.'

'And what about our office?'

'That'll be in the farmhouse kitchen,' said William. 'The missus wasn't too pleased, but she realised it had to be.'

'We've just got the implements to number then, and the small tools ring to set up. Have you got that wagon rope and the stakes we talked about?'

'Yes, they're all ready in the barn.'

The small tools, pitchforks, sledge hammers, muck forks, beet forks (with rounded ends to the tines), ditching spades, sack barrows, baler twine, salt licks, small electric motors and spare parts for the implements would not be lotted, but sold from a roped enclosure in the sale field. They would stay indoors until the morning, in case any light-fingered visitors came in the night.

'Alf, will you go and set that up, while Bill and I lot the implements.'

He and I walked round the field, with Bill sticking lot numbers on to the lots of machinery and equipment, while I listed each one on the sale sheets. When this was done I went back to see William.

'We've finished for today. The weather forecast looks good for tomorrow.'

'I thought it was going to rain tonight.'

'Well they say so, but it's due to finish around 6am tomorrow, and if that turns out to be true it'll be just right for us. The farmers won't be able to work on the land until it dries out – so the day's free for them to come to the sale.'

'I hope you're right' added William, 'I can do with all the help I can get.'

'We've had quite a lot of enquiries about the main lots,' I said.

'Yes, I've had five or six people come to look at the tractors and combine.'

'We'll see you tomorrow then, bright and early. You'll have your sheep dogs ready, won't you?'

The next morning we arrived at 6am to find William and Robin waiting. William looked anxious, which was not surprising, because a big part of the money he needed for his retirement depended on a successful sale.

'Bill, will you and Alf go and number the cattle,' I said. 'You'll find it's more difficult than you think, but Alf will keep you straight.'

They had to go to each group of cattle, put a dollop of glue onto the haunch of one of them, and then slap a lot number on to the glue. The excited cattle run round in circles, determined to avoid the attentions of these strange men and their glue pot, so what seems a simple job always takes longer than expected.

'The lot numbers we use for the cattle are much more impressive than those I stuck on the implements' said Bill.

This was certainly true. The implement lot numbers were white and insignificant – like cloakroom tickets – but their cattle counterparts were very grand – much larger and oval, with 'Weatherill and White' printed in red and black around the edge.

'After you've done that, will you write in chalk on the doors of the loose boxes, the lot number of the cattle inside, and how many there are – such as "Lot 1 - 5 Steers"? Then collect the tools and small equipment from the barn and take them out to the roped ring in the field. Use the old tractor and trailer.'

Stan had already driven off in the office car to put out the roadside direction signs, which were pieces of white cardboard bearing the message 'Weatherill and White – To the Auction', with a hand pointing in the required direction. He had to hammer two stakes into the roadside verge and fix the signs to them with drawing pins. They were essential when the sale was being held in such an isolated location as Lodge Farm, and he put one up at the end of the drive and at every crossroads and road junction within a mile.

William introduced me to another of his men who would direct the traffic to the car park in the adjoining field. It's necessary to supervise a car park at a farm sale, because farmers are not the most considerate of men and invariably want to park their vehicle as close as possible to the exit. Since the entrance and exit are usually through the same gate, this means that if nobody's in charge, the first ten vehicles will be parked in a semi-circle inside the entrance gate, and no one else will get in.

'Alf, will you put out these "To the Pay Office" signs around the yard please. We don't want the buyers to be in any doubt where they have to pay! William, have you got your dogs ready? We've come to the critical bit.'

Most of William's Border Leicester ewes had lambed and it was essential that the lambs should be sold with their correct mothers: if a ewe is sold with a lamb that isn't hers, she will reject it, and the lamb won't survive. At a recent sale of ours the entire flock of sheep had been driven into the sale field and penned, before the owner tried to match the right ewes with their lambs. It was obvious after the sale that he hadn't done this successfully, and the buyers had to bring their sheep back to the farm the next day and wait until the ewes found their own lambs. They were understandably very unhappy, and some claimed for the costs they had incurred. I didn't want this to happen here.

William had brought his flock to an adjoining field yesterday, and he, Robin and I went there with the two dogs.

'They're good dogs – this'll go like clockwork,' he said.

I wanted to believe him: time was short. I'd seen how wrong things could go, and it was so important to get this right. The dogs followed his commands, ushered one of the youngest ewes into the corner of the field by the gate, and two lambs ran to her. A second young ewe was treated in the same way, and this continued until ten similar ewes and their lambs had been isolated: these were then driven into a pen in the sale field. The process was repeated for all the ewes, starting with the youngest and continuing with the older ones, which took a long time, but eventually all the mothers and their lambs had been penned. The rams, sheders (which are one year old female lambs) and in-lamb ewes followed, and the flock was ready for sale.

There was only half an hour to go now, and I went to check that the office arrangements in the farmhouse were satisfactory. On my way I met Oliver

Weatherill, who had just arrived.

'There's no direction sign on the road from Swaythorpe to Little Glen' he snapped. He didn't mention that he'd passed two other signs before then, and knew where the farm was in any case.

Ella and George were sitting in splendour in the kitchen behind a large scrubbed pine table, each with a steaming mug of tea and a buttered scone, freshly baked by Mrs Hall.

'It's all right for some,' I said, 'are you ready?'

They obviously were, and I set off with Stan to the sale field, pleased to see that there were now a lot of people about. We were ready to go.

Threshing Machine

Chapter 6

No Hearing, No Eyesight and No Parents

Stan and I walked to the heap of scrap iron in the far corner of the field to begin the sale. He rang a brass hand bell on the way, and stood beside me when we got there, holding the clipboard and sale sheets. His job was to record the price paid for each lot, let me know if there was a reserve price, and if anyone had left an 'absentee bid'. Several clients had already viewed the sale and were interested in buying a particular lot, but couldn't get to the auction. They let us know the price they were prepared to pay, and this was entered on the sale sheets so that we could bid on their behalf.

The weather forecasters had been proved right, and it was fine after a steady drizzle in the early morning, with a watery sun doing its best to peek through the clouds. A good number of people followed us across the field, and I stood by the heap of iron with Stan, and William's grandson Arthur. He would take each completed sale sheet to the office in the farmhouse so that Ella and George could write out the buyers' bills. The three of us were overshadowed, however, by a fourth figure, leaning casually on his walking stick, with one foot on the pile of metal.

'Morning Robert, are you in good voice?' said Tom Cash – the godfather of the local scrap iron dealers – who was wearing a battered tweed suit over a red waistcoat and gleaming brown boots. He had achieved a position of dominance in the trade over many years, which was now unchallenged: a few fawning acolytes stood around him, hoping to be given some 'crumbs from his table' during the sale. Tom could make or break any young man in the area who hoped to make a living from buying and selling scrap iron.

'Good morning Tom, good morning ladies and gentlemen,' I began 'as you know we're selling today under instructions from William Hall, who is retiring from farming. Our office is in the farmhouse and we shall be pleased to see you there at the end of the sale: a receipted bill is needed before any lots can be taken out of the field. I must also remind you that, in accordance with the Lincolnshire custom, 5% commission will be added to the purchase price of all lots.'

It had been the custom in the county for generations, to add commission to the price paid for machinery and equipment at auction sales, which meant that buyers paid the auctioneer's charges instead of the seller. The custom didn't apply in neighbouring counties, so we always made this announcement before a sale so purchasers from outside the area didn't get a nasty shock when they got their bill.

(How times have changed since those halcyon days. Both buyers and sellers pay the auctioneers now – and rather more than 5%!)

'How much may I say for Lot 1 – the scrap iron? Give me £20.'

It was worth at least that.

'£20!' exclaimed Tom in mock horror – 'I'll give you £2.' His followers tittered.

I thought of the hours it had taken us to make this heap.

'£5, or we'll leave it where it is,' I said, knowing that if Tom didn't buy, he'd make sure no one else did, and the iron would stay in the field.

'Go on then,' he said with a show of reluctance. As I expected no one else dared to bid, so I banged my stick down and sold it. Stan wrote the price down, and we continued with my authority reasonably intact. Most of the redundant implements were knocked down to Tom for very little, although he graciously permitted some of his retinue to buy an occasional item.

Next came the lots of 50 wooden fencing stakes, and I announced that the purchaser of the first lot had the option of taking the next two at the same price. The first two buyers chose to do this, leaving only one more pile to be sold.

Who should buy this, but Granville Hart.

'I'll take the next two lots at that price,' he said.

These lots were new galvanised iron field gates – worth far more than the stakes.

'Oh no, you won't!' I said. 'I didn't offer an option when I sold that last pile.'

'I thought you said we could take the next two lots at the same price from now on.'

I wasted no time in arguing. Everyone knew Granville, and there was a hint of a smile on his face. He knew exactly what had been said, and I carried on resolutely, selling the two gates, followed by the tumbrels which had caused such excitement yesterday. The company was growing steadily as the sale progressed: farmers knew that the principal implements wouldn't be sold until around noon, and many had stayed at home to finish their chores before setting off. I sold about sixty lots of general equipment before we reached the more important machinery, where Oliver was waiting to take over. He was a good auctioneer, red-faced and short in stature like his father, with the same commanding presence.

'Well done Robert – things are going well,' he said.

'Praise indeed,' I thought, as Stan handed the sale sheets to me so I could take over as clerk, while he went to help in the office.

After the scrap iron had been sold, Tom Cash adjourned to the bar, but as the godfather of the scrap trade left the scene, his counterpart from the agricultural machinery world took over. From humble beginnings Fred Black had built a large and successful business buying and selling tractors and agricultural machinery. He was powerfully built with a personality to match, wasted little time in social niceties and had a prodigious capacity for drink. He also had greater powers of persuasion than anyone I have ever met. The saying 'he could sell snow to Eskimos' certainly applied to Fred Black.

There is an Act of Parliament that prohibits buyers from acting as an organised group at an auction. This illegal practice is known as 'forming a ring', when a number of buyers agree between themselves not to bid against one another, which stifles competition and keeps prices low. At the end of a sale these buyers adjourn to a quiet place and hold a second auction of the lots they have bought, dividing the additional proceeds between them.

Although unlawful, the ring flourished in south Lincolnshire at the time, and as far as agricultural machinery was concerned Fred Black was the acknowledged ringmaster. Tom Cash maintained his position by ensuring that his minions faced financial ruin if they stepped out of line, and was prepared to use physical persuasion. Fred's operation was much more sophisticated: his associates stood in different places around the company and if prices were low they bought the lots in rotation. Fred emphasised his authority by taking his turn when the most valuable machinery was being sold.

Farmers often talk about the merits of respective auctioneers, and I remember Reg Weatherill discussing this once.

'To be a good auctioneer,' he said, 'there are four essential qualities. You must be audible, know the value of what you're selling, conduct the sale at a good pace and keep the buyers in good humour'.

Unfortunately Reg's age and health did not permit him to sell at farm sales now, but Oliver was having a good day. The farmers were bidding well and the high prices meant that Fred's group wasn't buying much.

There were two ploughs in the sale, one almost new and the other very old: I saw that a bid of £100 had been entered on the sale sheets for the old plough, which was to be sold first. John Bramwell, a farmer from the next village, couldn't come to the sale and had told us to bid up to this figure. When we came to this plough I showed the note to Oliver, and he opened the bidding at £25. No one else bid and Oliver sold it to him.

William's three tractors, baler and combine were the last lots of machinery to be sold. He had put reserve prices on these, because their total value was more than all the other lots in the field, and the success of the entire sale depended on how much they would make. He was concerned that no farmers would be interested and couldn't risk Fred and his cohorts buying them cheaply. Fortunately William was a popular man – and a lucky one – because neighbouring farmers competed with others from further afield, and they all sold well.

Now it was my turn, as the junior auctioneer, to continue the sale by selling the small tools, spares and stores from inside their roped enclosure, and Stan came out of the office to help. These items were not lotted, and after each sale, the item was handed to the buyer. It said much for the honesty of the neighbourhood and for Stan's efficiency in writing down the prices and buyers' names, that there was rarely any difficulty in getting paid.

This was not my favourite part of the sale: I stood in the middle of the enclosure with the buyers gathered outside the rope in a complete circle, so that bids came from every direction and were difficult to spot. Farmers take great delight in making 'witty' remarks about auctioneers, particularly young ones, and if I missed a bid, loud protests and comments could be expected. I have heard it said that the position of an auctioneer can be compared to that of a parson in his pulpit, but this does not take into account the nature of the audiences. It's unusual for a parson to be interrupted in his sermon, firstly by an accusation that he has no hearing, then no eyesight – and finally no parents. An auctioneer expects it.

There is another complication during this part of the sale. When I was 'writing up' the sale sheets before the auction, and came to a contraption in the field that I'd never seen before, I could ask the farmer what it was. In the small tools ring the items aren't entered on the sale sheets, so there are no descriptions to rely on, which can be embarrassing. I hoped this wouldn't happen today – but after I had sold the first ten lots of batteries, sacks, spades and forks, Bill held up a tool I'd never seen before.

'How much may I say for this lot?' I said.

'What is it?' shouted someone.

I hesitated – fatally!

'It's a thistle puller,' shouted another.

'No, it's a staff for leading a bull by the nose,' said someone else.

'Send him back to school,' cried a third.

More ribald comments and much hilarity followed, until the auction was in danger of getting out of control – an auctioneer's ultimate disgrace.

'You can't expect me to know everything,' I said, 'not like Denis Hale over there. Let's get on, we've got the sheep and cattle to sell'.

This quietened them and I sold the rest as quickly as possible to avoid any more awkward questions. It still took me over half an hour to sell everything in the roped ring, none of it being very valuable, and I could see that Arthur and Oliver were beginning to look anxiously at their watches. However the end came at last and Arthur Weatherill, Oliver's elder brother, walked over to the sheep pens. He was taller and broader than Oliver, lacked his exuberance, but had no difficulty in showing any displeasure in quiet, forceful language.

'Good afternoon ladies and gentlemen,' he began 'I'm sorry that this is the last time Weatherill and White will sell livestock for William Hall. He has been a client of ours for many years at the cattle market, and when he entered sheep or cattle we knew we should see quality. Just look down these sheep pens for yourselves: what more can I say?'

Several farmers nodded enthusiastically when they heard this last phrase, hoping that Arthur had finished his peroration and would get on with the sale, but the Border Leicester ewes did look well with their white faces and 'aristocratic Roman' noses. Their lambs stood inside the semi-circle of wire netting beside each pen, to avoid being trampled underfoot by the anxious ewes. The Suffolk rams – or tups as they're known in Lincolnshire – were evident at the end of the row with their distinctive black faces, which would be passed on to their progeny.

Arthur began the auction.

'I shall sell this first pen of ten ewes per head, and include their lambs in that figure: they have fifteen lambs between them, so every bid you make is for two and a half animals.' Several farmers looked confused at this point and scratched their heads, but he continued, 'these are the youngest ewes in the sale, so they have a long life in front of them: they're right in mouth and bag.'

This meant that their teeth and udders were in good condition. As a sheep ages, its teeth gradually drop out and eventually, when they've all gone, it can no longer 'chew the cud' and feed itself. This is the end of a ewe's breeding life and it will be sold for slaughter. If the teats in a ewe's udder are defective it cannot suckle its lambs properly.

The prospective buyers were either dealers or farmers: the latter knew William and were prepared to accept what he said about the condition of the sheep, but the dealers weren't. They climbed into the pens, much to Arthur's annoyance, to have a close look and examine their teeth. They needed to buy, and sell on quickly at a profit, and were anxious to use any ploy to lower the price.

'There's a tooth gone here guv'nor,' said one.

William climbed into the pen to look at the sheep in question.

'She has one chipped tooth,' he stated, which the dealer knew, but hoped he might deter some possible buyers.

'This one's limping,' said another.

'You'll limp if you don't get out of the pen while I'm selling,' said Arthur, in a rare show of annoyance.

William's flock had a good reputation and the bidding was very competitive with excellent prices being made. The youngest ewes were sold with their lambs in the first twelve to fifteen pens, and Arthur then announced that the rest were 'right in the bag only', meaning that their udders were in order but their teeth had started to go, and these lambs were likely to be their last. One pen of in-lamb ewes came next, followed by two pens of sheders which William had planned to introduce into his breeding flock. His three Suffolk rams came last, the first two stated by Arthur to be 'good stock getters' sold to local farmers: the third, and oldest, received no such accolade and was sold to a dealer.

The company then moved out of the sale field to stand round the cattle ring, the combination of straw bales and people making a stockproof circle. Arthur and I made our way to the nearby wooden rostrum which had been brought from the cattle market.

'I told you before I sold the sheep,' said Arthur, 'that William was a good stockman, and you can see the evidence again in these cattle. They're grand animals which the butchers will be very pleased to have in a few months time.'

Bill walked to the loose box housing the first group of cattle, and several farmers formed an alleyway from there to the ring. He opened the door and out ran the five, two-year-old Hereford cross steers; they were good-looking cattle with the white faces characteristic of the breed. Bill followed them into the ring and kept them moving to help the buyers decide on their value. When the sheep were sold the youngest breeding ewes were the most valuable, but the oldest and strongest cattle were offered first as they were nearly ready for slaughter and would make the most money.

Philip Manson, a cattle dealer and wholesale butcher from Nottingham, had called in on his way back from the market of the day, and was interested in buying them to fatten up on his farm, but first he had a question.

'Arthur, why do you always build your ring on high ground and make us look up at the cattle?' he shouted to general amusement. 'You make them look twice as big'.

'Philip,' replied Arthur 'when we have your sale I promise that we'll build the cattle ring on a big mound and have the buyers standing in a pit.' There was more laughter.

'That's all right then,' said Philip with a smile. He had made his point, and the sale continued.

He bought the first five, and then the three Aberdeen Angus heifers, after which both lots were driven back to their boxes. The sale continued with the younger cattle and finished with the calves, all of which were bought by local farmers.

'That concludes the entertainment,' said Arthur 'I'm sure we all wish William a healthy and contented retirement. Thank you all for coming – we shall be pleased to see you in our office in the farmhouse, to settle your accounts.'

We left the rostrum and Arthur gave out vouchers to buyers who had been good customers. These entitled the holder to a drink and sandwich from the bar, to which Arthur and Oliver made their way. I was heading for the office when I was stopped by Denis Hale, a tall stooping man with a melancholy expression, whose name I had used to get me out of trouble when I was selling in the small tools ring.

'Do you remember the water tanker that Fred Black bought?'

I told him that I did recall this large four-wheeled tanker which had once been the back part of a petrol delivery lorry, but was now modified to be towed by a tractor.

'Well transfer it to me will you: I've done a deal with him.'

Fred had bought the tanker in the auction, but agreed that Denis could have it and pay us the sale price instead – Fred would have screwed a good sum out of him before agreeing to this. Denis was a livestock farmer and would use it to cart water to his isolated fields.

'Yes of course,' I said, 'it'll be very useful to you.'

'It's a wonderful buy,' he said, looking furtively over his shoulder to ensure no one was listening 'Fred says it's lined with silver.'

'My word,' I said, trying to look suitably impressed and marvelling that Fred could convince anyone with such a story, although he had picked an easy target in Denis. His neighbours still talked of the time when he went into his local pub and saw a corn merchant who owed him a lot of money

'I'll sort him out this time,' he announced and strode purposefully across the room, holding him in earnest conversation before returning a few minutes later.

'Did you get your money?' they asked.

'No,' said Denis 'he's a bit hard up at the moment so I've lent him £100.'

Before I reached the office I met John Bramwell, who had just arrived.

'Did you get that plough for me?' he asked.

'Yes we did – for £25.'

'Splendid! I've brought my tractor, so I'll pay my bill and take it home.'

There was a queue of farmers in the kitchen waiting to settle their accounts, but Stan and Ella were managing well, so I started to add up the totals on the sale sheets. William would want to know as soon as possible how much the sale had realised. Then I heard John Bramwell's voice from the doorway.

'My plough's gone!' he said.

He and I went out into the sale field and, to my relief, the plough we had bought was still there, and I showed it to him.

'I didn't leave a bid on that pile of junk,' he said furiously 'I wanted the new one. Anyway who would pay £25 for that: it's not worth a tenner.'

I apologised for our mistake, explained that the new plough had been sold to another buyer and asked him to come back to the office with me so I could return his cheque. This he did, making sure every step of the way that I knew his views on the competence of auctioneers in general and our firm in particular. As I was looking for the cheque, Oliver and Arthur came in from the bar and had to listen to his grievances, delivered even more graphically, as he explained that he had rung our sale office that morning to leave his bid, and specified that he wanted the new plough.

Oliver didn't like being spoken to like that, and looked round angrily for someone to blame. That someone was me.

'What on earth did you think you were doing?' he said.

There was no point in defending myself in front of a client, so I simply repeated that a mistake had been made, apologised again and returned his cheque. He was nearly out of the door when he turned round and said

'Who sold that old plough?'

'I did,' said Oliver.

'Well it's strange that when you thought you had a bid of £100, the bidding went as high as £25: everyone knew it was worth £10 at the most. The underbidder must have been a fool!'

He then left the office, but Oliver was determined not to let the matter drop as he realised that the firm would have to pay William the price for which the plough had been 'knocked down', even though it hadn't been sold.

'Who took that phone call from John Bramwell?' he asked.

Stan and Ella said nothing, and all eyes turned to me, before Arthur said quietly, 'I did. I came into the office when Robert and Stan were in the field and Ella was busy, so I took the call. I must have entered his bid against the wrong lot on the sheets.'

This was too much for Oliver who was looking for someone to blame, but wasn't prepared to have a row with his older brother.

There was still a lot to do. The totals of the sales sheets and bills had to be balanced, and some buyers hadn't paid, so we needed to check that we could trust them before their lots could be released. I went to retrieve all the direction signs and came back half an hour later to find that all the bookwork had been done, and that Arthur, Oliver, Ella and Stan were sitting round the kitchen table, which was now cleared of papers, and covered in food. William stood at one end, carving generous slices from joints of ham and beef.

Come and sit down Robert,' he said, 'you've done a first class job.'

I sat down contentedly. It had been a good day.

Chapter 7
Listen to those Budgies

William Hall had lived in Lodge Farmhouse for 40 years, but when he retired he wanted more people around him and bought a cottage in the village.

'I shall never get all our furniture into that little house,' he told me before his farm sale, 'what shall I do with the rest?'

Most farmers had a problem, with their surplus furniture when they retired. Some got rid of it in their dispersal sale, but it never seemed right to me to see beds, tables and chairs standing forlornly on the lawn in front of the farmhouse, while neighbours walked around making sarcastic comments.

'I don't think we should sell it here,' I answered. 'There won't be enough to attract furniture buyers, so I suggest we take it all to our Grantham saleroom.'

'I think you're right,' he said. 'I'll let you know when we've decided what to keep and then leave it to you.'

The building that we used as our furniture saleroom was barely worthy of the title. It was a plain, single-storey structure in the cattle market, built of red brick, with a tiled roof and small-paned iron windows, which until the 1930s had been known as the 'Lincolnshire Horse Repository'.

The firm's furniture expert was Ken Greening, a lovely man with a brilliant mind, but incapable of much physical exertion as he had lost a lung through tuberculosis. He met his wife in a clinic where she was undergoing similar treatment. His father was a gamekeeper who couldn't afford to send him to college, so he studied for his professional exams by postal course, and won a medal for getting the highest marks in the country – a remarkable achievement as he was competing against full-time college students. He applied to Weatherill and White for a job, and Reg took him on, partly out of feelings for a fellow sufferer, because he too had chest problems after being gassed in the First World War. The partners soon realised how fortunate they were to have such talents available to them 'on the cheap' –his physique couldn't withstand stress so he was never likely to press for a partnership in the firm.

He was a voracious reader with a wonderful memory, and became quite an authority on furniture, paintings and silver. He also had a wicked sense of humour which I enjoyed to the full during my articled years, when he was very kind to me and patient with my many mistakes. I learnt more from him than anyone, and he told me something of the history of the firm.

'Weatherill and White was founded in 1860,' he told me during one of our trips to look round a property, 'and its success was built on two main activities – management of agricultural estates and the sale of horses. When the First World War began, horses were in keen demand by the Army for haulage work, and as it continued casualties became so high that prices rose to alarming levels. They made up to 300 guineas in our sales – a guinea being £1 plus 1 shilling (£1.05) – which was the price at that time of a small house in this area. Selling horses was a lucrative business. The owner received the £1, and the auctioneers kept the shilling as their commission, so when that horse made 300 guineas, we earned £15 – a big sum in those days.'

The Lincolnshire Horse Repository was a large rectangular building which had once boasted a handsome rostrum at one end where the auctioneer sat in elevated splendour. There was a bank of tiered seating for the buyers and spectators along one side in front of which the floor was surfaced with old railway sleepers where the horses were 'shown', as the Shires had been at our farm sale. Before and after the sale the horses were held in two rows of wooden stables attached to the Repository.

The partners of Weatherill and White had over the years much preferred accumulating money to spending it, so after the horse sales finished the sleeper floor remained intact, and the former stables were used for storing furniture. The old high rostrum was taken away and replaced by a much more prosaic one halfway down the building opposite the tiers of seating – now used on sale days by buyers of bric-a-brac, rather than horses. Wooden benches stood on the sleeper floor to provide extra seating, but buyers soon discovered that quick sideways movements could result in splinters being lodged in unfortunate places.

During one of our chats Ken told me what to expect on sale days.

'You'll find the first two rows of benches are occupied by the same women at every sale. I think of them as the Grantham equivalent of the tricoteuses during the French Revolution, who knitted beside the guillotine while heads rolled. You'll find they contribute about as much to the auction, as those French women did to the Revolution: they don't come to buy, but to gossip, chatter and have free entertainment. Sales seem to be their main interest in life – each woman sits in the same place every time, and woe betide any stranger who takes their seat: they only stay away if they, or their cat, are really ill.'

Jim Baker, one of the regular buyers, who always stood next to the rostrum, said to me during one sale

'Listen to those old budgies.'

'What do you mean – budgies?' I asked.

'Well, whenever I buy anything they all look at one another and say "cheap – cheap".'

Ken was not physically able to sell by auction and the Weatherill family were not interested in furniture, so I began to sell and became more knowledgeable under his guidance. He told me that the firm's policy was to hold "run of the mill" sales every three weeks, including a few lots worth over £100 to attract good buyers, but keep better items back for antique sales every other month.

'You'll find that selling at antique sales is exciting,' he continued 'although we don't have many lots that make over £500, but auctioning at an ordinary sale can be very tedious. You'll sometimes see a report on the television of a sale at one of the major London auction houses, and there's the auctioneer sitting smugly at the rostrum selling an important painting, and chanting "£1 million - £1.2 million - £1.4 million" in a bored monotone, before selling at £2.2 million to general applause. You'll feel like throwing something at the set when you remember that only that morning you were flogging your guts out trying to get £5 for a sofa.'

At a farm dispersal sale nearly everything belongs to a single vendor, although two or three neighbours may have entered a few lots of surplus machinery. In most antique sales many of the lots are entered by dealers who have bought goods elsewhere and hope to sell at a profit. However, in a general furniture sale of 500 lots there can be easily 60 vendors, ranging from individuals with one or two lots, to the executors of an estate selling the complete contents of a house.

Meeting executors or solicitors to get instructions to sell the entire furnishings of a house was an interesting part of the work, but not without its hazards. When I first went to the firm, Reg Weatherill told me that in this job I would soon discover the meanness of the human spirit, and I often remembered that, particularly when I was asked by relatives to meet them at the home of their recently deceased parent. We were often asked to be there immediately after the funeral, which seemed far too hasty, but some relatives had often travelled a long way, and had no wish to spend a moment longer than necessary with other members of the family, who they rarely met and couldn't stand.

By the time of the funeral the relatives had made it their business to find out what the deceased parent had stipulated in their Will, and usually, apart from a few specific bequests, the estate –including the house and contents – was to be shared equally among the children. In most cases the beneficiaries didn't want the property for themselves, and quickly agreed that it should be sold, with the proceeds divided between them. The contents, however, were a different matter: they occasionally agreed how they should be divided, but this was rare.

Ken or I would be summoned to meet the family and their solicitor at the house, and the bickering would begin.

'Mother always wanted me to have that bureau.'
'No she didn't – she said I could have it.'
'When did she tell you that? You haven't been near her for years!'

'That oil painting of sheep grazing on the moor is one of a pair with the landscape that father left me.'

'No, it's one of a set of three, and I have the other two.'

'That silver tea set's mine. Mother borrowed it five years ago.'

'No it isn't. I remember her bringing it out thirty years ago, when the vicar called.'

And after more of the same, the questions would start.

'What's the bureau worth?'

'About £200,' I would reply.

'And that mahogany chest of drawers?'

'£150.'

'I'll take the bureau as part of my share, and Henry – you can have the chest of drawers.'

'I hate that chest: it smells of mothballs. The bureau has sentimental value for me: I remember sitting there and writing down what I was going to say when I asked my wife to marry me.'

After more muttering from several members of the family that he'd have been a lot happier if he'd not proposed and kept his mouth shut, and as tempers got more frayed, the solicitor would ask for my advice.

'I suggest that all the contents are brought to our salerooms and members of the family can bid for the lots they want at the sale. They needn't pay for them then – we can deduct the bill from their share of the estate.'

The solicitor would say that this seemed reasonable to him, and after further muttering and grumbling, the family would appreciate that they were never going to agree, and this was the sensible thing to do.

After the solicitor had confirmed these instructions, we would begin listing the contents, deciding which lots to save for an antique sale, and what to sell at one of our regular auctions. We didn't sell modern clothing and needed the family's consent to give it to a charity. Fur coats could be valuable, but we didn't handle those either because there might be problems from animal activists – something we could well do without in the middle of a busy auction. The sale of birds' eggs, stuffed animals and birds is subject to stringent regulations, and we preferred not to include them.

Family members that lived nearby usually volunteered eagerly to clear any food and drink from the house. The generation whose estates we dealt with at the time had endured wartime rationing, and often hoarded stocks of tinned food, which were divided with alacrity between the relatives.

Arthur said to me one day, soon after I came to the firm 'Relatives of the late Miss Smythe are calling tomorrow to pick up the keys to her house, because they want to take away any food, drink and perishable items. She's the last survivor of a local brewing family. Will you go and help them, and then bring the keys back.'

The relatives arrived in a large car, and I drove with them to her imposing Victorian house. They didn't speak to me, but went straight to the cupboards in the spacious kitchen and pantry, removing all the full bottles and unopened tins and packets, which they curtly told me to take out to the car: the half empty tins and bottles were left on the kitchen table. After an exhaustive search they left in their heavily laden vehicle, regretting there was now no room to give me a lift back to the office. They told me to put the rubbish in the dustbins and said as they drove away...

'Help yourself to anything that's left.'

'Thanks a bunch,' I thought, having watched their painstaking hunt through the house, and not fancying part tins of custard powder and mouldy remnants of tomato ketchup. I had a last look round the house after clearing up, and as I was closing a cupboard in the pantry noticed something that had escaped even their eagle eyes. Behind it was a second cupboard, and when I opened this, there were three tins of Baxters Game Soup, two bottles of good claret, two tins of peaches and a box of fancy biscuits. In view of their last instructions and arrogant attitude, I had no qualms in taking them home – and very nice they were too!

When we listed the contents of a house we had to label everything carefully, so we knew who the items belonged to when they were mixed with other lots in the saleroom. The goods have to be valued, because an estimate of the tota worth of the estate has to be given to the Inland Revenue before the executors can implement the Will. After the sale the actual proceeds will supersede this provisional estimate, so the valuation has to be conservative to avoid an excessive tax assessment, but not so low as to appear ridiculous when the sale results are known.

If the deceased had a car we asked the local main dealer to give us a valuation based on the mileage and year of manufacture. If it was valuable, we sold it privately or to the dealer, if not we included it in one of our auctions, where the general public seemed keen to buy old cars at a good price.

Ken's knowledge did not extend to jewellery, so if an estate included any rings, brooches, earrings or necklaces, we called in Peter Christopher, a local jeweller. I took the lots down to him and we sat in the office behind his shop with the jewellery in a pile on his desk, while we chatted.

'That's an interesting motor' I said to him once, pointing to an oil painting of a shiny red racing car on the wall behind his desk.

'You must know I'm a car fanatic,' he said. 'That's my Ferrari – it came second in the Italian Mille Miglia race, and... oh, excuse me, there's someone in the shop.'

He left, but was back in two minutes. I suspect that customers were an unwanted intrusion into our conversation, and he hadn't tried hard to sell them anything.

'Now where was I – yes, I've driven it many times in vintage races – Spa, Silverstone, Monza. Did I tell you about the time when a wheel came off on the first bend…,' and off he went on another long and entertaining tale.

Eventually we got down to business and he would examine each item, making careful notes before deciding on the value, which was the price he was prepared to pay. He had a thriving trade in antique jewellery and often didn't charge a fee for his valuation, providing he had prior notice of the auction so he could come and bid for the better pieces.

We were often asked to go out and value individual items of furniture, paintings, china or silver, so the owner could decide whether to include them in one of our sales. These visits were more often depressing, than a cause for celebration. Ken said to me one morning 'I've got a trip into the country for you this afternoon; I can't go because I've got another appointment. Will you go and see Mrs Cousins at this address; she wants a valuation of a painting she's been left in Granny's Will.'

My hopes were high when I drove into the village close to Grantham and found a delightful house with extensive grounds, and I remained optimistic, even after realising that her dogs enjoyed complete freedom inside it. However, any lingering hopes of a missing masterpiece were dispelled when I saw the reason for my visit.

'I'm very sorry Mrs Cousins, but this isn't an original oil painting; it's a print from a well-known one called "The Monarch of the Glen" by Landseer. It's difficult to distinguish between a painting and a print,' I said, trying to be tactful 'but it's worth very little I'm afraid.' It was also very faded.

She was a delightful person and very apologetic for getting me out on a 'wild goose chase' as she called it. She insisted that I stay for coffee and a biscuit, so we went into the kitchen where we continued our conversation, while I fought off the moist attentions of various dogs, pulled dog hairs off my biscuit, jacket and trousers, and sipped my dog-flavoured coffee. I left the house thinking I had earned nothing, but not knowing how profitable it would prove to be.

A few months later I had a telephone call from Ron Bellman.

'I'm instructed by the executors of a woman who lived at 4 Church Close, Great Napton. The house is rented so I just need to know if the contents are worth anything: I have the keys here. The relatives are all in the north of England and haven't been in contact for years.'

'Thanks very much, Ron.'

'Don't thank me,' he said, 'I don't think there's any money for you in this one.'

I went out to Great Napton and found the property, which was a modern semi-detached bungalow, part of a small, warden-controlled housing development built for elderly people by the local council: I feared that Ron's assessment of the earnings from this job was right. There was little of note in the bungalow, except – unbelievably - a set of eight mahogany dining chairs, including two carvers – with the lower rail in the back of each one carved in the form of a rope. This design became popular after our naval victory at Trafalgar in 1808, so these chairs dated back over 150 years. They almost filled the sitting room, and there was hardly any space for the old lady to have any other furniture in this tiny bungalow, but she was obviously determined to keep these precious chairs at all costs: perhaps an ancestor had been a seafaring man – even fought in that epic battle. The set made a big price in one of our antique sales, and the buyer – who was a good client and lived in Great Napton – asked where they had come from. He couldn't believe that such gems had been preserved in such modest surroundings 'on his doorstep'.

After this sale Ken came into my office one morning and said:

'Have a look at this,' handing me a letter. It was from the Treasury Solicitor in London, written in the stilted prose so beloved by civil servants. It was headed:

'In the matter of John William Henry Smithson deceased'
...and continued...

'We have to inform you that the above named person of Field Cottage, Little Walton near Grantham died intestate on September 2nd, 1963. All investigations and publicity to find a living relative have proved fruitless, and in accordance with the relevant Acts of Parliament and statutory regulations, his estate reverts to the Crown.'

'The Treasury Solicitor proposes to instruct Weatherill and White to act in this matter, subject to a satisfactory response to this letter. Will you provide an estimate of your fee and expenses, for undertaking the following:

1. Inspecting the property, which we understand to be freehold, and providing us with a valuation on an open market basis with vacant possession: a location plan is enclosed.

2. Preparing a schedule of the contents of the property, and advising whether, in your opinion, the likely sale proceeds will exceed the costs of removal.

3. The sale of the property by public auction

    I beg gentlemen, to remain your obedient servant
Nigel H. Clutterbuck
Assistant Solicitor'

Ken replied to this missive, and ten days later we were told to go ahead. The small detached cottage wasn't easy to find, as it stood in the middle of a paddock outside the village. There was no vehicular access, so we followed a footpath across the field into the little garden, unlocked the back door and went into the kitchen. It took a while for our eyes to adjust to the darkness, and longer to realise what we were looking at. We could see nothing but a mass of cardboard boxes, stacked one above the other, almost to the ceiling. We managed to squeeze between them into the living room – where the situation was just the same!

The small sitting room was also piled high, and when we went upstairs there were still more boxes, and it seemed that they were all full. The late Mr Smithson obviously had a mania for buying new goods from newspaper advertisements: perhaps a visit from the postman eased his loneliness. It seemed that after each box had been delivered, he simply opened it, looked at the contents, and then added it to the piles. We could see electric kettles and percolators, magnifying glasses, garden gnomes, secateurs, commemorative plates, foot baths, slippers and sets of books. Preparing a full list was going to take a long time, so we advised the Treasury solicitor of the situation, and told him we were confident that the sale value of the goods would exceed the removal costs.

About a week later we heard again from Nigel who, before begging to remain our servant for a second time, instructed us to proceed with the sale of the cottage and contents, so I contacted John Ward and asked him to bring the goods into our salerooms. He ran a small removal business in Grantham and we used him for all our haulage. The business had been started by his late father Fred, who delivered vegetables around the town in a horse and cart, but unfortunately was a little too fond of alcohol, which once brought him before the local court.

The newspaper account of the proceedings related that Fred, having finished his deliveries on a market day and drunk far too much at lunchtime, clambered with difficulty on to his empty cart to go home. The horse heard him singing merrily and realised that she was the only one of the pair that would remember the way. When they reached a crossroads, Fred stood up and put his arm out to indicate he was turning right: the horse knew better and turned left, whereupon Fred fell off the cart, landing at the feet of a watching policeman. The magistrates, when considering the prosecution for being drunk in charge of a horse and cart, had difficulty in concealing their mirth when listening to the policeman's evidence, and imposed no penalty, but warned Fred severely as to his future conduct.

I went out to the cottage after John had removed the first load of boxes from the ground floor, and was surprised that I could now see a Georgian mahogany pedestal card table, a Victorian desk known as a Davenport and an oak coffin stool in the sitting room. It was also possible to see a display cabinet in the living room containing several nice pieces of china, silver and plated ware. We kept these better lots for an antique auction, and sold the boxed goods in one of our regular sales.

Nigel received a substantial cheque!

Goss Cottages

Chapter 8

An Expensive Pram

Some firms, like ours also act as bailiffs, and follow the orders of a Court by removing goods from people or businesses that can't pay their debts, and then selling them by auction. Administrators usually instruct these firms to sell the assets of businesses that have gone into receivership, and they deal with a wide variety of goods, selling the contents of a furniture warehouse one week, machinery from a welding workshop the next, and then the contents of a shoe shop. We weren't in this business – I couldn't imagine any of the Weatherills as a bailiff – but we did have special sales from time to time, usually of collections built up by an individual over a long period. Ken said to me one morning, 'We're off to Sleaford this afternoon to see a client's collection.'

'What sort of collection?'

'Wait and see.'

Later that day we pulled up outside our Sleaford office, and Ken led the way to a nearby shop.

'Good afternoon George,' he said, 'I've brought Robert with me, so let's have a look.'

We went into the stockroom at the back, where three large tables were covered with pieces of china.

'Come and see some Goss ware, Robert,' said Ken. 'You're the expert George, but I hope you won't mind if I tell him something about these pieces – hopefully he'll be selling them soon.'

'Be my guest Ken, I'm only sorry I've got to sell them, but we're retiring from the shop and I shan't have anywhere to keep them.'

'William Goss was a manufacturer of china in the early part of this century,' said Ken, 'and he mainly made small white china models of buildings or objects carrying the name and coat of arms of a British town or city – perhaps a lighthouse with "Plymouth" printed on it. There are a great many of those here, but since they sold well as souvenirs a lot were made, and apart from a few rare ones, they're of modest value – say £4 to £15 each.'

George nodded his agreement.

'But at the far end of this table, is the important part of this collection. William Goss also made a number of small coloured china models of buildings, such as "Burns Cottage", "Shakespeare's House", and "Anne Hathaway's Cottage". They all have the name on the bottom and are very attractive, but as you can see they're only the size of a small box of matches, and the factory made different quantities of each one, depending on the

55

number they thought they could sell. They're all very collectable, but in some cases only a few were produced, and taking breakages into account, these have become scarce and valuable. George has twenty different model cottages, and only about thirty five were made, so we'll have to do some research.'

We listed the white commemorative pieces of china and the model cottages and then went back to the office to consult our reference books. We found that some of his cottages were rare examples, and agreed with George that we would produce an illustrated catalogue and hold a special sale within one of our antique auctions. We advertised in the local and national press, and in the Goss collectors' magazine – known as 'The Goshawk'. There was widespread interest, and specialist dealers came to the auction from all over the country, resulting in some astonishing prices.

As one of the dealers was leaving the sale he said to me, 'I go all round the country buying Goss china in the finest salerooms, and today I've seen one of his cottages make a world record price of £400 – in Grantham Cattle Market!'

Miss Cornwall was the last member of a family that had run a chemists shop in Grantham for several generations, and before her retirement she asked us to go and see her.

'This is an Aladdin's cave,' said Ken as we looked at the racks of small mahogany drawers with glass knobs and chemical abbreviations like "Mag Sulph" on the front, and the blue glass bottles with matching stoppers and similar inscriptions. They reminded me of my father's shop before he modernised the interior in the late 1950s, like many chemists.

'But these are the stars of the show,' continued Ken. 'I've admired them since I was a boy – look here...'

He indicated about thirty, pale biscuit-coloured Lambeth stoneware drug jars, with embossed coats of arms. They would have been a feature in any museum, but she had approached the local one, and they didn't seem interested. We held a 'sale within a sale' featuring the Lambeth jars and the other equipment, which aroused a lot of interest locally and nationally, the jars making around £60 each.

There was nothing special about today's sale however; it was one of our regular auctions, which we held every three weeks to dispose of the mundane items that had accumulated in our salerooms. I learnt that, just like farm sales, these auctions had to follow their own unchanging pattern, and although they were always referred to as 'furniture sales', they included a wide variety of goods. The first lots to be sold were displayed in the yard – mowers, garden equipment, bicycles, ladders, prams, timber and tools. Then came the miscellaneous items in the saleroom, which were crammed into boxes under the tables – paperbacks, pottery, records, souvenirs from seaside holidays and kitchenware. The next lots were set out on the tables and included china, glass, books, metalware, ornaments and bric-a-brac. Prints and pictures would follow, and the sale ended with the furniture, which was laid out at one end of the building.

At our antique sales there would be good garden ornaments outside, and the lots on the tables would include china figures, silver, plated ware and jewellery: we produced a lotted catalogue for these sales but not for the ordinary ones. All our auctions were held on a Wednesday morning, starting at 11am, with viewing the day before and on the morning of sale.

On the Monday before a sale the goods were lotted by Bill and Alf, which involved sticking small adhesive paper numbers on to lots that had hard surfaces, and on to labels tied to such items as rugs or soft furnishings. I then wrote up the sale sheets, entering a description of each lot and the identification number of the vendor. The outside lots, which had been stored in the former stables, were taken out into the yard early on Tuesday morning and the sale was ready to be viewed.

Auctions seem to fascinate people, and a constant stream came to our view days. Some came to every auction, some to look at a particular lot they had seen advertised, and some to look at their neighbour's possessions, which they knew were included in the sale. We always had a good attendance of bric-a-brac dealers, often women who wanted a rewarding hobby while their husbands were out at work, or retired people who hoped to convert a pastime into a source of income. They bought from auctions and sold in shops, market stalls or country fetes, making little money, but kept going in the hope of finding something of real value among the general run of mediocrity. Occasionally they did, but in pursuit of this 'holy grail' spent endless hours examining in minute detail the contents of every box and tray of china, glass and linen in each sale. It was our job, of course, to ensure that we didn't sell anything valuable without appreciating its worth.

Some years ago Alf brought me a small box that had been left at our salerooms by people from a local church who were asking for advice. In it were two circular decorative pottery items that had been donated to one of their jumble sales, and I took them to Ken.

'They're pot lids,' he said. 'They were made about 100 years ago as covers for pots of hair grease, and handsomely decorated to make the product look attractive. The pots were usually broken or thrown away, but the lids kept as decorative ornaments, and they became collected over the years, the value depending on the condition and rarity of the design. Both of these are in good order, but the scene on this one's called "The Village Wedding" and I know it's very common and not worth a lot.'

'The other one's much more interesting: it's decorated with a portrait of the nineteenth century statesman Sir Robert Peel; you can see from this why people said that his smile was like moonlight glinting off the silver handles of a coffin! One of the London auction houses had a special sale of pot lids last month – I've got the catalogue somewhere, if I can find it... yes here it is, let's have a look. Well, bless my soul!'

'What is it?' I asked.

'Here's a lid with a portrait of Sir Robert Peel, and it made £200. I'll ring them up', which he promptly did.

'Is his right hand holding a scroll of parchment, or resting on a cushion?' asked their expert.

'He's holding a scroll,' said Ken.

'Oh dear,' came the reply, 'that one's very common – worth about £10. It's the one with his hand on the cushion that's rare, and made £200.'

We told the church people about this and included the two lids in our next auction, realising a useful £20 for them – certainly better than selling them in their jumble sale!

When we were talking about the pot lids, Ken said, 'You'll find that the value of chattels is very dependent on the fashion of the day: pot lids are all the rage at the moment, but two years ago you could hardly give them away. Everyone wanted fairings then – and before you ask, they're small naïve pottery figures that were given away as prizes at fairgrounds: the most common one shows a couple getting into bed, with the caption "Last into bed put out the light". Buyers paid a lot of money for them but the market's collapsed now. They'll have to wait a few years before they're in fashion again.

'The value of antiques varies in the same way; oak furniture will sell well for a few years then go out of favour and Victorian mahogany furniture will be "in". The value of silver tea services and coffee pots varies wildly from year to year, depending on the scrap value.'

We were ready to start today's sale: Anne was in her mobile van, doing a brisk trade in bacon sandwiches, cups of tea and coffee. We suspected that our customers wouldn't mind which auctioneer sold at our sales, but only Anne would do as caterer. Stan rang his bell and the small company walked across the yard to a bundle of garden tools, where I started the auction with our current articled pupil, Henry, as my clerk. He was the son of a farmer client, and we feared that he was only showing an interest in our profession because he thought it would be easier than farming.

His father had built up a large farming enterprise through attention to detail, and a forthright attitude to any problem. The main topic of conversation in the cattle market recently had been about a group of travellers who had parked their caravans on a green lane that ran through one of his farms. In view of previous problems, he wasn't happy about this, but went to see them to say they were welcome, providing they did no damage, and in particular kept their dogs under control, as he had sheep grazing in fields nearby.

All was well for a couple of weeks but then, when he went shepherding one morning, he found that five of his ewes had been worried by dogs; three were dead and the other two injured so badly they had to be put down. In his fury he lifted two of the carcasses onto his broad shoulders and strode through the middle of their camp to show the damage their dogs had done, shouting that if they were still there the next day he would drive a tractor straight through the lot of them. He was completely out of order, but the travellers took him seriously, left that night and set up camp in another green lane about five miles away.

Unfortunately for them this lane ran through another of his farms, and this time he said nothing, but arrived in a tractor with a front end loader and began to move straw bales, leaning them against the other side of the hedges on each side of the lane.

'What are you doing?' they asked.

'I'm going to set light to these bales in 24 hours,' he told them.

Fortunately for him, they moved on again.

Henry, like his father, was inclined to give us the benefit of his opinion on any topic that arose. He had been the clerk at only two auctions, when he said to Stan...

'Selling by auction is a piece of cake.'

'You think you could do it, do you?' asked Stan.

'No problem. I could do it tomorrow.'

Stan told me about this, and after talking it over with Bill and Alf, we decided to stage a one-act drama at this sale to put him right. I gave the usual pre-sale announcements – that auctioneers' commission would be payable in addition to the purchase price, that no lots could be removed without a receipted bill, and that all lots in the yard must be removed immediately, as tomorrow was cattle market day. I then said, 'Right Henry, over to you,' and handed him my stick, while Stan took the sale sheets.

He recovered quickly from the initial shock and started well, making £3 for the tools, and satisfactory prices for the next few items. His confidence, never fragile, grew as he continued down the row, until he arrived at Lot 23 – a pram. We had received no bid for it in the last two sales and the vendor had left the area, so it was bound for the council tip, but Henry didn't know that. Nor did he know that we had persuaded three dealers, a large elderly man, a young man and a forceful woman to take part in our little play.

'May I say £1 for the pram?' said Henry.

'Yes,' said the large man.

'£5,' said the youth.

'£10,' rejoined the former.

'£20.'

'£30.'

'£50.'

The two 'bidders' were now glaring fiercely at one another, and all conversation stopped as everyone stood in amazement looking at this pram that was making so much money. Henry was becoming more and more bewildered as this worthless lot attracted such bidding.

'£60,' continued the large man.

'£80,' replied his younger opponent, and so it continued until the bidding got to £250. Then the large man (right on cue) shouted angrily to Henry,

'I don't think this young man can afford to pay this kind of money.'

'I'm not bidding for myself,' came the reply. 'Edith Stacey of Alford Street told me to buy it, whatever it made.'

'She told me to buy it as well,' said the other, 'this is ridiculous.'

'I'm certainly not going to stay here and be made a fool of,' said the youth, and the two men stormed off.

'Well!' said Henry who had been listening open-mouthed to the exchange, and was so confused that he hadn't banged his stick down to confirm a sale to either of them, 'we'll move on to the next lot then.'

But – as they say at the opera – the drama isn't over till the fat lady sings, and the forceful woman stepped forward.

'I entered that pram in this sale. You had a bid of £250 and you let it go. I want your confirmation NOW that I shall be paid that amount in full. My husband is the Chief of Police'

I had been watching (and admiring) the drama from afar, and strolled over at this stage to ask Henry if everything was all right! After listening to his embarrassed explanation I assured the woman that the matter would be settled to her satisfaction, and asked Henry to finish selling the outside lots, which he did, but not in the same confident manner. I think he eventually found out what we had done, but by then he had decided that his father's job wasn't so bad after all, and enrolled in an agricultural college.

The auction continued in the salerooms, with Jim Baker leaning on the rostrum beside me, and the tricoteuses all in position chattering animatedly about the price of prams nowadays. I sold the miscellaneous items heaped in boxes beneath the tables, (we never used the word 'rubbish', but it often came to mind). Then came the better lots of china, glass, brass, copper and general goods, which were displayed on trays – not the sheep hurdle variety, but the circular tin ones seen in public houses. Each tray was held up by Bill or Alf so that the contents could be appraised by the company as they were sold. For some reason glassware always sold well at these auctions: an articled pupil at another firm told me that on sale days he augmented his meagre wages by buying a few dozen wine glasses from Woolworths, and dividing them into lots for auction. He reckoned to double his money!

A routine furniture auction is not a gripping spectacle, so it's essential that the auctioneer sells quickly to keep the company's attention. It was quite warm in the saleroom, and I remembered another piece of advice from Reg Weatherill.

'If people are bidding slowly, knock one or two lots down while they're still making up their minds. That'll liven them up.'

Some of the bric-a-brac dealers were taking an age to decide whether to bid, and I realised it was time to put his advice into practice. The bidding for a tray of ornaments had reached £5, and a woman was wondering whether to bid again, when I banged my stick down and announced…

'£5 – Jim Baker.'

'I was going to bid again,' she said.

'Sorry madam, you'll have to be quicker!'

I repeated the exercise with another slow bidder, and suddenly everyone was on the edge of their seats bidding furiously. Jim Baker chuckled – 'that's the way, keep them at it,' he said.

He could afford to be on my side when I was trying to speed things up, because he had his own private way of bidding. He had his hand behind the boarded façade of the rostrum and pressure on my right knee meant a bid from him: I would have found sales much more exciting if Jim had been female!

The auction continued with two sets of encyclopaedias, copper kettles, a warming pan, pewter tankards, a brass companion set, an oak book trough and a chandelier with matching wall lights. Next came some rugs, rolled up in a bundle.

'What have you got there?' I asked.

'Two sheepskin and two goatskin rugs,' said Bill.

'Here's the next lot, ladies and gentlemen,' I announced 'four skin rugs.'

The tricoteuses didn't titter this time. They guffawed, and so did everyone else.

'Can you rephrase that?' said Jim.

I tried to carry on as though nothing had happened, but my bright red face told another story!

The pictures and prints were displayed on the end wall of the saleroom: there were a few sets of hunting prints faded by exposure to sunlight, several amateur oil paintings, two modern embroidered samplers and three framed maps of Lincolnshire that looked old but weren't.

William Hall had come to see his furniture sold near the end of the auction. We had kept back a roll-top bureau and an oak chest for an antique sale, but here he had a pine dresser, a reproduction refectory table, a mahogany chest of drawers and some stick-back kitchen chairs. The main buyer in this part of the sale was Joe Flight, an American who had relatives in south Lincolnshire and realised during one of his visits that reproduction furniture didn't make much at auctions here, but was sought after back home. He started a business buying these lots, filling a container and shipping it to the States where he would rent space in various cities and advertise 'British Period Furniture for Sale'.

William's furniture sold well and he said...

'I'm glad I took your advice and brought it here.'

'Well I'm pleased that I was right and you had a good sale. It doesn't always happen!'

I walked across the yard after the sale, past the cattle pens, to the small brick building that we used as an office for the cattle market and saleroom. A queue of buyers was waiting for their bills, which were being prepared by George and Ella, while a coal fire burned dully in the grate in a forlorn attempt to ward off the late afternoon chill. The buyers were soon dealt with and I looked through the bills as I had done at the farm sale: there were no problems and I was about to leave when Ella said:

'There was a telephone call for you from a Mrs Cousins. I told her you were busy in the saleroom, and she asked me to let you know that she has told Lady George you are a good auctioneer, and you may be hearing from her.'

I remembered the pleasant, doggy hour I had spent with Mrs Cousins, and her faded print of 'The Monarch of the Glen'. It was good of her to recommend me to a friend, but as I walked back to Oak House I doubted if it would lead to anything, and thought no more about it.

Lambeth drug Jar

Chapter 9

Send the Meat on Later

Ken was very interested in local history, and this became a passion of mine. His main interest was in shards of ancient British pottery that had been discovered in various villages, and how they helped to identify which tribes had lived there. When we were travelling to a job and he held forth on this topic, I tended to switch off and admire the scenery, but I did listen to him once when he was talking about the history of the Grantham area.

'The ancient Britons chose wisely,' he said, 'when they created their settlement here by the river, with hills rising to the north, east and south, and only the one level access from the Vale of Belvoir to the west. Many centuries later the daily London to Edinburgh stagecoach ran through the town and it was recognised that the hill on its northern side was the steepest incline between the two cities. The higher ground to the east and south of the town is heathland, which is now farmed intensively, but in the early nineteenth century before the Enclosure Acts, the only food it produced was meat from vast rabbit warrens. The heath was so hazardous for travellers in the eighteenth century that an inland lighthouse – a tower with a large brazier on the top – was built about thirty miles north east of the town, to guide them on their journey. The roads were simply rough tracks, and rife with highwaymen.'

This didn't tell me much about the agricultural history of the district, and why there was a cattle market in the town. However, Arthur took me with him one day to take particulars of a farm we had for sale, and as we left the town we drove past a number of large plain brick buildings with many floors and small iron-framed windows. They looked like Victorian prisons, but obviously weren't, so I asked him about them.

'When the heathland around Grantham was ploughed,' he said, 'the soil was stony and easily worked, and farmers called it "light", whereas clay land was "heavy" and difficult to cultivate. The heath grew good crops of barley, particularly the varieties from which malt is made, so Grantham became a centre for its manufacture before it was moved on to the traditional brewery towns to make beer. Those massive buildings are maltings, and were built in the nineteenth century: barley was spread on the floor, turned frequently, and then heated in a kiln to produce the malt. The industrialists who built them realised that the more floors they could cram into each malting, the more barley they could process, so the height of each floor was restricted to around 1.5 metres, and generations of people worked there with bent backs. Perhaps your comparison with a prison wasn't so far wrong.'

'So most of the land around Grantham was arable,' I said. 'How did the cattle market get established?'

'There was still a lot of heavy land around the town,' replied Arthur 'particularly to the north, and much of this was down to grass. Although the ploughed heathland was ideal for malting barley, the crop couldn't be grown every year, as disease would spread and yields would drop. It was essential to rotate the crops on a three- to five-year cycle, and sheep would be grazed in the intervening years, either on temporary grassland, or on root tops after the main crop had been cleared.

'Before artificial fertiliser was produced, land was manured by the dung from sheep and cattle. The sheep consolidated the light land with their hooves as well as manuring it, and this was thought to be very important in producing a good crop of barley the following year. In fact this compaction was so highly regarded that the heathland became known as "sheep and barley land", and the part played by the sheep was referred to as "the golden hoof". As a result store sheep were brought here from other parts of the country to be fattened, and considerable numbers were kept in the area. This was before the days of rapid transport, so when they were mature they had to be sold locally.'

'So that's why our cattle market started,' I said.

'Well for centuries sheep and cattle were sold at country fairs, or at weekly sales in the unmade streets of towns: you can imagine the filth and chaos this caused. Many shopkeepers had entrance doors with upper and lower halves, so the bottom part could be closed to keep animals out. The larger villages had periodic fairs, but the only survivor in this area is at Corby Glen. When the railways came in the 1870s, they brought tremendous change. Cattle markets were built in towns close to the new railway stations so that buyers could move livestock all over the country. Grantham followed the general pattern, and was particularly fortunate as its station was on the main London to Edinburgh line.'

A stream called the Mow Beck ran through the land that was developed for the cattle market, ans was enclosed within a long culvert. After heavy rain a mass of rubbish sometimes blocked the entrance to this, so that our sheep pens flooded – as illustrated by Terry Shelbourne in a cartoon in the Grantham Journal.

As I worked in the cattle market during my articled years I learnt that many neighbouring markets sold store cattle and sheep, as we had done at William's sale, and fatstock – which is livestock for slaughter. Since there were so many fat sheep in the area, and also a lot of cattle being fattened, our market established a good reputation as a "fatstock market", but over the years the firm didn't make enough effort to attract farmers to sell their store animals as well.

Although the nearby railway was invaluable to the wholesale buyers for taking their livestock away to the cities, very few animals were brought in this way. For the first fifty years of the cattle market's existence there was almost no mechanised road transport, and livestock was brought in from a very limited area. Cattle and sheep were driven there, pigs arrived in horse-drawn carts, and horses were ridden or led to the Repository.

The main line railway passed on a high embankment beside our market. Soon after I came to the firm, I got to the market one Thursday morning with another clerk and we noticed that the ground had slipped severely at the top of the embankment leaving one of the rails exposed, but inter-city express trains were still hurtling by. We telephoned the Permanent Way Inspector at the local station, but it was at least an hour before four men in yellow jackets made a leisurely appearance. We watched with disbelief as one of them checked the stability of the rail beside the crumbling edge of the embankment by pressing gingerly on it with his foot, which seemed an inadequate test compared with the weight of a freight train. However, it was soon apparent that drivers had been told to go slowly along this stretch, and a few days later heavy metal shuttering was built into the embankment to stop any further erosion.

Grantham cattle market lay near the centre of the town, about a quarter of a mile from the railway station, with two entrance gates from Dysart Road. By the 1960s the amount of traffic on the roads meant that it was too dangerous to drive livestock into or out of the market, so some farmers brought their animals in small trucks or in trailers towed behind tractors, but most came by haulier's lorry and left in the same way. One firm "Hameys" was dominant, and on a Thursday their green lorries seemed to form a constant procession into and out of the market.

A large building built of brick and stone extended along the road frontage, housing the covered cattle pens, and behind this was a series of open pens divided by iron fences. At one end of the cattle building stood a tall wooden structure housing the sale ring, which was enclosed on three sides by tiered wooden seating, like a small amphitheatre. Fat cattle were brought individually from the covered pens on to a large weighbridge, which stood beside the ring and had an overhead dial to record their weight.

After each animal had walked on to the weighbridge, a gate was closed behind it and the weight shown on the dial was announced by the auctioneer, who sat at a high wooden rostrum overlooking the sale ring. The clerk, sitting beside him, recorded this and then the front gate of the weighbridge was opened releasing the beast into the ring: a drover kept it moving round so the buyers could make their assessment and bid accordingly. When the auctioneer's hammer fell to confirm a sale, the animal was let out of the ring into the open pens. The drover had two short sticks with cloth wrapped round the ends, one dipped in red paint and the other in blue. As each beast left the ring he dabbed on the appropriate paint mark for each buyer, so the cattle could be easily sorted before being taken away. Phil Manson's cattle had a blue mark between the shoulders, while Sid Howitt's had a red dab on the top of the tail.

I had a friend, Jim, who worked for a similar firm in a nearby town, and often met him for a chat, when we would compare notes about how our respective markets were run. I was astonished at the difference.

'My boss sells the cattle: he's very informal and likes everyone to call him Eric.'

'Good grief,' I said, 'the senior partner of our firm sells the beast as well, but if any farmer or buyer called him Reg, I'd expect a bolt of lightning to strike him dead! He's Mr Weatherill to everybody.'

'Does he let the buyers stand inside the ring while he's selling?'

'He certainly does not. He wouldn't start the auction if they were!'

'Eric likes vendors to stand on the rostrum beside him while he's selling their cattle: he doesn't mind the odd dig in the ribs when they want to move the price on a bit, but he'd much rather they gave him a reserve price. Is Reg the same?'

'No, he's not! He won't have anyone but the clerk beside him, and doesn't allow vendors to bid for their own cattle. He doesn't encourage reserve prices either, because he thinks it's a slight on his skill as an auctioneer, and in any case he regards it as a privilege for any farmer to sell his cattle at Grantham market.'

'Is he good at "trotting"? Eric's a master at it.'

It's common practice for a cattle market auctioneer to bid himself without authorisation from the owner, if he thinks that an animal isn't making a satisfactory price. This is known as 'trotting', and can be easily done at a furniture sale where most buyers are inexperienced and don't realise what's happening. In a cattle market there are only a few buyers, many of whom go to five auctions a week, and they know immediately if an auctioneer is bidding. They grudgingly accept that he has a duty to sell the animals at a reasonable price, and providing he's conducting the auction well, and doesn't overdo it, they tolerate an occasional bid.

'Reg wouldn't contemplate it, for the same reason that he won't do any house selling. He considers himself to be a land agent and a professional person, not one that soils his hands with commercial transactions. He believes that an auctioneer is there to oversee a trading situation, but certainly not take part; it just wouldn't occur to him to bid himself.'

On another occasion Jim and I were discussing bidding techniques.

'Have you realised,' he said, 'that if a member of the public stood behind the auctioneer at a furniture sale he would see nearly all the bids, because most people call out, gesture, or nod their heads,'

'I'd never thought about it, but yes, that's true,' I replied, 'but they'd find it very different at a cattle auction.'

'That's right,' said Jim 'he or she would wonder where on earth the bids were coming from, because cattle buyers don't reckon to use unnecessary energy. One buyer at our market stands by the ring resting his hands on the top rail, and bids by lifting one finger about an inch (13mm) into the air. Others bid by winking, twitching their mouth, and sometimes by putting their tongue out!'

'Yes, we get most of those,' I said, 'it shows how important it is for an auctioneer to know his clients. You've got to know the type of beast that each buyer wants, and who's likely to bid when the next animal comes into the ring. We did have one buyer from the south Midlands who was very useful to us because his mouth twitched all the time. We could always take it as a bid and knock a beast down to him: if he denied bidding we just apologised and sold it again.'

In those pre-metric days cattle were sold per hundredweight (cwt); there were twenty of these to the ton. I saw a letter in a national newspaper from a woman who said that she had attended a cattle auction for the first time, and saw to her surprise that the bidding for a good beef animal had only reached £9. This seemed very cheap to her so she put in a bid of £10, which won the day. She went to the pay office with two £5 notes to settle her account, only to find to her horror that the figure she had bid was the price per cwt, and her bill for this 10 cwt animal was £100. She explained her mistake to the auctioneer, and said in the letter that he was quite nice about it and agreed to cancel the sale. I have no doubt that what he actually said when she'd gone was very different!

The two principal buyers in our market were Philip Manson and Sid Howitt, both successful wholesale butchers in the same city, but very different men. They were both ruthless, but Philip was quiet and charming with it, whereas Sid was foul mouthed and aggressive. They were business competitors, but realised that since they both attended the same markets every week it would be stupid to bid against each other. Their object was to buy cattle as cheaply as possible, not drive the price up by competing.

Like the tricoteuses at furniture sales, cattle buyers always occupied the same places around the sale ring, and these two took the dominant positions. Philip stood opposite the weighbridge, just outside the gate through which the cattle left the ring, and had the first view of a beast as it walked onto the bridge. Sid stood beside the bridge and was the only buyer who could reach through its bars to feel the flesh of an animal and assess the quality of the meat. The other wholesalers, dealers and local butchers stood around the ring or sat on the tiered seating.

Dealers who who bought cattle and sheep and then sold them on to wholesale butchers, gave us most problems over the years. Sometimes their clients would take delivery of the livestock and then go bankrupt without paying, or the dealers would receive payment and then decide to go bankrupt before paying us. I was talking about this with Jim who had firm views as to the financial viability of cattle markets.

'Running a market,' he said, 'is like going out into the street, finding two or three really doubtful people and lending them £100,000 each.' I could see his point.

Grantham had several shops run by individual butchers and nearly all of them bought livestock from our market, but Philip and Sid made this as difficult as they could. Most of them had enough customers to sell the meat from one beast every week, and each favoured a different type of animal: Fred Forest always bought a heifer weighing around 8cwt, but Colin Hyder only purchased well fleshed steers weighing over 10 cwt. The auctioneer knew this and would look for a bid from one of them when a suitable beast came into the ring. Philip and Sid knew it as well, and would bid vigorously against them, making sure they paid a high price. They wanted local butchers to buy from them, not direct from the market.

Although the two of them loved to 'dish it out' like this, they hated to be on the receiving end, and Sid showed it more than Phil. If he started the bidding for a beast and a local butcher bid against him, he soon got angry, and pointed remarks would be made about the other's parentage.

Sid also made his feelings known to vendors who sent in cattle that should have been fat enough for slaughter, but weren't. I remember him shouting out as a very lean animal came into the ring...

'Who the hell brought that in?'

'It's mine,' said a farmer from the tiered seating.

'Will you send the meat on later!' said Sid.

Years ago Fred Forest's father, Albert, had worked for another butcher, but told him one day that he was leaving to open his own shop.

'But Albert' said his employer, 'how will you manage?' You've never bought a beast in your life: you won't know how much to pay.'

'When I'm using my own money I shall b..... soon learn,' he replied.

The great joy of working in the cattle market was meeting the characters that came into the place. There was always a slight atmosphere of conflict between buyers and auctioneers, because the former were there to buy livestock as cheaply as possible, while we had a duty to make the best price for our vendors. The market was a commercial forum and a place of business for buyers, but it was more than that for farmers: a trip to the market was a morning away from their daily, often monotonous toil. It was a chance to listen to the latest gossip, talk about commodity prices, and 'set the world right' with their friends. Farmers spend a lot of time working on their own, during which they form firm opinions on most topics – which they are prepared to defend at length, despite any inconvenient facts to the contrary.

At our market on a Thursday they learnt how Farmer A was recovering from his illness, and how Farmer B's marriage was faring – 'I never thought it would last'. Every scrap of gossip spread fast, the main culprits being the salesmen of seed, fertiliser and feedingstuffs, who came every week to meet their existing clients and cultivate new ones. The most successful were those that could pass on the best news – in confidence of course. After a furtive glance over his shoulder one would say to a client...

'I heard the other day that XYZ Ltd (usually a competing firm of agricultural merchants) is in financial trouble. Mind you, I'm not one to gossip, and it may not be true.'

"D'you think the Auctioneer will allow us anything for shrinkage"
Flood in Grantham Cattle Market by Terry Shelbourne

Of all the characters that came into the market, Peter Surtees was the one who stood out. He came from a family of shopkeepers, and served with distinction throughout the Second World War, but after that experience resolved to never again accept an order from anyone. He became a farmer and found that he had a natural aptitude for tending livestock, and for training horses and their riders, but when he took more land he concentrated on his farming and the horses had to go. He had a flock of pedigree sheep which won many prizes, and his ram lambs were in keen demand throughout the area. He also raised quality pigs and exceptional turkeys.

He was a fine raconteur with colourful language, featuring one short Anglo Saxon word used in many forms. The conversational hub of the market was Anne's tea van, which had a canopy on one side providing minimal cover in wet weather. Farmers and buyers would gather here for her tea, coffee and bacon butties, and to complain about current price levels. I remember Peter reminiscing one Thursday about the Army advancing through France in 1944. His platoon of tanks was in the vanguard, and in the evening the men were told to dig a trench and put their sleeping bag in it for the night. He continued

'For the first few nights there was no way the newcomers to our platoon were going to do this – after an exhausting day they weren't going to dig a f… … trench – they'd sooner sleep on the f…… ground. Then some Messerchmitts flew over one evening and shelled us: that night they dug like f…… moles.'

He drove into the market one Thursday in his old Rover car, and on the front passenger seat sat an old ewe looking ahead through the windscreen, like an aged and bewildered aunt – which she probably was. After he had let her out through the passenger door I said to him 'You're giving her a good ride.'

'Well,' he said, 'if I didn't have the f…… sheep, I couldn't afford the f…… car, so the f… er's entitled to ride in comfort.'

After his wartime experiences he hated all officials with a passion. A neighbour told me that when Peter was ploughing an outlying field about 300 metres off the public road, a man in a dark suit made his way with difficulty across the furrows to the tractor.

'Can you tell me where Mr Surtees lives?' he asked.

'Yes,' said Peter, 'go back to the road, turn left and his house is the first you'll come to on the right. It's about half a mile.'

The hapless official made his way back to the road across the ploughed field, his shoes collecting more and more mud. Half an hour later he was back.

'Why didn't you tell me that you were Mr Surtees?'

'Because you never f…… asked me!'

The sheep grader certainly represented officialdom, and Peter was rarely happy with his decisions. On one occasion the grader grasped the back of one of his sheep as usual, to assess the depth of body fat. However, he was slow to make a decision and repeated the exercise three times on the same animal. This was too much for Peter.

'You're supposed to grade the f…… sheep' he shouted, 'not give them a f… … medical!'

Chapter 10

Here's a Grand Pig

I had sold at farm sales for a couple of years, and would have liked to auction on a Thursday in the cattle market, but the partners told me I wouldn't do this regularly for a long time. When I began my articles, my Thursday job was with the sheep, and although I helped out occasionally with the cattle, I did this for many years, and loved it. Before my first market Stan was deputed to 'show me the ropes', and took me to the area where the sheep were sorted and the rows of sale pens, laid out parallel with the railway embankment.

He explained, 'The sheep are unloaded into the sorting pens, where they are "drawn" into suitable lots. "Drawing" doesn't mean sitting behind an easel with a pencil, but sorting into groups of similar appearance, size and quality: white-faced lambs are separated from black-faced, well-fleshed animals from those that are leaner, and big ones from little. It's critical that this is done well if the sheep are to make a good price. Buyers come here looking for a particular kind of animal for themselves or their clients – possibly lean, black-faced sheep weighing up to 41kg. For them to be interested in a pen of lambs they must all be similar: if the animals are very different they won't bid.

'After they're drawn into suitable lots, usually of ten animals, each group is driven out of the sorting pens onto the weighbridge, to be examined by a grader, employed by the Ministry of Agriculture. The government pays a subsidy on the sale of every beast, sheep and pig, and it's the grader's job to certify that each animal is good enough to qualify for this payment. The amount of the subsidy isn't based on a sheep's liveweight, but on the "estimated dressed carcass weight", which means that having weighed the sheep, the grader has to assess what the weight of the carcass will be. He calculates the killing out percentage of well-fleshed animals at around 50% of their liveweight, but less for leaner sheep. If the animal is very bony or too fat, the grader will reject it, and no subsidy will be paid.

'The grader's decisions are controversial because they affect the amount the owner is paid, so heated arguments often take place. He's usually a man with butchering experience who goes to several markets each week, and is quite capable of standing up for himself – if a farmer is completely unreasonable, he can refuse to grade any of his sheep, which means no subsidy. After they've been weighed and graded, they're released from the weighbridge and driven to the next empty pen.'

This was my job for the first couple of years, and is not as easy as it sounds. The pen can be 50-60 metres from the weighbridge and the sheep can be driven there easily if the alleyways are clear, but farmers invariably gather there to talk, and complain about the many things that are wrong with the world at the time. When the sheep see these people standing in their way, they stop, get confused, and try to turn back. If they succeed in getting past the person who is driving them, they get mixed up with the group that's following, which makes everyone angry, except the gossiping farmers who caused the trouble in the first place.

One of our regular sheep vendors was the farm manager of a large estate just outside Grantham, including a fine stately home set in a park which boasted a golf course. This was grazed by a herd of deer, and a flock of sheep made up of two breeds – Cluns which were white with black noses and black patches in the fleece, and Welsh Mountains which were small and entirely black. Neither breed was chosen for its economic merit, but because they looked good in the park, and Mr Bellamy the eighty-year-old shepherd did his rounds each morning to ensure that all was well. I was lucky to be there early one spring morning to see his pony and trap emerging mysteriously from the mist, and it was a sight I shall never forget.

When I first encountered the Welsh Mountain sheep in the market, I was driving them towards their pen with no problem, until they came to the inevitable farmers chatting in the alleyway. They turned, and I discovered that they were not only small and black, but extremely agile, as they leapt past my ears and charged through my legs.

'The little devils must have fed on golf balls!' I thought, as they jumped and bounced all round the market with me in hot pursuit.

Our peak period for selling sheep was between January and March, because many local farmers and dealers bought lambs in the autumn from northern England and Scotland, and brought them home to be fattened. They took some to the fens in eastern Lincolnshire, where they were fed on the remnants of cabbages and cauliflowers that remained in the fields after the crop had been harvested. Others were fed on the leaves of sugar beet, left on the ground after the crop had gone: it was essential that these were allowed to wilt for several days, as they could be poisonous if eaten fresh. Kale and fodder beet were also grown to provide winter feed, and although store sheep were usually quite small when they arrived, they grew rapidly on this diet and made a good price early in the New Year, when the supply from grassland areas had finished.

In the 1960s we sold up to 2000 sheep a week in our peak period, but this number diminished until there was a resurgence in the popularity of the market in the 1990s. One famous day I sold around 3500 sheep – which gave rise to another Terry Shelbourne cartoon.

After I had driven the sheep to their pens for about two years, Oliver said to me one Wednesday 'As you know, Harold writes down the weights of the sheep, but he's given his notice, so we'd like you to do that from tomorrow.'

This was another job that wasn't as simple as it looked. I was now promoted to a small wooden hut beside the weighbridge, where I had to write down the weights of the sheep in duplicate on official forms supplied by the Ministry of Agriculture. The top copy was taken away by the grader and enclosed with his report to the regional office, and we used the second copy as a sale sheet. The hut had an open hatch at the front overlooking the weighbridge, and behind this was a shelf used as a writing desk: the wind and rain always seemed to blow directly into the hut, playing havoc with the flimsy Ministry forms and the carbon papers between them.

The wind and rain were not the only problems! I had to count the number of sheep on the weighbridge, record their actual weight, and the estimated dressed carcass weight assessed by the grader. It was also part of my job to provide each vendor with a card giving the pen numbers and weights of his sheep, which he would use to record the sale prices. I needed to concentrate hard to avoid making mistakes, but unfortunately I was rarely alone in the hut. There were usually two or three people with me, one of whom would be the vendor of the animals being graded...

'You're being a bit harsh with them, grader,' he would say. 'The butcher who bought my sheep last week said they killed out real well.'

'He won't say that this week,' the grader would reply.

Then the door would open, the resulting gale scattering all my paperwork.

'Have you got my card?'

'Yes, here it is,' and the door would close, only to reopen after a few seconds for someone else to walk in.

Then Granville Hart would walk onto the bridge, quite oblivious of the fact that he was stopping any other sheep from being weighed.

'How is it,' he would shout, with his face as red as a beetroot, 'that my neighbour got here later than me, yet his sheep have been penned before mine?'

I had learnt a little about client management in my two years.

'But Mr Hart, you complained last week that your sheep were too early in the sale, so I thought that's what you'd want.'

The auctions started with the pigs at 10.15am, followed at 11 o'clock by the sheep, with Oliver as auctioneer, and he made his entrance around 10.30am when we'd been busy for three hours. The first pen to be sold was decided by lottery: we kept a bag of numbered wooden beads and a farmer was asked to draw one before the sale, to determine where we started. This was not a popular job, and after Granville's recent outburst I asked him to do it, which he did with some reluctance. Mercifully the one he drew out meant his sheep were in the middle of the auction, so another 'explosion' was averted.

After the draw Oliver went to the first pen, and I followed ringing the inevitable brass bell. During the sale I had to call out the name of each vendor as we came to his sheep, and the weight of the animals in the pen; after they were sold I recorded the sale price and the name of the buyer. This needed more concentration than was necessary at a farm dispersal sale, because the pace was much quicker, with around 120 lots sold in an hour. At a farm sale we wrote down the information on our own sale sheets, which were small and made of thick paper, but in the market we had to use the government-approved sheets which were large, and as flimsy as tissue paper. They were a nightmare in the rain, when I either had to shelter under an umbrella, or cover them with layers of blotting paper. It was a cold job in winter, and mittens were essential.

In many markets the sheep auctioneer and his clerk walk along a board above the pens, and sell the animals from there. This must be much easier for the clerk than it was for me as I walked with Oliver in the alleyway between the pens. I had to stay close to him so that he could hear me when I shouted out the weights, and wouldn't make a mistake when writing down the buyer's name and the price paid. Several pens included an odd sheep that had been rejected by the grader as too fat or too lean, and this had to be sold separately. I was in big trouble if I didn't tell Oliver that there was one of these in the next pen.

There were more difficulties to be faced! The gossiping farmers who had been obstructive when the sheep were being driven to their pens, were still there in the alleyways. They hadn't yet solved the problems facing the farming industry, and saw no reason to move just because an auction was taking place. Most of the buyers stood by the pens so they could lean over the rails and feel the backs of the sheep, to judge the quality of the meat. Some stood facing Oliver in the alleyway on the far side of the pens, but many preferred to be beside him, so that they could bid by digging a finger into his ribs, while giving the impression they weren't interested. The area around the auctioneer was very congested, with buyers, chatting farmers, and vendors trying to write down the selling prices of their sheep.

The alleyways were also used by people simply trying to get from one end of the market to the other, and when they were added to the melee, the space in which the auction was being held became even more crowded. I was in the middle of all this, trying hard to push my way through the company, hear what was going on, record the outcome of the auction, and not get bawled out by an irascible auctioneer. It was like trying to write poetry in the middle of a rugby scrum!

Pigs are not my favourite animals! Cattle and sheep can be driven quite easily to their allotted places in the market, if there is no third party interference. Pigs cannot – probably because they are more intelligent. If a sheep runs towards you, it can be caught by its fleece, and persuaded to go in the required direction. A beast can generally be turned back by waving one's arms and making encouraging noises, but a pig keeps coming! When it hits you there is nothing to get hold of, and it usually escapes between your legs. This is probably the origin of the saying used in Lincolnshire describing a bandy-legged man – 'He'd never stop a pig in an entry!' (An 'entry' is the local name for the passage between the back yards of terraced houses.)

Stan Rowan liked pigs, and was the clerk in charge of them: he told me on that first day how the auction was organised.

'They're sorted and sold in a similar way to the sheep. We have a set of metal numbers mounted on rods, which are dipped into red paint; a lot number is stencilled onto the back of each pig in the collecting area, and then they're weighed and driven to their pen, where there are usually no more than three in each lot. As with the sheep, the Ministry grader had to decide whether the animals qualified for the Government subsidy. They're sometimes rejected on quality grounds, because they're too fat, and sometimes because a female is "in pig" – meaning pregnant.'

The Government grader George, who looked after the sheep and pigs, was a big burly man, a former butcher who stood no nonsense. He never felt the cold and put it down to constantly rinsing his hands in cold water during his years in the shop. His reminiscences were very entertaining, and I remember him telling me...

'I once examined a female Welsh pig that had been brought into the market for sale: this breed has particularly large, floppy ears, which fall forward over its face. I rejected it because I thought it was in pig, and when the owner came he was furious. He swore and declared that the pig couldn't be pregnant – it had never even seen a boar. I said I believed him, because its ears covered its eyes!'

Arthur was the pig auctioneer, but some years later when he was on holiday, I was told to sell them. My knowledge of pigs was minimal, but I tried my best to get good prices by exaggerating the qualities of every animal I was about to sell. This didn't go down too well with the buyers.

'Here's a grand pig,' I announced before selling a particularly large and unattractive animal.

'Robert,' said Ian Base, one of our main buyers 'you wouldn't know a good pig if it fell on you.'

I think he was right!

The Christmas Show was the highlight of the cattle market year. Most markets called these annual events 'Fatstock Shows', but we changed the name of ours to the 'Grantham Christmas Prime Stock Show'. This was because most housewives didn't want much fat on their joints, and farmers were trying to satisfy their customers' requirements by producing ever leaner livestock. Our Show was organised by a committee of farmers who decided what classes of livestock there would be, and then helped to run proceedings on the day. There were usually six cattle classes – three for steers and three for heifers, depending on their weight. The sheep had light and heavyweight classes for continental and British breeds, while the pig classes catered for single animals and pairs of differing weights. All animals were judged on their suitability for butchers.

Another of the committee's tasks was to decide which three buyers should be asked to judge the various classes. It was an honour to be approached, but the accolade was mitigated by the farmers' expectation that, having chosen the Champions, the judges would then buy them at an inflated price.

Training cattle for a Show is a long and arduous process. A beast has to be docile, and allow its handler to lead it up and down in front of the judge and crowds of onlookers which requires endless patience and hundreds of hours of practice. The animal must learn to tolerate continual brushing and grooming so that it will appear in peak condition on the big day. The results of these efforts are spectacular when the magnificent animals are led into the straw-covered ring to be judged. The winner and runner-up from each class are awarded rosettes, and go forward to form a final group from which the judge selects a Champion and Reserve Champion. He has to be a strong character as frequent comments can be heard from the watching farmers:

'He'll never pick that one.'

'The black steer limps'

'That black heifer's got a wonderful back end. The Hereford's far too gutty.'

Having made his choice the judge steps forward to shake the hand of the successful owner, and hands him the Champion's rosette.

Our committee did not encourage 'pot hunters' – farmers or dealers who go from Show to Show winning prizes, and are not seen again until the following Christmas: they insisted that entrants must be regular vendors at the market. Furthermore the Champion beast had to be sold in the market, and not taken on to another Show. Despite these restrictions the standard of entries in our Show was always very high, because we had a nucleus of clients who took immense pride in their animals and were keen to 'do battle' with each other every year, although there was little financial reward. The winner of each class would receive about £10, while the owner of the Champion beast would get £50, a higher selling price and a silver cup, which he held for a year. The farmers prepared and showed their livestock to demonstrate excellence in their work, to be acknowledged as 'good livestock men', and to share a sense of achievement with their family and employees.

When the judging had finished, the photographer from the Grantham Journal would take a picture of the Champion and its proud owner, after which the animal was examined closely by the farming fraternity.

'Why on earth did he pick that one? The black steer's far better.'

'I've seen him judge before. He always picks a heifer.'

'It's a disgrace. I've got four beast better than that at home.'

After all the chatter, the Champion was auctioned first, with the owner usually putting some £10 notes on its back to encourage the bidding, before it was bought by the judge at a figure well above its commercial value. If he was a local butcher this was an onerous financial burden, but it was good publicity when he displayed the rosette in his shop window, giving the impression that he bought nothing but the highest quality beef throughout the year. His name would also feature in our Show Report in the local newspaper beneath a photograph of the Champion.

I was talking with Jim about the value of this publicity to a shopkeeper, and he said, 'All his customers want a joint from the Champion, and he's able to charge a bit extra for the privilege. It's remarkable how many joints come from that one beast!'

The Christmas Show was the one market of the year when Philip and Sid adopted a low profile. Neither would agree to be a judge, partly because their expertise would be open to general scrutiny, but more importantly because they would have to buy the Champion for a substantial figure, which was contrary to their creed of buying everything at the lowest possible price. They hardly ever bought even a class winner, as this would mean paying a bit extra.

The cattle were the 'glamour animals' of the Show, but the sheep and pig classes were contested just as keenly. Over 200 sheep were entered with the main classes being judged in pens of three, and the owners spent many hours trimming their fleeces to make their backs look broad and flat. One regular entrant was a bachelor farmer for whom sheep were an obsession, and as he proudly brought in his entries each year, the other owners would look at them in admiration, groan quietly and say to one another…

'William's done it again!'

He always wore a flat cap, beneath which was a good fringe of hair. It became a much anticipated feature of the Show to see him go into the cattle ring, as he usually did, to collect the cup for the Champion sheep, and take off his cap. Only then was it revealed that above this luxuriant fringe he was completely bald. I heard one farmer say, 'No wonder his head's gone like that – it never sees daylight. He spends all night and all day with his sheep and his cap's never off!'

Many sheep farmers liked to support the Show, but not go to the trouble of preparing their livestock, so we had a special class for five untrimmed animals.

Competition in the pig section was fierce, with a mysterious white powder applied liberally to the entries, in an attempt to improve their looks. Strange white flat sticks, like paddles, were used to usher them into their straw-lined pens.

The Show was keenly anticipated, well attended and much talked about afterwards – particularly, the merits of the various entries, and whether the Champion beast was as good as the winners in other markets. The partners of the firm entertained the judges, stewards, committee and leading farmers to lunch afterwards at a local hotel. The staff was not invited, so we adjourned to a nearby pub to celebrate another successful event, a 'curtain raiser' to Christmas festivities.

I remember speaking to one of our regular clients at the first market in the New Year:

'Did you have a good Christmas?' I asked.

'Yes,' he said, 'I love Christmas – it's a shame it only comes once a year. Jesus should have had a brother!'

Corby Fair by Joe Flauto

Chapter 11

The Innermost Mystery of the Profession

Between October and January Reg Weatherill and his sons spent most of their time shooting. Many agricultural valuers did the same, and it was generally accepted in the profession that any contentious jobs in the winter should be postponed until February at the earliest. During the rest of the year, however, the partners undertook a wide variety of agricultural work, including sales and lettings of land, farm dispersal sales, tenantright and stocktaking valuations, and the management of landed estates.

One March morning during my second year at the firm I had been out on a mortgage valuation with Ken, and we were walking back into the office as Arthur was going out.

'I want you to come with me tomorrow, Robert,' he said, 'it's time you came on a tenantright valuation. We'll set off at 9 o'clock.'

'Thank you,' I said, 'I'll be ready.'

'My word,' said Ken, as we climbed the stairs. He didn't do agricultural work and was sceptical of the social pretensions of those who did. 'You're going to be baptised into the innermost mystery of the profession.'

I learnt over the years that he was right, and this is just how a tenantright valuation is regarded by agricultural valuers. It is an enigma to which they are the sole guardians, a secret rite jealously guarded by the practitioners and conducted in a mystic language. The concept is simple. When a tenant leaves his farm, usually at the end of his tenancy, he needs to realise the assets he has accumulated over the years. His machinery is sold at a dispersal sale, and his livestock either there or in the open market. His grain, and produce, such as hay, straw and roots, are sold to merchants or other farmers in the usual way. However, although his tenancy is coming to an end, he is obliged under the terms of his lease, and in accordance with good farming practice, to cultivate and sow the land as though he were staying. He will not be there to realise the benefit of this and is entitled to receive payment from the incoming tenant. This asset, together with any improvements he has made to the farm, is known as 'tenantright'.

A tenantright valuation is not just an assessment of the payment due to an outgoer. A tenant undertakes in his lease to keep the land in good condition and free from weeds: he must also maintain hedges, fences, ditches and gates in good order and, depending on the terms of his tenancy agreement, paint and repair the farmhouse and buildings. If he doesn't do this, it is obviously unfair for the liability to be passed on to a new tenant, and since the landlord is rarely prepared to put his hand in his pocket, the cost of doing the work must be assessed. This figure is known as 'dilapidations' and will be deducted from the tenantright payment due to the outgoing tenant. The incomer will then start his tenancy with similar maintenance obligations to those imposed on his predecessor.

The next morning I was ready to leave the office promptly with Arthur. He was a stickler for punctuality, and if I wasn't there on time, he would go without me.

'We're going to Hillside Farm, Stackby,' he said. 'The village is about ten miles south of Grantham; it's a strange place – no heart to it, just a few scattered farmhouses. This farm and most of the land in the parish belongs to the Fairfield Estate, which Oliver manages.'

I knew that we were the land agents for this large estate, which was managed from an office in Fairfield village, where Oliver lived in one of their houses.

Fred Coke was the outgoing tenant of the 300-acre farm; he and his wife were elderly and childless, and had decided to retire. There had been many applications for the tenancy of the farm and Oliver decided to let it to David Tims, a young man who rented a smallholding near Lincoln, and had recently married the daughter of one of our farmer clients. He asked Arthur to act for him in the tenantright valuation, which was a wise move, as Weatherill and White would be the agents for his landlord, and it was sensible to 'get in their good books' as soon as possible. Tenants on the estate who didn't use the firm for their professional work, and didn't sell their livestock in Grantham market, always suspected that they were at the bottom of the list when they needed a new farm building. Fred Coke had instructed Eric Shiller, a Leicestershire valuer of long experience, to act for him.

David Tims drove with us to Hillside Farm on this dank, cheerless day, and Mrs Coke welcomed us into the farmhouse, where Fred and Eric were already sitting at the kitchen table.

'Good morning Eric, morning Fred,' said Arthur, 'I've brought Robert Brownlow with me to hold my hand. I think you know David Tims.'

'Good morning Arthur. Nice to meet you again David, and you young man,' said Eric as we shook hands. Fred stayed at the table, looking worried: this was an important day for him.

'There didn't seem any point in Oliver coming with me to represent the landlords,' said Arthur, 'I'll look after their interests, as well as David's.'

The landlord's agent usually came to a tenantright valuation to satisfy himself that the property was being properly maintained.

'I'm sure you will!' said Eric with feeling.

Both valuers produced their notebooks and put them on the table. Weatherill and White prided themselves on theirs, which looked like bibles and were nearly as thick, with glossy black covers having the name of the firm and a serial number written in gold on the front. A copy of the Tenancy Agreement lay on the table, as this was the contract between Fred Coke and the landlord, setting out the terms on which the farm had been let. These terms were based on a standard pattern imposed by statute, and didn't vary much from one farm to another. The Agreement also included a plan of the holding and a Schedule of all the fields, with their individual areas.

The two valuers met seven or eight times a year representing different clients, and had been good friends for a long time, but they had to be careful not to show it, as both clients wanted to see them fighting hard to achieve the best possible settlement. They knew the area intimately, and in particular that the land at Hillside Farm had been quarried for ironstone about 15 years ago. The soil had been removed during this process, and replaced afterwards, but the land would take many years to regain its original fertility. It was a sheep and barley farm – the land wasn't good enough for potatoes or sugar beet.

After a cup of coffee, Eric Shiller started proceedings by referring to the Agreement on the table.

'The first entry on the Schedule is – "House and Buildings – 1.342 acres".'

Both valuers wrote this down in their notebooks. There was no claim to be made at this stage so it was a pointless exercise, but a necessary part of the ritual. The Schedule must be followed! He moved on to the second entry

' "Home Paddock –1.817 acres": have you done any work there Fred?'

This was a small grass field next to the farmstead, which years ago would have been grazed by the cow that provided milk for the family.

'I've chain harrowed it,' said Fred.

They both wrote down the name and area of the field on the left-hand page of their book, and underneath that, 'Ch. H' to indicate the work that had been done. The right-hand page was sacrosanct at this stage – it would be used to enter dilapidation claims when they walked round the farm. The process continued.

'Next on the Schedule is "Near Pasture – 9.648 acres",' said Eric.

'That's arable now,' said Fred.

'Did you get the landlord's permission to plough it?' asked Arthur.

This was necessary under the terms of the Agreement.

'Yes,' said Fred.

'When?'

'Five years ago.'

'In writing?' asked Arthur.

'No, I asked Oliver in the market.'

'I don't think that's good enough,' said Arthur 'I shall have to speak to him about that.'

'What crop have you sown there?' asked Eric.

'Winter wheat,' replied Fred.

'What crops did you grow before that?' asked Arthur.

'Let me see – wheat again last year and a one-year ley before that.'

This was important because three successive wheat crops were thought to exhaust the fertility of the land, and if Fred had done this he would have incurred a dilapidations charge. A one-year ley is a mixture of grass and clover that is either mown for hay or grazed, and then ploughed up.

'What cultivations have you done since the crop was harvested?' asked Eric.

'I ploughed it,' said Fred 'then disc harrowed twice, medium harrowed once, rolled it, combine drilled, and then light harrowed.'

Arthur wrote these cultivations down, using the obligatory abbreviations that had been handed down for generations within the firm:

'T.Plo' (meaning tractor ploughed). This abbreviation was designed to indicate that a tractor had been used to pull the plough instead of a horse. No horse had pulled a plough commercially in the Grantham area for at least twenty five years, but this was not a sufficient reason for the firm to change its ways.

'2 Disc H'

'H' (Harrowed)

'C Roll' (Cambridge rolled)

'C Drill' (A combine drill applies seed and fertiliser to the field at the same time)

'SH' (seed harrowed – a light harrow after the drill)

'What seed did you use?' asked Eric.

'One and a half hundredweight of Capelle to the acre.'

'And how much fertiliser to the acre?'

'Two hundredweight of ICI number one.'

All this information was entered in the valuers' books.

Eric continued 'The next field is Middle Close – 12.642 acres.'

'That's fallows,' said Fred.

'Bare fallows?'

'Yes.'

This meant that the field was being given a rest this year, with no crop being grown. It was a condition of most tenancy agreements that a proportion of the farm should be fallowed each year. Sometimes a green crop, such as mustard, was grown and then ploughed in to benefit the land – this was known as a 'bastard fallow'. Although no crop was being grown, it was important that the field was cultivated while being rested, so that weeds didn't grow.

'What work have you done?' asked Eric.

'I ploughed it, disced it twice and medium harrowed once,' was the reply.

This was also written down.

'Oh, and I mucked it,' came the afterthought.

This meant that manure from the cattle yards had been spread there after the animals were let out in the spring. This mixture of straw and dung added 'body' to the land, as well as providing beneficial nutrients. It was the custom in Lincolnshire to pay outgoers for the work done in spreading the manure, but not for the commodity itself, as happened in other counties.

'Was the manure carted straight out from the yard?' asked Arthur.

'No, from a hill,' replied Fred.

Manure could be taken from a cattle yard to the field in two ways. It could be loaded on to a spreader which would be towed directly to the field by a tractor: this has a flat bed with chains that move the manure slowly to the back, where revolving tines propel it with some force over a considerable area. Farmers who are aggrieved at a large rates bill from the local Council, or an unreasonable account sent by the Electricity Board, have been known to tow one of these fully loaded machines at speed past the relevant offices, giving them a coating not anticipated by their architects!

The other method of emptying a cattle yard was to cart the manure out and heap it in a convenient place to form a 'muck hill', which would be spread later. Fred had done this, and was entitled to be paid for carting it to the hill, and from there to the field.

'How many loads to the acre?' asked Eric.

'About twelve.'

Arthur entered in his book the time-honoured abbreviations describing this work:

'12 loads FYM p.a. 2C&S' (12 loads of farmyard manure per acre, twice carted and spread).

Our client David Tims had said nothing so far, and I was beginning to wonder if he understood what was going on, but I needn't have worried.

'There's a bit of twitch in that field,' he said.

Twitch is a variety of grass with vigorous roots that spread in all directions, and becomes a major threat to crops if left unchecked. One of the objects of leaving a field fallow and cultivating the bare land, is to eradicate weeds, and if some twitch was still growing Fred would have to pay for its removal.

'We'll have a look at that when we walk round the farm,' said Eric.

Arthur noted David's comment in his book, while Fred frowned, indicating his displeasure at the very suggestion that there might be any weeds on the farm.

The next field was 'Top Close – 9.862 acres'.

'That's Tenant's Pasture,' said Fred. 'I've chain harrowed it and put on 2 cwt of Nitro Chalk to the acre.'

The field was shown as arable in the Tenancy Agreement but Fred had sown it two years ago with a mixture of grass and clover to provide pasture for his sheep and cattle. He intended this to provide good grazing for several years and was entitled to be paid for it on leaving the farm. The figure would need to be agreed between the valuers, depending on the quality of the crop.

The ritual continued until all the fields listed in the Tenancy Agreement had been entered in the valuers' books, with details of the cultivations done, the growing crops and the seed and fertiliser used.

'Now let's have a look at the fertiliser bills,' said Eric.

These were the accounts received for fertilisers that had been applied to the land: they were piled in an untidy heap on the table.

'I haven't got the bill yet from Hunters for the 5 tons of Nitro Chalk that went on the grassland last week,' said Fred.

'Send it to me when you can,' said Eric 'and then I'll pass it on to you, Arthur.'

The tonnage and cost of the fertiliser used during the last six months was noted from the accounts, and written down by both valuers. Arthur told me to check when I got back to the office that the tonnage from the bills tallied with the amounts applied to the various fields.

Fertilisers are put on to the land to add nitrogen, phosphate and potash, essential nutrients for the growing of good crops. Scientists have played into the hands of agricultural valuers by decreeing that each of these constituents benefits the land for a different length of time: nitrogen lasts for only one year, potash two years and phosphate for three years. The monetary value of these residual values has been assessed by the scientists, and an outgoer is entitled to be compensated accordingly. Most fertilisers are compound, containing differing percentages of the three nutrients, which has given agricultural valuers the opportunity to prepare tables, exclusive to the profession of course, showing the value of every ton of each proprietary fertiliser applied over a three-year period.

Eric took the fertiliser bills so that he could prepare a schedule of these residual values calculating the payment due to his client, and then forward it to us: the accounts received for seed corn were also noted. A list was prepared of the feedingstuffs fed to the livestock over the last two years, because in passing through the animals the food is converted to manure, which then improves the land. The friendly scientists have also calculated a monetary value to this benefit, providing another arrow to the agricultural valuer's secret quiver.

'Is there any hay or straw to be valued?' asked Arthur.

'Yes, there are two bays of hay in the Dutch Barn,' replied Fred.

'Have you sold any hay during the last year?' asked Arthur.

A tenant was not permitted to sell hay off the holding during the last year of his tenancy: it had to be valued over to the incomer.

'No.'

David Tims made another of his occasional contributions.

You sold a trailer load in the market two Thursdays ago.'

'Oh yes, I'd forgotten that.'

This was entered in the books, after which Mrs Coke made a welcome entry with cups of tea and a large home-made cake.

'That's good timing,' said Eric 'we're finished here and ready to walk round the farm.'

'Let's have a look round the house first,' said Arthur.

He needed to check that Fred and his wife had kept the inside of the house in good condition, as they must do under the terms of the tenancy. We finished our tea and most of the excellent cake before going to look at the scullery, and then down three steps to the dairy which was at a lower level to keep it cool. This had a floor of small red quarry tiles, and a narrow raised brick platform, known as a 'thrall', around three walls. In past years when a pig was killed, this was used for storing the many by-products provided by this versatile animal. A large wooden tray called a cratch, used for salting the bacon, still stood there, and the hooks in the ceiling were once used for hanging hams.

Another door from the kitchen led to the front hall with its handsome mahogany staircase: at the far end was the main front door to the house which was rarely used, and on each side of this lay the sitting and dining rooms. The latter had a large oak dining table with eight matching chairs, while the sitting room contained a mock leather three-piece suite, a sideboard and a china cabinet, but it was obvious that both rooms were only used on special occasions. Upstairs were four bedrooms, the main one having a carpet and an oak bedstead with matching furniture, but the other three were sparsely furnished having only iron bedsteads, minimal furniture, and simple peg rugs on the floor. As I walked around one of these beds my foot clanked loudly against the chamber pot lurking beneath, to the general amusement of everyone but myself.

The only bathroom boasted an iron bath standing impressively on its four feet, and a matching basin, but the toilet occupied a room on its own, as it should, for it was a masterpiece of its kind. The toilet bowl bore the name of its maker Thomas Crapper, and was ornately decorated with birds and flowers in blue and white, the whole surmounted by a highly polished mahogany seat and cover. The cistern, which was also cased in mahogany, stood proudly beneath the ceiling, with a long chain hanging down: it was all I could do to leave the room without pulling it, just for the thrill of seeing this magnificent contraption in action.

We finished our tour back in the kitchen. Fred and his wife had spent their lives working hard on the farm, but could not have enjoyed much comfort in the house, apart from this room which was its welcoming hub and heart.

'I'm satisfied with the way the house has been kept, Eric,' said Arthur. 'It's still a foul day outside, and it's going to be a wrench leaving this warm kitchen, but we'd better go and have a look round the farm. You take the notebook, Robert: you can do the writing from now on.'

Chapter 12

Forty Loads of Manure

We put on our wet weather gear and went out into the yard to start our walk around the farm. Arthur noticed immediately that the farmhouse garden was knee deep in weeds. Fred should have kept it in reasonable order, but not many farmers are interested in gardening – a spade seems very small when you've been ploughing all day!

'That needs digging,' said Arthur turning to me, 'note it down.'

Fred had walked quickly across the yard hoping we wouldn't see the garden, but since that hadn't worked he suddenly realised he had a claim to make.

'I put up that interwoven fencing dividing it from the yard,' he said.

'That's a tenant's improvement,' said Eric, 'you're entitled to be paid for that.'

Arthur muttered that Fred had only done it to hide the weeds, but told me to make a note. We walked on across the concreted yard, passing a range of brick buildings.

'There's grass growing in those gutters,' said Arthur 'write that down Robert.'

Fred should have cleaned them out and would have to pay for the work to be done.

'I've made some improvements to that wagon hovel,' said Fred.

The building had been a two-bay open-fronted cart shed with a central brick pillar, but now boasted a pair of corrugated iron sliding doors.

'When did you do that?' asked Eric.

'About two years ago.'

'That's another improvement the landlord should pay for.'

'Note it down,' Arthur told me, 'and I'll ask Oliver if he gave permission for the work to be done.'

Fred pointed to a diesel tank in the corner of the yard.

'David asked me not to include that tank in my sale. He said he'd like to buy it and the diesel as part of this valuation.'

David confirmed this, so we needed to establish how much fuel it contained. Fred found a step ladder, and I clambered on to the top with a long stick and 'dipped' it. We agreed the contents at 150 gallons and this was duly entered in the notebooks.

We continued into the stackyard and paused beside the Dutch Barn that covered the stack of hay bales Fred had mentioned earlier.

'Is this meadow hay?' asked Arthur.

It would be worth less if it came from a long-established meadow rather than a newly sown ley.

'No, it's from the new seeds in Top Pasture,' replied Fred indignantly.

Each valuer took a handful and smelt it. Good hay should smell sweet and fresh, but the gesture was performed more to impress their respective clients than in a quest for knowledge.

'Count the bales, Robert,' said Arthur.

I looked at the stack with mounting panic, then realised what I had to do. I counted the number of bales at ground level, then the number of layers, and multiplied one by the other to arrive at a total of 912 bales. Arthur opened his bag with a flourish and pulled out a large spring balance – a narrow brass cylinder with weight markings, beneath which was a short chain with a hook on the end. He threaded the hook beneath the strings of a bale and lifted both balance and bale into the air. The reading showed a weight of 45lbs (20.4kg). The exercise was repeated several times and I recorded the average weight.

'That's about 18 tons for the entire stack,' said Eric, who seemed to have accepted my calculation of the number of bales without question, but his benign exterior masked a shrewd brain and he had been watching me carefully.

'Robert can check that in the office,' said Arthur with a smile.

We left the stackyard and walked into Home Paddock.

'Where's the gate?' asked Arthur.

'I don't need one,' said Fred. 'I only mow this paddock for hay, so there are never any cattle there. Opening and closing a gate every time I left the yard would be nothing but a d… nuisance.'

Arthur said to me, 'Write down "gate missing".'

Eric said nothing. He knew his client would have to pay for a new one.

Home Paddock was enclosed by a well-trimmed hawthorn hedge, which Fred pointed out with pride, but unfortunately he had no claim to make, as he was obliged under the terms of his Tenancy Agreement to keep fences and hedges in good condition. Eric drew attention to a large heap of manure in the corner.

'I suppose you'll want paying for the labour in carting that out of the yard,' said Arthur, and then turned to me, 'How many loads are there in that heap?'

I looked at him blankly.

'A load is about one cubic yard,' he said, 'estimate the volume by pacing out the area on the ground and multiplying that by the height.'

I did that. The heap measured about four paces by five paces, with an average height of two yards, giving a volume of forty cubic yards. The two valuers were standing to one side chatting, so I went over to tell them.

'Write down "40 lds FYM to hill",' said Arthur, and Eric nodded: I was beginning to realise he was only too happy to look on while I did the legwork.

We continued through the gate at the far end of the field into Near Pasture which, as we had previously noted, was growing wheat. The gate and posts were in good order, and on each side of these was a ditch, which Fred had recently cleaned out. An underground pipe had been laid beneath the gateway to act as a culvert, but water was standing to a height of about three feet to the left, while the other side was dry.

'This culvert's broken,' said Arthur.

'It's just blocked, it only wants rodding,' replied Fred.

The deficiency was noted. David was asked to investigate and report on what he found.

'It's a good crop of wheat,' said Eric.

This was generally agreed and we walked through it towards the next field, Middle Close. There were several gaps in the hawthorn hedge dividing the two fields which had been filled by stretches of post and rail fencing. Some of this was in poor condition so we walked along the hedge counting the lengths that needed replacing, a 'length' being about two yards (1.83m).

'I think there's eight new lengths needed,' said Arthur.

'I make it six,' said Eric

It was no surprise when they agreed that seven were required.

We climbed over one of these fences into Middle Close but my weight was too much for the ash rail and it collapsed beneath me, to the hilarity of all, except Fred, who muttered darkly about some young men that should be on a diet. This field lay on the western edge of the farm and the boundary hedge loomed in front of us: it was more like a row of young trees, standing about 15 feet (4.57m) high. Arthur asked if this hedge belonged to the neighbour or to Hillside Farm, and Fred confirmed with some reluctance that it was his.

'Oliver told me not to trim it,' he said, 'he wants me to keep it high to improve the quality of the shooting, and that suits me because it gives shade for my young cattle now the field's down to grass.'

Landlords rarely include shooting rights when letting a farm. They can't prevent a tenant from shooting rabbits, because he's allowed to do so by Act of Parliament, but tenancy agreements usually stipulate that he's not allowed to shoot any pheasants or partridge. These rights are reserved by the landlord and either exercised by him or let off separately. Tenants hate this – not only are they obliged to watch the landlord's birds growing fat by stuffing themselves with corn and grass they have grown, but they have to keep their temper while parades of sportsmen and beaters march across their farm. Both Fred and David were well aware that on this estate the shooting rights were let to the managing agents – Weatherill and White!

If a tenant does shoot game birds on his farm it amounts to poaching – an offence considered by landlords to be quite as grave as mugging a bishop. A hundred and fifty years ago it was regaeded even more seriously and the penalty was transportation to Australia. Today this would be considered more of a jaunt than a punishment, so landlords deal with the matter by raising the miscreant's rent as soon as they can, and placing him at the bottom of the list when improvements are needed to his buildings. This retribution tends to outweigh the secret admiration the culprit will have earned from his neighbours.

It is beneficial to have high hedges on land where shooting takes place, because when game birds are driven over them, they fly at a height that provides 'good sport' for the guns ranged on the other side. The higher birds can be made to fly, the better the sport provided. A pheasant or partridge that flies towards a gun at knee height is not 'playing the game'.

Arthur accepted the explanation for the height of this hedge without question, but as we turned away and walked across the field we could see the patches of twitch, that David had mentioned in the farmhouse.

'That needs pulling out. Note down that six acres in this field need harrowing a couple of times,' he said.

The hedge between Middle Close and the next field, Top Close, was similar in height to the one on the boundary.

'Oliver told me not to trim that one as well,' said Fred.

I rather doubt that,' said Arthur, who had shot many times over the farm. 'We often drive the birds over the boundary hedge but never over that one.'

He turned to me, 'How long is that hedge, in chains?'

A chain is a unit of measurement twenty two yards long. There are ten chains in a furlong and eight furlongs to a mile.

'About four chains,' I estimated.

'That's not far out. Write down "four chains of tall hedge to cut and lay".'

Cutting and laying a hedge is very skilful work, usually done by specialist contractors. Unwanted species, such as elder and ash, are removed to leave only hawthorn bushes which are drastically pruned and reduced in height. The stems are cut in half vertically and bent over parallel to the ground, one above the other, and then the top of the hedge is bound together using some of the discarded material. The final product has a stockproof base which provides new growth over the years and forms an excellent hedge.

I wrote in the right-hand page of the notebook opposite the entry for 'Top Close'.

'Hedge to Middle Close - 4ch C&L.'

Fred dashed forward to unfasten the gate, and held it open for us to go through into Top Close. It was the quickest he had moved all day, but his hasty chivalry couldn't disguise the fact that there was no bottom hinge to the hanging post, and the clapping post on the other side was leaning outwards at an alarming angle.

'New hinge and gatepost required,' said Arthur.

The ditch on the far side of the field had been dug out recently and Fred had spread the excavated soil in a thick layer, about five yards wide, inside the field. The work had been done in wet weather, so there were deep ruts in the grassland where the machinery had operated. Arthur told me to note this, and Eric heard him do so.

'I hope you're not suggesting that we pay you anything after we've dug out that ditch,' he said loudly, 'I could understand you making a fuss if we hadn't done the work.'

'You can't expect my client to pay for filling in ruts and levelling heaps of soil which your client has left behind,' replied Arthur.

'You're being completely unreasonable,' said Eric, 'and when we meet to settle this valuation, I shall have more to say.'

Fred Coke was delighted that his valuer was showing such inflexibility on his behalf, but had not seen the wink which accompanied Eric's forceful words. However friendly two valuers may be, and however much they may agree during a tenantright valuation, there are times when each of them must demonstrate to his client that he is firm of purpose.

Arthur was too strait-laced for amateur dramatics, but I had heard from a pupil at another firm about a tenantright valuation on a small farm, where Eric was acting for the outgoer and John, a valuer from a rival firm, for the incomer. The two were close friends. The incoming tenant already farmed a large area of land, so acquiring this smallholding was a matter of little consequence to him and he didn't attend the valuation. However the outgoer was very interested in the proceedings as he hadn't been able to save much for his retirement, and the outcome was very important to him. He was lame, so after the valuers had finished in the farmhouse, they told him that he needn't walk round the land with them – he watched their progress anxiously from the stackyard. The pair walked through the fields noting down the dilapidations and agreeing everything on the spot, in the best interests of their respective clients.

When they had completed their tour they returned to the small grass field by the farmhouse, where they could see the outgoer in the distance, waiting and watching. Eric said to John:

'My client thinks he's been badly treated by the landlord and expects me to fight hard for him. You've been very fair in this valuation, but my client's going to expect a bit of a show. Are you ready?'

The two valuers turned to face each other, and Eric shook his fist dramatically at John. The gesture was reciprocated and the sound of raised voices carried across the field to the stackyard. After a few minutes the 'altercation' finished, and the two men walked back separately.

'It's been a struggle,' said Eric to his client 'but I've agreed a reasonable settlement for you.'

'Yes, I could see what a terrible argument you were having,' said the outgoer, very satisfied with his valuer.

We continued our walk around the farm, noting other hedges and ditches that needed attention, and more gates and fences to be repaired or renewed.

There were a few areas of land affected by twitch or chickweed, but generally the growing crops looked well. Eventually we arrived back at the entrance drive to the farmhouse.

'I think we're finished,' said Eric.

'What about the cottage?' asked Arthur.

'The man who was living there left three years ago,' said Fred, 'and I set a chap on who lives in the village, so I don't need the cottage any more. David's employing the same man, so he won't need it either. The landlords can take it back and let it to someone else.'

David agreed that this was so.

'You haven't told the landlords you don't want it and since it's still on your tenancy agreement you're liable to keep it in good order,' said Arthur. 'Let's go and have a look.'

As Fred trudged reluctantly back to the farmhouse to fetch the key we walked round the outside of the semi-detached cottage, which was built of red brick and stood beside the public road close to the farm entrance. The other half of the pair had been let off separately by the Estate, and the contrast between the two was stark. The neighbouring cottage had an immaculate garden and gleaming paintwork but this one was a sorry sight. The garden was uncultivated, several window frames were rotten, and all the outside woodwork needed painting. When Fred got back with the key we could see that the inside was just as bad – the place was filthy, decoration was needed, patches of ceiling plaster had fallen down, and there were mouse droppings everywhere. I made copious notes.

'Why on earth didn't you tell Oliver three years ago that you didn't need it?' asked Arthur. 'The Estate could have done a deal with you and taken it out of your tenancy before it got into this state.'

Fred mumbled that he meant to do something but hadn't quite got round to it.

As we walked back to the farmhouse Eric and Arthur agreed to meet again at our office in three weeks time to settle the valuation. Arthur told me to be there as well.

The following day he gave me the valuation book and told me to work out the payment due to Fred for the fertiliser used on the land, the seed sown, and the feed eaten by his livestock. I had to calculate the weight of the hay in the Dutch Barn, and the amount due to him for cultivations. He gave me a schedule of prices, which had been agreed by agricultural valuers at County level, for work to fences, hedges, ditches and gates. This gave the cost of cutting and laying a hedge as £6 per chain, replacing fences £1 a length, and digging out ditches £1.10 shillings (£1.50) per chain. I was to work out the complete dilapidations claim from the notes I had taken while walking round the farm, and told to take my calculations to him the day before Eric came, so that he could check my prices and arithmetic. I did this, and after he had made some alterations we were ready.

Eric duly arrived, but Arthur had two other valuations to settle with him, so it was a little time before he called me in to his office.

'This is the young man that's done all the work,' he said.

'Well we'd better see how close we are,' said Eric.

He produced his assessment of the payment due to Fred for fertiliser and feedingstuffs, which was very close to my figure and quickly agreed. There was no disagreement on the cost of the seed sown, and a price per ton was settled for the hay. Our total for the value of the cultivations was lower than Eric's, but he had used a high figure for ploughing at a considerable depth. Arthur insisted that it was impossible to cultivate so deeply on this farm and Eric conceded the point, agreeing a figure close to the one we had suggested.

The negotiations became more contentious when we started to discuss the dilapidations payment due from Fred, and Eric wouldn't agree many of our claims, saying they were much too harsh. He told us forcefully that even where the claim was justified, the figure we expected was far too high. He specifically referred to the spoil spread from the newly excavated ditch in Top Pasture, and refused at first to pay anything at all. He asked what his client was supposed to do with the surplus soil – put it in wheelbarrows and deliver it to the Estate office! He also said it was quite unreasonable for the landlords to expect one hedge in Middle Close to be kept high to improve the agent's shooting, and then claim a dilapidation payment when the adjoining hedge was maintained in the same condition. The discussion became quite heated, but common sense prevailed and an overall dilapidations settlement was agreed, but closer to his figure than ours.

The various payments due to the outgoer were added together, and the dilapidations settlement deducted to give a net sum payable by David. The valuers would now notify their respective clients of the settlement, and the fee they proposed to charge.

Now that the business was over, the conversation turned to the problems incurred during the last shooting season, and the prospects for the next one. Arthur told me that I could go, and get on with my other work, so I said goodbye to Eric, who got up to shake my hand.

'I gather that you prepared the claims for your client,' he said.

'Yes,' I replied, 'under supervision.'

'Well,' he said, 'they were honest and fair, even though they were weighted on his behalf. I think you'll make an agricultural valuer.'

I had wondered if this meeting would simply be a token one between two friends, with a compromise agreement reached in a few minutes. I had learnt that an agricultural valuer must always look after his clients' interests to the best of his ability. It was a lesson I tried to carry forward into my own career.

Chapter 13

I've Never Seen a Better Crop

The sun was shining – I was looking forward to the day and walked to the office with a smile. I had three stocktaking valuations to do for farmer clients during the morning, and another meeting in the afternoon to assess some crop damage. I loved to be outside – a day in the office was a penance.

As I walked through the front door Ella gave me a cheery greeting, but added a warning, 'Keep out of Oliver's way this morning. I think he's got out of bed the wrong side!'

I went upstairs to my office. Soon after Oak House had been bought by Reg Weatherill's grandfather, part of the first floor was converted to a property saleroom. Several large estates in the area were being forced to sell land at that time, and we needed extra space for these major auctions. Sales on this scale didn't last for long, so the saleroom was divided into three offices – Oliver had the biggest at the far end, Ken Greening the middle one, while mine was the third and smallest.

Reg Weatherill had already sorted the morning's letters and there were three waiting on my desk, one to do with a house we had for sale, another from a seed merchant giving information I needed for a stocktaking valuation, and the third with entries for the next furniture sale. I used our brand new internal telephone system to speak to Joan Housfield...

'Joan, would you come in and take some letters please?' We dictated letters to the secretaries, who noted them down in shorthand before they were typed.

'Oliver's just rung and wants me, so I'll come when I can,' she replied abruptly.

Joan worked for both of us, and made it abundantly clear that he had priority: she shared an office with Avril and Gwen, who were secretaries for Reg, Arthur and Ken. For many years Reg insisted on having a male secretary, in fact he refused to have any women in the office, but had now bowed to the inevitable. I had a rather prickly relationship with Joan, and always felt that she resented working for the most junior qualified member of staff. I had to be careful though, because I had been courting her best friend Sarah for several months.

Since I couldn't get on with my correspondence, I went downstairs to see Stan Rowan, 'How many bills are outstanding from the last furniture sale?' I asked, 'it's time we paid out the vendors.'

'Everyone's paid,' he said, 'and the cheques will be in the post tonight. But I've a lovely story to tell you.'

Every Monday he collected rent from tenants of the houses we managed, walking round the town with a leather bag like a bus conductor's hanging from a strap around his shoulders. He enjoyed his rent round. He loved chatting up the old dears in their terraced houses, as well as drinking umpteen cups of tea – with something stronger on offer at Christmas! Rents were statutorily controlled at a very low level so collecting them was barely profitable, but when a house became vacant we had it to sell, which made the exercise worthwhile.

'It happened last Monday,' he said. 'One of my tenants is a retired sailor, a great big fellow with a beard and tattooed arms, and I don't look forward to visiting him. He seems to think that paying rent is an affront to his dignity, and when I knock on his door he generally tells me very loudly where I can go and how quickly! If we took him to Court it would cost a lot, and he'd probably be told to pay a few shillings a week off the arrears, so we send him a notice to quit every three months and then he pays up, but I still have to call every week.'

'He lives in a small terraced house,' continued Stan, 'and last Monday I walked through the gate into his tiny front garden, and saw a great big Alsatian dog standing there. "That's all I need," I thought knocking on the door with some trepidation, but he opened it and asked me in. The dog followed. "How much do I owe?" he asked. I gave him the total figure of the arrears, and he gave me a cheque for the lot straight away. "There you are," he said, "now get out – and take your b..... dog with you"!

'I'm thinking of hiring it full time,' said Stan, 'if only I could find the owner.'

We were having a good laugh at this, when Oliver rushed into the room.

'Have you worked out that valuation I gave you yesterday?'

'Not yet,' I replied.

'Well it must go off tomorrow.'

I now appreciated Ella's warning, and promised he would have it by then. It was the annual stocktaking valuation of a gentleman farmer who sat with Oliver on the committee of the local Hunt, and so was high priority.

Our conversation was interrupted again by Ella...

'I've got Gordon Wright on the telephone for you.' He was the secretary of the Stumblers Cricket Club.

'I'm one short for the match this evening. Can you play?'

'I'd love to'.

I left Stan and went back to my office to fetch the notebooks I needed for the stocktaking valuations: these were the same 'bibles' that we had used for David Tims' tenantright valuation. Reg only did stocktakings for our most important clients, but Arthur and Oliver did over a hundred every year. Twelve months ago they decided to lighten their load and suggested to twenty five smaller clients that I should do their work in future, a gesture I greatly appreciated.

My first appointment was with P.J. Oldershaw at Church Farm, in the centre of Blaisby village, a few miles north of Grantham. This was a visit I enjoyed, because Mr Oldershaw – I never discovered his Christian name and would not have presumed to use it – followed a traditional system of farming that had varied little over the decades. He and his family lived a frugal life on this small and scattered farm. He had started with very little money but over the years had painstakingly managed to buy and rent several fields around the village, taking additional areas of grasskeeping in the summer. Under this arrangement an owner allows a farmer to graze his grassland during the summer months, on condition that he will give it up in the winter, so that no formal tenancy is created.

He raised high quality beef cattle which were always in keen demand at our market. During the winter they were kept in various small, open and covered yards around the farmhouse, which were enclosed by ranges of low brick buildings used to house calves, and sows with their litters. When the young pigs were weaned from their mothers they were moved to other loose boxes, or ran freely with the cattle and hens in the yards. The Oldershaws sold eggs from the farmhouse as well as potatoes, which they grew on the farm. They also grew wheat which was sold, grass for grazing and hay, and barley which was ground up to feed the livestock.

Mrs Oldershaw greeted me at the back door 'Come in Mr Brownlow,' she said, 'he's waiting for you.'

She took me into the kitchen, where hams hung from the ceiling, and eggs stood in trays by the sink ready to be washed. We went on through the living room with its large pine table, and Aga cooker with shining saucepans hanging from the beam above, to the parlour where the master of the house was sitting at a mahogany table, and to my surprise his son Trevor sat beside him. I knew that he was at least forty, and had managed the farm for a long time, but this was the first time he had been allowed to 'sit in' at this annual valuation. Evolution was slow at Church Farm.

P.J. was a short, jolly, pear-shaped man with an enormous stomach, beneath which was a pair of trousers held up by braces: he was wearing a white shirt with thin black stripes, but no tie. When I first came to the firm it was common to see farmers at the cattle market wearing a shirt like this with no collar and fastened at the neck by a gold stud, the outfit being completed by a black waistcoat and flat cap. Mr Oldershaw's shirt had no gold stud, but it was smart and freshly laundered, as he rose from his chair to greet me. 'Good to see you Mr Brownlow; you know Trevor of course.'

I confirmed that I knew him well, and we shook hands before deploring the recent spell of terrible weather. This is an inevitable prelude to any conversation with a farmer, whether it has been wet, dry, warm or cold, and Mrs Oldershaw then brought in tea and biscuits and we began our work. The purpose of a stocktaking valuation is to establish the value of a farmer's assets at the end of a financial year, so that an appropriate figure can be shown in his annual accounts. This figure will affect the amount of income tax he pays for that year – the greater his assets, the more tax he may have to pay. It can therefore be in a farmer's interests to understate these assets if he thinks he can get away with it.

We started with the tenantright, where the procedure is just the same as in a valuation at the end of a tenancy. I used the previous year's valuation book as a guide and went through the various fields, noting down cultivations, fertilisers applied and seeds sown. A thick file of invoices stood on the table, and I went through them to extract the actual cost of these commodities, and the quantity of bought feedingstuffs eaten by the livestock. The animals also needed to be valued, so I noted the prices paid for pigs, hens and cattle brought onto the farm during the year. The Oldershaws kept all the farm accounts in this one file so I had to leaf through all the other invoices – for, weed killer, Wellington boots, slug bait, baler twine, diesel oil and repairs to machinery. I always felt I was snooping into their private affairs while doing this, but quite enjoyed it all the same. On some farms I would find receipts from the butcher, dressmaker, grocer and wine merchant – but no doubt these got mixed up with the business accounts by mistake!

I knew from past experience that at least once while looking through the bills, I had to pause and say 'My word, Mr Oldershaw these costs keep going up,' at which his jolly face would cloud over, he would suck in air through pursed lips, shake his head and say:

'It's serious Mr Brownlow, very serious.'

Having looked at all the bills and made my notes, I asked, 'What tonnage of corn and hay do you have in stock?'

They looked at one another and Trevor said, 'We've fed most of it to the livestock during the winter, but there's about five tons of hay left in the Dutch Barn, and three tons of barley in the granary to grind up for feed.'

His father looked at him proudly: we all knew these were conservative estimates, but I entered them in my book under the heading 'Produce and Stores' – another time-honoured Weatherill and White tradition. I asked what quantities of petrol, diesel and purchased feed were in stock, and entered these under the same heading.

'How many head of poultry do you have?'

'A hundred old hens and the same number of pullets bought at point of lay about three months ago,' P.J. replied. I had seen the bill for these earlier.

After we'd finished in the farmhouse it was time to have a look at the livestock. The small covered yard housed a few older cattle that would soon be ready for market, with some store pigs and hens running amongst them. In a nearby loose box lay a sow with a litter of eight tiny piglets nestling close to her with an overhead lamp giving extra warmth during their first few days. The bigger yard on the other side of the house held several in calf cows and younger cattle, with calves and store pigs in the surrounding buildings. I listed these in my book, and then took Trevor in my car to two fields on the edge of the village where there were more cows with calves, and some strong store beast which had just been let out of the yards. I took him back to the farmstead and then drove to my next appointment realising what a pleasure it had been to visit the Oldershaw family again, and how I admired their reliance on hard work and traditional farming.

My next visit was to Frank Branscome at Lodge Farm, Steeple Ford which, like most Lodge Farms, lay well outside the village, and about half a mile off the public road. I drove into the yard overlooked by the gaunt stone house with its 'cold' blue-slated roof, so different from the cosy warmth of Church Farm, and after I had knocked several times, Frank came out to greet me.

'Sorry to keep you waiting,' he said, 'I was getting the bills ready and thought the wife was here to open the door.'

We went into the large, sparsely furnished kitchen and sat down at the table which was covered in scattered papers. There was no neat file of documents here, which wasn't surprising as Frank didn't give the impression of being organised. He was short, with thick-lensed glasses, wearing brown corduroy trousers and an old jacket with faded leather patches at the elbows. He had old brown socks on his feet, having left his boots outside the door as demanded by his formidable wife. Other farmers told me that Frank had been 'a bit of a lad' when he was young, but he was given little chance to stray nowadays. He married his wife when they were both middle aged, and she gave up her job as a hospital matron to channel her considerable vigour into looking after Frank and 'keeping an eye on him'.

We talked about the weather, as convention required, before discussing other matters, including the price of livestock and the way farming was being reported in the national press. One of the more lurid tabloid newspapers was running a campaign to support British farmers, and Frank said that because of this he was now permitted to have it in the house. I gathered his wife would not normally have allowed it through the farm gate.

'I'm trying to read their articles on buying British food,' he said, 'but I'm finding it difficult to get past those photographs of girls with nothing on.'

He giggled loudly and his eyes gleamed behind the thick glasses, but the merriment died abruptly in his throat as the door opened and Mrs Branscome swept in.

'Good morning Mr Brownlow – what are you two laughing at?'

'Just something that happened in the market dear,' said Frank.

'Oh,' she said suspiciously 'Have you offered Mr Brownlow a cup of coffee – and look at those untidy papers. Really Frank, you must get organised.'

I assured her that I wouldn't have a cup of coffee, having had one at the last farm, and Frank muttered something under his breath about needing to have the bills spread out so he could see what was there. We started to write up his valuation which was similar in principle to the last one, except that Frank's rented farm was mainly arable, with no cattle or pigs, although he did have a flock of 120 ewes and their lambs,. Last October Frank had bought one of Peter Surtees' Suffolk rams and his ewes had lambed well this spring, or 'had a good fall' as he put it, averaging over one and a half lambs each.

When his wife was out of earshot Frank whispered to me…

'Do you know why we've got so many lambs?'

I shook my head.

'I reckon our new ram saw those photos in our newspaper and that's what turned him on.'

He chuckled heartily again, and having finished the valuation, I left him to his supervised bliss.

My last morning appointment was with William Morgan at Ridge Farm which was not far away. The farm was well named because it stood on a ridge overlooking Grantham, and seemed to attract the coldest winds from all points of the compass; it was always cold at Ridge Farm. William's house was small and stood beside a busy main road. He was a sprightly man, well over retirement age, and like Frank Branscome wore thick glasses, but there any similarity ended – I can't imagine that William was ever 'a bit of a lad'. He was a sheep man through and through, having a considerable flock of ewes with their lambs, and bought stores throughout the year so that he always had sheep to sell.

'Do you know Mr Brownlow, I sold sheep in Grantham market every single Thursday last year,' he said proudly.

The farm was heathland and, like the Oldershaws, he grew wheat for sale, and barley which was mainly fed to the livestock. The land was suitable for sugar beet, so he let out two different fields each year to a neighbouring farmer, who had the machinery to grow and harvest it.

Behind William's house lay the farmyard with two fine stone barns, one of which had a splendid doorway, probably indicating that years ago it had been a roadside tavern. Its once handsome façade was now concealed behind timber and corrugated iron shelters which he used for housing a few calves, and for lambing his beloved sheep.

The valuation followed the same pattern as the others, but this time conversation was minimal. It was remarkable what gossip I learnt when doing my stocktaking valuations – who was having an affair with whom, who was 'very ill but never shows it', and who was in financial bother. I learnt nothing from William – he just talked about sheep.

After leaving him I snatched a quick sandwich at the Coach and Horses at

Great Somerton, the village where the Stumblers had their cricket ground, and, although I didn't realise it then, the place where I would build a house and live for over thirty years. Dan Robinson who lived and farmed in the village sat in his usual position on a stool beside the bar. He was very keen on his cricket and had founded the Stumblers club by laying out a ground in the paddock behind his house.

'Are you playing tonight?' he asked.

'Yes, I'm looking forward to it.'

'Well make sure you win. I've had my chaps mowing the ground this morning, so it all looks good.'

We carried on talking about cricket and the current price of sheep, before I had to leave for my next appointment, about four miles away.

Robin Smythe had an arable holding which, like Ridge Farm, lay beside the busy road from Grantham to the east coast. There was a bad bend in this road as it passed through his farm, and at least once a year some driver decided not to bother with it, and drove straight through the hedge into one of Robin's fields. What had been a good roadside hedge now had several lengths of fencing filling gaps made by uninvited vehicles.

He kept his farm in immaculate condition, and the grass verges on each side of the tarmac drive leading to the house were beautifully mown, with standard rose trees at regular intervals. Mrs Smythe had noticed me coming down the drive and was waiting at the door to take me to her husband. His sense of humour was soon apparent, as fastened to the door of his office was a pottery lustre dish with an inscription on the bottom which faced every visitor and announced 'Prepare to meet thy God'. He was a good farmer, and obviously organised his office work well, because I noticed that there were no papers lying about on his desk, before he led me out to his Land Rover.

Two days ago, early in the morning, a lorry taking vegetables from the eastern fens to wholesalers in Derby had ploughed through the hedge beside the bad bend, and into Robin's field of winter wheat. Heavy rain had softened the land and the lorry sank up to its axles. It was stuck so fast that the recovery vehicles couldn't winch it out from the road, and two tractors had to be driven into the field to provide extra power. This made a terrible mess and Robin, being such a neat and tidy farmer was not pleased.

'I reckon there's about half an acre of the crop ruined,' he said, 'and I can't leave the land in this state until harvest. When it dries out it'll be as hard as concrete; I've got to tackle it now.'

This meant that more of the crop would be destroyed when his machinery went in to do the work.

'It looks a good crop of wheat,' I said.

'I was only saying to the wife last week that I've never seen a better crop in this field,' he replied .

I expected nothing else, having learnt from Granville Hart and others that when it comes to making a claim from an insurance company, any animal that has met an untimely end was sure to be the finest the farmer had ever owned, and any damaged crop would certainly have yielded a remarkable tonnage. We went through the figures that would form the basis of our claim, working on a yield of 3.5 tons to the acre to assess the value of the lost crop, and adding further sums for the cultivations needed, and for planting a fresh length of roadside hedge. The young hawthorn plants – known as quicks – would need to be protected by wire netting on each side, to prevent damage by deer, hares and rabbits. I thought to myself while writing this down that further damage was much more likely to be caused by another lorry, than by any of these creatures. Robin gave me details of the haulage firm that owned the lorry, and their insurance company, and I assured him that I would add my fee on to the claim so he would have nothing to pay.

'Don't negotiate with them,' he said as a parting shot, 'I'm sick and fed up with these b..... lorry drivers, who either fall asleep or don't look where they're going. Make the b....s pay.'

When I got back to the office I wrote out the detailed claim for Joan to type, and sent it off to the haulage company. Three weeks later a cheque arrived from their insurers in full settlement of the figure I had claimed, including our fee. I suppose a national insurance company would regard our claim as very small in comparison to many they received, and it was simply not worth their time to employ another valuer to argue about it.

Chapter 14

Possessing many Original Features

When someone from my profession is asked what he does for a living, he will reply:
'I'm a land agent', or
'I'm a chartered surveyor', or
'I'm an agricultural valuer'.
He will not say – 'I'm an estate agent'.

There are two main reasons for this – and the first is to do with status. Land agency, agricultural valuing and estate agency are the main sources of income for a typical market town business such as Weatherill and White, but land agency is by far the most prestigious. I began to realise this during my articled years, and asked Ken why it was.

'Well,' he said, 'it's to do with one's standing in the community. A land agent often has his office in the outbuildings of a stately home, which may be dilapidated but gives an up-market address: he is also able to fraternise and shoot with the gentry on almost equal terms. The owners of landed estates generally prefer to employ 'one of us' as their agent, which isn't difficult because this part of the profession has been infiltrated by the aristocracy due to massive social change during the last hundred years. In the 1800s the eldest son of a noble family inherited the title and estate, the second son went into the army or navy, and the third (if there was one) took holy orders. A career in the church no longer has the same social status, so the third son disregards any religious inclinations he may have, goes to agricultural college and becomes a land agent. He can then expect with confidence to be offered a post by a landed estate, or by a national firm keen to take advantage of his family connections.'

'So where do an agricultural valuer and an estate agent stand in the pecking order?' I asked.

'An agricultural valuer cannot aspire to the eminence of a land agent,' replied Ken 'but he does conduct his business from an office, and is therefore regarded as a professional person. Estate agents don't operate from an office, but from a "showroom" with glass display windows at the front. This is trade – and trade is not a suitable occupation for those in the higher echelons of society.'

Reg Weatherill was one of many in our profession with this attitude, although when times were hard in the agricultural sector, they did condescend to take their share of the income earned from selling houses.

The second reason for the gulf between estate agents and the remainder of the profession is that they get a very bad press, being portrayed as devious, grasping and untrustworthy. I am biased of course, but have not found this to be so, and often think back to Reg's advice that in this job I would soon discover the meanness of the human spirit. How right he was! I'm not a natural cynic, but after spending some time selling houses, I soon became one. Estate agents simply hold up a mirror in front of their customers, and when the latter find the reflected image not to their liking, it's the agent that gets the blame.

To illustrate this, after a person has viewed a house and is interested in buying, he or she will make an offer to the selling agent. If the offer comes from a first-time buyer and is acceptable to the vendor, the sale can be referred immediately to solicitors for the contract to be prepared. Very often, however, the prospective purchaser has his own house on the market for sale, and the agent must ask if he has a buyer, because he can't sign a contract for another house until he's sold his property. The answer that the agent usually gets is,

'Yes, I have a cash buyer for my house, and the sale is in solicitor's hands.'

I learnt very quickly that this information needs checking, and four times out of ten is untrue. There is either no buyer, or someone may be interested but haven't sold their own house. The prospective purchaser knows this of course, but when confronted by the facts, is likely to say:

'I'm very surprised that you should doubt what I say. I spoke to my solicitor (or estate agent) and he assured me that my house was sold. I will speak to him again immediately.'

Another favourite habit of buyers, when the housing market is difficult, is to make offers for three different houses, and if they are accepted, have three contracts sent to their solicitor, after which they take their time to decide which to buy, if any.

The faults are certainly not all on one side. When house prices are rising, a vendor will accept an offer, but say to his estate agent 'I know you've instructed solicitors to prepare the contract, but keep the house on the market.'

If a higher offer is received the agent is legally obliged to notify the vendor, who will usually accept it and cancel the first sale. This is 'gazumping' and the client himself never tells the original buyer he has changed his mind. He gets his estate agent to do it.

When house prices are falling and a sale has been agreed, a buyer will receive the contract, have it checked by his solicitor and then, just before signing, tell the vendor that he'll only proceed if the price is reduced. This is known as 'gazundering', a very appropriate term in Lincolnshire where a chamber pot used for relieving oneself in the night is called a 'gazunder' because it 'goes under' the bed. It seems right that an unsavoury receptacle and an unprincipled practice should share the same name.

A few vendors and purchasers, having agreed to a transaction at a given price, stand by their word, but most don't, and it's the estate agent that gets the blame. The plain fact is that if the general public stuck to a basic code of morality, the practice of selling houses would have a better image, and the reputation of estate agents would be much improved.

Weatherill and White had always considered themselves to be a professional firm – certainly not estate agents, and it isn't surprising that while they had this attitude they weren't instructed to sell many houses. The few they had were handled by Arthur, or by Ken, who in addition to his furniture expertise was our specialist in valuing houses. I went with him occasionally when he took details of a property we had for sale and enjoyed it, so when I was employed by the firm he said to me:

'I've had a word with Arthur, and now you're "on the staff" we'd like you to take over house sales.'

Similar firms to ours in nearby towns had realised long ago that estate agency was profitable, and used their good local reputation to achieve a dominant position in selling houses. Weatherill and White's attitude over the years meant that not only did we have a very small stock of properties for sale, but other firms had seized the opportunity to open an office in Grantham, and now dominated estate agency in the town.

Our sale brochures were very basic. We prepared a brief description of a house, with its location, measurements of the rooms, and the mains services connected. This was typed on to a stencil that was fastened to the revolving drum of a duplicator, and a number of poor-quality copies produced for distribution and exhibition in the office. The display facilities at Oak House were terrible, just a sash window on each side of the front door, with the lower halves obscured by black gauze. I suppose this was put there to reflect our past attitude as a professional firm that didn't want the general public looking through its windows. Our duplicated sale brochures were fixed by paper clips to the top of the gauze, and hung forlornly at a variety of angles, so a passer-by found it difficult to grasp that we were actually trying to sell houses. The ancient enamelled signs that we put up outside the few properties we had for sale were black and white, and announced hopefully that the property was 'To be Sold'.

I was the first person in the firm to take a real interest in house-selling, and it was obvious that our image was awful, and gave no one any incentive to employ us. I spoke to a graphic designer in the town, and he produced designs for new sale boards, brochures and letterheads, which the partners discussed, after which Arthur told me, 'We'll agree to the new sale boards and brochures, but we don't want the letterheads changing.' That was a step too far!

Oak House was listed as being of architectural importance and the windows couldn't be enlarged, but we took the black gauze away and installed wooden racking so we could display photographs of properties. The new sale boards, brochures and window display made a big difference to our image, and started the long process of making us competitive with other estate agents in the town. An advertising promotion, or an improvement in presentation, brought quick results in estate agency and I enjoyed this: gaining new agricultural clients was a lengthy business.

When working in estate agency there are two lessons to be learnt quickly. Firstly, everyone is an expert on house prices. When a patient consults a dentist and is told 'You need a filling in your right-hand top molar' – he doesn't argue with the diagnosis – even if he was able to speak through a mouthful of fingers.

If a plumber investigates a damp problem, and reports 'The wet patch on your kitchen ceiling is caused by a faulty radiator valve in the front bedroom' – the client doesn't tell him he's talking rubbish.

However when an estate agent views a house and advises, 'In my opinion this property is worth £150,000 on the open market at the present time,' he is often asked if he's in his right mind.

'Don't you know,' says the householder 'that Mrs Sharpe's house, which is next door but one and quite a bit smaller, made £165,000 only three months ago, and prices have risen since then?'

That brings me to the second lesson – never take any notice of information you're given about property transactions. We did many valuations for mortgage purposes, and probably knew that Mrs Sharpe's house had actually sold for £140,000. We couldn't disclose this because our information was confidential, and the householder's opinion is unshakeable; he knows his information is correct because he got it from the landlord at the local pub!

Learning the job takes a long time, and mistakes along the way can be painful. I learnt an early lesson when we were instructed by a farmer client to sell his late parents' house in Carthorpe: it was a delightful property built of the local ironstone with an attractive front elevation and three acres of gardens. The house stood on the edge of the village, but unfortunately the front windows were only two metres away from a busy road. On the other side of this road lay part of the garden, overlooked by the main windows, beautifully landscaped and known as 'The Golden Acre'. It was a feature of the property, but the road had to be crossed to get there.

Ken and I went to take particulars of the property and I took some photographs, which we had started to use on sale brochures as part of our new image. I discovered that a view of the house from the far end of The Golden Acre showed the attractive front elevation beautifully, and I also realised that if there was no traffic, this shot didn't show the road at all: it seemed that the front door of the house opened directly on to The Golden Acre. I thought this was very clever and used the photograph on the front of the sale brochure, but soon realised how stupid I'd been. The first few people to view the house reacted furiously, thinking with every justification that we had tried to mislead them.

"....2,506, SOLD.   2,507, SOLD.   2,508, SOLD.   2,509, SOLD.   2,510, SOLD."
A record sheep entry in the Market by Terry Shelbourne

I never forgot that lesson, but I wasn't on my own at the time, because estate agents were often criticised for exaggerating the charms and minimising the faults of properties in their brochures. The law courts condoned this to some extent by ruling that such descriptions were 'puffing statements', and should not be relied on as facts: they applied the principle 'caveat emptor', or 'let the buyer beware'. Their attitude is, quite rightly, very different now.

When a politician wishes to attack a colleague publicly but not be accused of disloyalty, he or she uses 'coded language', which journalists have great fun in deciphering. It was just as enjoyable at that time to decode an estate agent's vocabulary.

A house 'possessing many original features' had had nothing spent on it for years. One 'suitable for modernisation' or 'in need of renovation', may well have been derelict. Prospective buyers viewing a property 'in poor structural condition' could well find a pile of bricks!

I once took particulars of a country cottage that we had to sell, and found that outside the back door the ground was covered in knee-high grass and bushes: I got some innocent pleasure, and felt justified in noting in the brochure that the property had 'a natural garden'.

Those days have long since passed and estate agents have been legally obliged for decades to describe properties accurately –'warts and all'.

Jim and I enjoyed many hours at our occasional get-togethers thinking up silly descriptions for houses, and joking about the latest names we had seen.

'Do you know,' he said, 'we've been asked to sell yet another "Dunromin" – I've lost count of the number I've dealt with. I can't understand how people can be so unimaginative – I certainly shan't retire to "Dunsellin", and has a vicar ever settled down in "Dunpreachin"?'

'I found a new one last week,' I replied, 'I went to look at a property, and took down all the details including the name, which was "Thistledome". I wondered why on earth the owners had christened their property after a weed, and part of a cathedral. It wasn't until I got back to the office that I realised it meant "This'll do me".'

'I've just said that "Dunromin" is unimaginative,' said Jim 'but we've got one property on our books called "The Bungalow". I wonder how much midnight oil they burnt thinking that up; I have a mental picture of a couple who both hated the names suggested by their partner, and eventually that was all they could agree on.'

'There's another favourite way of making up house names,' said Jim 'and that's by combining the Christian names of the people living there. A bungalow near my house was called "Tremarche" by the owners Trevor and Mary – not forgetting their daughter Cheryl!'

'Ken Greening's told me he'll never name his house that way.'

'Why's that?' asked Jim.

'He said it wouldn't do. His wife's name is Nell!'

Because of their agricultural work Weatherill and White had a stronger profile in rural areas than in the town, so that is where we tended to sell more houses. Visiting some of these country cottages was a real experience. On one occasion I went to view a semi detached cottage in Barthorpe, a small village north of Grantham, and met the owner, an elderly lady who had decided that she must sell up and go to live with her daughter. Her husband was ill and had already moved, so she greeted me at the door and showed me round the property, which had been kept in immaculate condition. In the kitchen a row of black enamel saucepans hung from hooks above the coal-fired iron range – the only source of hot water in the house, and willow-patterned plates stood on a simple pine dresser which matched the plain scrubbed table. As with so many country properties this was the room where the couple had spent most of their time, and the parlour next door was little used – perhaps when the vicar called, or when the family gathered on Christmas Day.

The single-storey extension behind the cottage had once contained the scullery and washhouse, but these had been converted to a bathroom, and a recently installed, sparkling, W.C. There were two bedrooms on the first floor. We walked around the front and back gardens which were long and narrow, and although kept in reasonable condition, had probably made the old lady realise it was time to move.

We sat in the kitchen after our tour and discussed the value of the property. She agreed with my advice, and told me to get on with the sale, after which she brought out the teapot and home-made cake. She told me how happy she had been in the cottage with her husband and children, and how sad she would be to leave. We talked about her forebears and the history of the cottage, which had belonged to the family for three generations, and I said that I thought the new toilet off the bathroom was a great improvement.

'Yes,' she said, 'we needed an inside toilet instead of that old coalhouse. Our privy used to be at the bottom of the garden, but it fell down two years ago – nearly killed my husband!'

I remembered seeing a pile of stones at the end of the garden, and tried to imagine her husband's predicament, since from her report of the incident he must have been in the privy when it fell. I wondered what he had done to cause the collapse! We continued with our chat before I drove back to the office smiling, but realising how lucky I was to meet such genuine people.

About two weeks later I was about to leave the office when a telephone call came from Ron Bellman. 'You're not going to believe this!' he said. Apparently a client, who also lived in Barthorpe, had recently died and Ron said he would be instructing us to clear out the contents of his cottage, and deal with the sale of the property.

'I've just had one of the neighbours on the phone,' he continued 'I gather she's the sort of person who knows what everyone in the village is doing, before they've done it. Not a sparrow falls to the ground in Barthorpe without her knowing!'

I wondered where this was leading.

'She told me that nearly every evening she'd see my client walking to the shed at the end of his garden with a torch. She thinks he's buried a hoard of money there.'

'Surely he was just walking to the privy.'

'He had a toilet inside the house,' said Ron. 'It seems very unlikely to me that he'd bury money in his shed, but now I've been told this story I've got to check it out. Why don't I pick you up tomorrow at 4.30, then we can go and have a look round, before I buy you a pint.'

And so the next afternoon a solicitor and a chartered surveyor (please note, not an estate agent) set out from Grantham with a spade to set many a lace curtain twitching in Barthorpe and seek buried treasure, but alas – none was found. The outside privy to this cottage had not collapsed, and it may be that the old man simply preferred the outdoor life to his indoor facilities. Whatever his preferences, we satisfied ourselves that if he deposited anything in his garden, it was not gold coins!

We wondered, on our way back to Grantham, if the busybody neighbour was still laughing at the wild goose chase she had organised for us. By the time we got to the George Hotel we had reassured ourselves that this fantasy had enriched her life, and who were we to deprive her of this simple pleasure. Arthur's bar at the George Hotel served draught beer out of silver plated tankards, and we had our noses deep into these, when Jack Barry walked in.

'I was talking to your friend Granville Hart yesterday,' he said.

'Oh yes,' I replied apprehensively, remembering our last meeting and wondering what was coming next.

'He told me that he bought a new tractor earlier this year and had a lot of trouble with it. The local dealer had it back in his workshop several times but eventually said there was nothing more he could do. Granville jumped on the tractor that evening and drove it through the night to the manufacturer's head office near London. When he got there he drove through the safety barrier, into the car park, up the steps and parked it so that it was touching the main glass entrance doors. No one could get in or out of the offices. He then walked off to get some breakfast, after telling the security man that the tractor was faulty, and he was on his way to fetch a journalist. When he came back an hour later a new one was waiting for him.'

'"You surely don't expect me to drive that all the way back to Lincolnshire", said Granville, so they delivered it to his farm on a low-loader, and gave him his first class rail fare as well.'

We agreed that Granville certainly knew how to get things done, and Ron said that it's always the squeaky wheel that gets the oil, but Jack hadn't finished.

'You've heard about Frank Branscome?'

'No.'

'You'll enjoy this. About six months ago contractors for the Gas Board were laying a high-pressure main through his farm. It's part of a national grid and the new pipe ran within fifty yards of his farmhouse, which did not have a mains gas supply. Frank had a brainwave. He went to the gang of men that were laying the main and asked if they would be prepared to "bend the rules a bit" if he paid them some cash. He asked if they would make a connection to the new pipe and provide a service to his house without telling the Gas Board, giving him free gas for life. The men said they would do it, but taking into account all the money he would save they would need a substantial sum; after some haggling they agreed on £1000 cash. They laid a pipe to his house and connected it to his newly bought gas cooker which worked beautifully. The money was paid, and the workmen continued on their way.

'About two months later the cooker stopped working: there seemed to be no gas. Frank couldn't ring the Gas Board because there was no official connection to his house, so he investigated matters himself. He dug down to the service pipe as it led away from the house, and the trench was about twenty yards long before he found that the pipe was not connected to the national grid, but to a buried gas cylinder!

'That was where Frank's gas supply came from, and when the cylinder was empty that was the end of his "free" service. The gang had moved on to another part of the country, and he realised it was no use trying to contact them, because they would certainly deny any knowledge of the matter!'

The pressure in the national grid pipeline is far too high to provide a direct service to an ordinary house and I didn't know whether to be pleased that Frank and his family had avoided an almighty explosion, or to feel sorry for him for when his powerful wife discovered the truth as she certainly would.

Chapter 15

A Torch, a Ladder and a Damp Meter

Ken Greening had a wonderful brain. When he sat the Final examination of the Chartered Auctioneers and Estate Agents Institute, he won a silver medal for getting the second highest marks in Great Britain. This was remarkable because he studied by postal course in the evening after a day's work in the office, and was competing against full-time students.

After serving in the army during the war he spent nearly a year in a sanatorium recovering from tuberculosis. He was fond of saying that he lost a lung, but gained a wife, because she had similar problems and was recuperating in the same hospital. His intellect should have qualified him for a top job in our profession, but the illness left him incapable of much physical exertion, so he had to be content to play a supporting role at Weatherill and White, and was invaluable as our expert in furniture, fine art and mortgage valuations.

He also had a wicked sense of humour.

'Anybody can be an estate agent,' he said. 'Once you've perfected a sincere expression and a winning smile, you can open a shop and sell houses; you don't need any qualifications, but valuations and surveys are a very different matter.'

It was essential even then to have qualifications to carry out professional work. Since passing my Final examination I was now an Associate of the Chartered Auctioneers and Estate Agents Institute, and entitled to use the letters 'AAI' after my name. My aim was to become a Fellow, but I needed at least ten years' practical experience before I could achieve that.

Since I had no family connections in the profession, it was important for me to become well qualified, so I also studied by postal course for the examinations of the Royal Institution of Chartered Surveyors. In due course I passed their Final examination and now had an 'ARICS' in addition to the 'AAI' after my name, but some years later the two bodies amalgamated, and three years of study were wasted.

There are several different types of surveyor, and the Royal Institution caters for them by having different divisions within the organisation. Quantity surveyors prepare detailed specifications of building projects, land surveyors specialise in maps and contours, and mining surveyors are experts in minerals. I passed my exams I in the Agricultural Division but transferred later to General Practice, because I was then doing a wide variety of professional work, and less on the rural side.

A general practice surveyor can inspect a property for many reasons, and each of them needs a different skill. He may be asked to value a house for sale, and this requires knowledge of the local market. A valuation for insurance involves assessing the cost of rebuilding the property, and understanding how it was constructed. He may be asked to prepare a full structural survey – a lengthy process involving a detailed report on condition, which presents practical difficulties. A full survey can't be done if a house has fitted carpets, because the floors are covered, and a surveyor can't report on the condition of woodwork that is concealed by plaster or floor boards. If the foundations of a property are exposed at one point and found to be satisfactory, the condition of the remainder still can't be guaranteed. For these reasons a structural survey report has to contain so many 'saving clauses', stressing that parts of the property can't be seen, that the final document is of questionable value.

Ken specialised in mortgage valuations of properties for Banks and Building Societies. He took a detailed record of each house and prepared a simple plan so he could work out the floor area. The cost of construction could then be easily calculated and adding this figure to what the site was worth, gave the value of the property.

He gained a good reputation from the mortgage companies, and was instructed by most of them to do their valuations in the Grantham area. I learnt a lot from him.

He was regularly instructed to value a house that was yet to be built based on plans supplied by the builder or architect, and his methods made this a straightforward task. Building Societies often financed a house while it was under construction by making payments to the developer at specified stages, and Ken would inspect the property periodically to report on progress. The stage payments were calculated as a percentage of the final value.

At that time Building Societies required a house buyer to pay for the surveyor's valuation but wouldn't let him see it, and this lasted for many years until one Society 'broke ranks' by sending him a copy, and the rest quickly followed suit. Before this change buyers often asked us to prepare a second report just for them, and we did this, on the clear understanding that we weren't carrying out a structural survey.

Ken told me when I first started, 'The essential tools you need when you're valuing or surveying a house are a torch, a tape measure or measuring rod, a damp meter, a pen knife and a sectional metal ladder. The ladder's usually in four sections which you screw together at the property – it must be strong so it can bear your weight, but light enough to be carried easily.'

'There are many defects that a surveyor's got to look for,' he continued 'but dry rot is the worst. It's a strange name for a fungus that thrives in damp conditions and stagnant air, but the name comes from the appearance of the wood after it's been attacked. All the moisture is sucked out, so that it dries, shrinks and cracks in a rectangular pattern before collapsing.'

He was warming to his theme, 'When you see this characteristic cracking, it's time to use your penknife. When the blade is pushed into healthy timber you'll feel some resistance when you pull it out, but when the wood's rotten there's none at all. You've got to use a small knife, and don't do it too often – preferably when the owner isn't looking. He won't be happy if he sees a dagger-sized knife being plunged repeatedly, and with gusto, into his skirting boards.'

Dry rot is generally seen in cellars, on the underside of timber floors, or in skirting boards and door architraves fastened to damp walls. If left unchecked, dry rot produces fruiting bodies, which are brackets, similar to those seen on dead trees in woodland. It is sinister, and reminiscent of science fiction stories where the world is being attacked by beings from another planet. There can be an attack of dry rot in a skirting board on one side of a room that will send out a strand beneath the concrete floor, which feeds on itself until it reaches woodwork on the other side, and another outbreak begins.

It's common to see limited damage in houses, but rare to see an extensive attack. On one occasion however I surveyed a large shop in Grantham that had been unoccupied for two years, and was appalled to see the extent of the dry rot in the cellar. The entire underside of the timber ceiling was covered in a blanket of white fungus, interspersed with orange fruiting bodies. It was frightening, and would have been very expensive to rectify: needless to say my client didn't take the shop.

Cellars are more common in older properties than in modern houses, and a surveyor feels at home there! There's no furniture to stumble over, the family dog is usually too scared to make the trip, and the fabric of the house is exposed, to be studied and criticised at leisure. Cellar ceilings are occasionally built of arched brickwork, but are usually the underside of the timber floors to the storey above. It is important to look out for hazards, because the lighting is always poor and sometimes non-existent. Hooks, once used for hanging hams, are often screwed to the ceiling beams and can give a nasty headache to the incautious surveyor!

When I was articled I went round a house with Ken and he asked me to have a look in the cellar which was disused. I went down the stone steps carefully, using my torch to illuminate the vaulted ceiling and the level floor in front of me. I stepped onto this floor – only to find that I was ankle deep in water. Another lesson learnt – most cellars are wet! Water accumulates there, and when left undisturbed for a long period, acquires a patina of dust that looks exactly like the surface of a stone floor.

Older terraced houses in the town were usually built with a cellar that had a grating at ground level at the front for coal deliveries, and Eric, a friend in the local Round Table, told me how he had used one:

'Last year we decided as our Christmas project, to buy coal and take it to needy pensioners: we had all seen delivery men working, and it seemed an easy job. Our hired lorry drew up at the first house and I wished the elderly lady the compliments of the season, then told her that we had brought a Christmas present. She was delighted, and I went to the grating and lifted it open. I trotted back to the lorry, swung an open-topped sack of coal onto my shoulders and staggered back to the house, before bending low as coalmen do, and jerking the sack up my back to launch the coal over my head and into the cellar. Unfortunately my technique was far from perfect and as the coal left the sack I felt every lump hit me on the back of the head!'

Surveyors must also look carefully for the common furniture beetle, or woodworm as it is generally known. Timber has an attack of woodworm when it looks as though it has been used as a dartboard, and there is a sprinkling of wood dust underneath. It is less serious than dry rot, but seems to make Banks and Building Societies very nervous. When we noted the presence of woodworm in a report they always told the prospective buyer to have the property inspected by a specialist timber treatment firm, whose advice they must follow. After one of these firms had treated the woodwork, they would issue a guarantee against a recurrence of the problem for a period of 10 or 15 years.

When woodworm holes are found, it isn't easy to decide whether the holes are old with no current occupants, or whether the pest is alive and attacking the timber. We therefore reported that we had found holes made by furniture beetle in certain areas, and recommended that a specialist firm should be consulted. It was amazing how often attacks – which we thought inactive – were considered to be alive by the experts, before they recommended a costly course of treatment.

Jim said, 'I think some of these specialists go into a roof space with a packet of drawing pins and a bag of wood dust, get busy and then come down shaking their heads and reporting sorrowfully that they've found woodworm.'

Ken was also eloquent on the subject:

'I once prepared a report on an old farmhouse, where woodworm had enjoyed themselves in the roof timbers for decades – I'd never seen woodwork eaten away to such an extent, and put that in my report. The client rang me afterwards to ask if the infestation was really as bad as I suggested. I said to him: "let me put it like this – the only thing that's keeping those roof timbers together is the woodworm holding hands".'

The client did not buy the house.

The roof space of a property is the area between the ceilings of the highest rooms and the underside of the roof. It usually houses the cold water tank, is full of junk, and unlike a cellar is not a surveyor's favourite place. In modern houses there are few problems, because the roof is supported by prefabricated trusses, has electric light and often a loft ladder for access. Sometimes in large, old houses the top floor was immediately beneath the sloping roof and used as attics to accommodate domestic staff. This is helpful because the structural roof timbers can be inspected in comfort.

In most cases, however, the access to a roof space is through an opening or 'hatch' in a first floor ceiling, which is covered over by a square of wood, or 'trap', resting on the surrounding frame, and this is where a surveyor's sectional ladder comes into play. Builders seem determined to put these hatches in the most unhelpful places. The obvious location is in the ceiling near the edge of a room, so that the ladder can be leant against the adjoining wall for easy access. This rarely happens. They are usually in the centre of a ceiling, and sometimes above a built-in cupboard which is so narrow that a child would find it difficult to squeeze through, let alone a portly surveyor.

To approach the hatch a surveyor screws together three or four sections of his ladder, depending on the height of the ceiling. It is then used to push the trap upwards, so that the upper rungs project a short distance into the roof space: this part of the exercise is usually trouble free. The ladder is then climbed, and the loosened trap pushed up further so it falls to one side of the hatch within the roof space, at which point the dust of decades is likely to cascade down the surveyor's neck. He then climbs through the hatch, torch in hand, for his first look round.

Wasps and hornets like to find their way between tiles or slates and build their intricate hanging nests on the underside of a roof. This is usually a simple matter of record for the surveyor, and an opportunity to admire the wonders of nature, but sometimes these ferocious insects are at home, and he has to rush down the ladder much quicker than he went up it!

Walking around in a roof space is hazardous, because the floor is formed by the ceilings of the rooms beneath, which are not load bearing. In a modern house they are made of wooden joists with plasterboard beneath, all covered by an insulating blanket of fibreglass. The joists are about two feet (0.6m) apart and will bear the weight of a person, but the plasterboard will not, so the surveyor must walk gingerly from joist to joist taking great care not to tread between them.

Roof spaces are often used for storage, although how some articles, like prams and pushchairs, are squeezed through the hatch is little short of miraculous. Christmas decorations, suitcases, unwanted wedding presents, piles of magazines and china tea sets handed down from parents, are also dumped there until they are needed, or more probably given to a jumble sale. A surveyor needs to check if there is any woodworm, rot or structural weakness in the roof timbers. All this rubbish lying about isn't helpful because it conceals much of the woodwork, but since the area is being used for storage, the owner may have laid boarding over the joists to make it easier to walk around. This should simplify matters, but not always according to Jim.

'My boss Peter,' he said, 'is the unluckiest man I know. He was carrying out an inspection for mortgage purposes recently, climbed his ladder and pushed open the ceiling hatch without incident. He was pleased to see that there was a boarded walkway over the joists down the complete length of the roof, and walked along it shining his torch on to the structural timbers. He was halfway down when he thought he saw some woodworm holes in a rafter. He leant to one side to take a closer look, but unfortunately the boards forming the walkway hadn't been nailed down to the joists beneath. As he leant one way the boards flew in the opposite direction, and he fell heavily between the joists and onto the plasterboard ceiling. This gave way and he found himself flying through the air before landing on a double bed in the room beneath. He had heard stories in pubs that involved jumping from the top of a wardrobe onto a double bed, but in this case it was unoccupied. Mercifully he wasn't hurt but had some explaining to do to the owner, and compensation to pay.

'His luck was no better on another occasion,' continued Jim, 'when he was instructed to survey a modern bungalow. The property was typical of its kind, built of red brick, with a tiled roof that extended over the bungalow and the attached garage. Peter walked round the outside but apart from some worn paintwork, there was little to criticise as he had expected from such a modern property, and inside it was similar. The previous owners had taken out all the furnishings and carpets so the fabric could be seen, and although decoration was needed there was little else to mention in his report. He went outside to look in the garage but couldn't get in, as the doors were locked, and the selling agents hadn't given him the key.

'He continued the survey by taking the sections of his ladder into the bungalow, screwing three of them together and pushing the completed assembly through the hatch into the roof space. This had electric light, and there was boarding over the joists, so looking round was easy, and he noted that everything was in order, except that the fibreglass insulation could have been thicker. At the far end of the roof space Peter noticed a second hatch between the joists, and realised that this was the access point from the attached garage. He had a brainwave! He couldn't get into the garage from outside, but he could lift this trap and inspect it from above.

'He did this, but unfortunately as he leant down through the hatch to have a look round, his surveyor's scales (which are short rulers for taking measurements from plans), pen, pencil and the front door key to the bungalow fell out of the top pocket of his jacket and down on to the garage floor. What was he to do? Being a man of resource he had a second brainwave! He went back to the first hatch, and pulled up the ladder, unscrewing the sections as he did so. He carried these to the far end of the roof space and assembled them, so that he could go down into the garage and retrieve his possessions. As he lowered the ladder through this hatch towards the garage floor however, his plan failed. He had not screwed the sections together properly, and the bottom one fell off! He was left in the roof space holding a ladder that was now only six feet long, looking down at the garage floor and his possessions, eight feet below.

'Peter realised that the time for brainwaves had passed. It was time for action! He dropped the rest of the ladder into the garage, and then swung ape-like from the hatch before letting go and falling to the floor. Unfortunately, he landed painfully on the metal sections, but regaining his composure, screwed them firmly back together and retrieved his belongings. He then made his way back through the two hatches and the front door before limping back to his car, a bruised and wiser surveyor.'

Subsidence (or settlement) is another defect for which a surveyor must be alert. Unless a house is built on solid rock it will move slightly, or 'settle', over the years, and providing this movement is small, and evenly spread over the structure, there are no external signs and it's not a problem. When part of a property sinks more than the remainder, cracks will appear in the external walls which a surveyor must note, and advise his client that there could be a problem. This uneven movement can be due to a variety of causes. The worst is where a property has been built over mine workings, and the roof of an underground seam gives way: houses have been known to disappear overnight. Mercifully Grantham is not in a mining area so I never had to deal with this nightmare.

Soon after I came to the firm, however, construction started on a new housing estate near the edge of the town on land that contained several springs. The developers were either unaware of this or decided to take a chance, although they should have noticed that a hole was being dug at a filling station across the road to install a new petrol tank, and the contractors had been pumping water out of it for three months. The first pair of semi-detached houses was built opposite this garage and had reached roof level, when suddenly the entire structure collapsed. Conscious of their image, the builders concentrated all their men on removing the evidence as quickly as possible, and within three hours there was no sign there had ever been houses there. They made sure that heavy steel piles were sunk into the rest of the site and there were no more incidents.

The main cause of subsidence in Grantham is running sand. The town stands beside a river and over many centuries several of the feeder streams silted up, so that no evidence remained on the surface. Houses were built over them, but the shifting sandy soil which formed the beds of these old streams was not load bearing and the structures subsided. As local experts we knew the location of these pockets of running sand, and could warn our clients accordingly.

Trees also cause settlement because the roots can spread out as far as the branches above, so if a mature tree stands close to a house, the roots may extend beneath the foundations. They take moisture from the soil which then dries and contracts, so the foundations subside, and the walls crack. The worst trees for this are Lombardy poplars, willows and cupressus, because they are fast growing and need large quantities of water.

Settlement is not confined to external walls. The ground floor of a modern house is usually constructed by laying a slab of concrete on top of 'hard core' – or compacted rubble. If the site is sloping, the depth of this rubble is greater under one side of the house than the other, to keep the floor level. If the hard core isn't properly consolidated, or if it includes pieces of timber that rot over the years, the rubble sinks and so does the floor. This can be easily spotted by looking for a gap between the concrete floor and the skirting boards, which are fastened to the wall.

The last of Ken's 'deadly sins' for a surveyor to find, was rising damp.

'Every modern house has a damp-proof course,' he said, 'which we call a "DPC". This is an impervious layer of material built into a wall about two courses of brickwork above ground level, and designed to stop moisture rising up the wall. It's now made of bituminous felt or asphalt, whereas slates or blue engineering bricks were used in the past. They can fail in places, or the adjoining ground level can be raised above them, so they become useless. Houses more than a hundred years old rarely have one, and often suffer from rising damp.

'Damp is usually obvious on the inside of a wall, because it stains the plaster, but to be sure – and in an attempt to impress – a surveyor uses a damp meter. This is a small black box with a battery inside and two metal prongs projecting from the end. The prongs are pushed into a wall and the theory is that the electric current passes more quickly between them if the wall is wet than if it is dry, and the meter registers not only the presence of damp but the extent of it.'

If rising damp is mentioned in a mortgage valuation the Building Society or Bank will insist on an expert's report, as with woodworm. A specialist company will then inspect the property and it is rare indeed for them to report that the problem is trivial!

Replacement damp proof courses were of two main types. One was electrical and purported to keep the damp in check by passing a current through the entire length of the wall, but in our experience was of doubtful value. The general method was to inject the wall at intervals with a clear liquid similar to that used between the wars for pickling eggs: this sets hard and forms a barrier to stop damp from rising up the wall. After completing the work the specialist firm issues a guarantee against recurrence for a twenty-year period, and this is highly valued by the mortgage company. An individual in Grantham set up a treatment company, and his guarantee was valued even more highly as it lasted for thirty years. Unfortunately he died after ten lucrative years of treatment, and his widow showed no interest in his business, and even less interest in considering any claims made under his guarantees.

Chapter 16
A Stuffed Owl and Magic Lantern

I realise now how badly I treated my parents before I was married, and how good they were to put up with it. At weekends I rushed home to Melton Mowbray, snatched a Saturday lunch with them, dumped my washing with mother, and rushed out to play cricket in summer and hockey in the winter. I then spent most of Sunday morning in bed before eating another wonderful lunch and dashing off to play more sport.

For my first two years in Grantham I travelled home by bus, and then bought a Lambretta motor scooter which I thought would be very stable, but was actually lethal in icy conditions. The headlight was dim, and on one memorable evening I was riding back home in dense fog, and decided to follow the white line down the middle of the road – only to find another scooter with a poor headlight doing the same thing from the opposite direction. Mercifully we didn't collide!

I was fortunate that my girlfriend Sarah needed a car for her work, which we used to go to pubs and do our courting on weekday evenings. She wasn't keen on the Lambretta. However a golfing friend told me one day that he was selling his Austin Healey 'frog eye' Sprite, a small sports car with an even smaller engine, and a soft top. We negotiated a deal and I became its proud – very proud – owner.

The seats were almost at ground level and it was not ideal for visiting farms – or farmers. Soon after buying it I drove into a farmyard to visit a client, and although I couldn't see him I could certainly see his Alsatian dog which raced out of the buildings and stood beside the car, showing its teeth and barking ferociously. I was looking up at the animal out of the car window, and it didn't take me long to decide against opening the door, so I drove out of the yard and came back an hour later, when the client was there, but thankfully not the dog.

'What have you got there,' he asked, nodding at the car, 'bird puller is it?'

Before I could answer, he continued 'I'll tell you what you'll need if you go courting in that – a fine night, and endless cooperation.'

I trudged to work one Monday morning – not my favourite part of the week – after a heavy weekend, wondering what the day would bring. Ella and George gave me their usual cheery greeting before I climbed the stairs to my office: the phone rang as I opened the day's letters.

'It's Lady George for you,' said Ella.

'Good morning Mr Brownlow,' said her ladyship 'Mrs Cousins has suggested that I contact you.'

I thanked my lucky stars that I had made that trip to see the worthless

'Monarch of the Glen'.

'As you know,' she continued 'I live at The Old Rectory, Cardingford and my late mother lived at The Hall.'

'Yes, I was very sorry to hear of her death,' I replied.

'Thank you, it was good of you to come to the funeral. I know she was always very satisfied with the way Weatherill and White did her agricultural work'.

'She was very fond of buying at furniture sales, and hated to get rid of anything. When her sister died ten years ago she brought nearly all the contents of her house back to the Hall, which was full to bursting anyway: now you can hardly move for the stuff. My brother and I only want a few pieces and have decided to sell the rest. The national auction houses have already been in touch.'

'I'll bet they have,' I thought. They probably didn't wait till the poor old dear was cold!

Lady George continued 'But they only want to take the best pieces and we don't think that's wise. We've had a family conference, taken the few things we want, and decided to ask two firms if they will act jointly in selling the entire contents. Mrs Cousins says that you have good sales in Grantham, and of course you're only a few miles away, so we would like you to handle the sale jointly with Henry Smythe and Sons of Bawtry.'

They were a leading regional firm of auctioneers and estate agents who had specialised for many years in the sale of fine art, and now ran one of the most successful provincial salerooms in the country.

'We shall be delighted,' I said, 'and thank you for the instructions.'

'That's settled then,' said Lady George, 'I've already spoken to Rupert Smythe and he's quite happy to work with your firm. Perhaps you'll get in touch with him, and then I'll look forward to hearing from you.'

Rupert was the senior partner and fine art specialist at Henry Smythe and Sons, and it was his reputation, particularly his knowledge of furniture, that had built their considerable business. He was an excellent speaker and I had heard him give wonderful lectures at junior auctioneers' meetings on the history of English furniture, from 'the age of oak', to 'the age of walnut', and then 'the age of mahogany'. I contacted him immediately, and we arranged to meet at The Hall in two days time. He was a delightful man, and if he was dismayed to find that his firm had to act jointly with us, he didn't show it.

On Wednesday Ken and I collected the keys from Lady George and drove the short distance to the Hall. The iron gates opened on to a gravelled drive which wound its way through a small park to the attractive stone facade of the Georgian house. Rupert arrived shortly afterwards, introduced us to his assistant Charles, and we walked round the house. As Lady George had said, it was crammed with furniture, and when we opened an occasional cupboard it was stuffed full of china, glass or silver. We knew we had to hold the sale as soon as possible, but there was a great deal of work to do before we could prepare a catalogue.

Although there was a lot to sell there didn't seem to be any individual items that would make many thousands of pounds, apart from a few oil paintings, which Rupert thought were valuable. He said he would do some research on these, and we agreed to allow two weeks to list all the contents and prepare a catalogue, another two weeks for it to be printed and a further four weeks for advertising. The sale would be held on a Wednesday in two months time, with viewing the day before.

The gravelled drive in front of the house formed a circle enclosing an area of grass – the ideal position for the marquee in which to hold the sale. As we walked round this area, there was a loud and continuous noise to the north which became louder and louder, and then deafening, as a Vulcan bomber passed overhead, so low that it seemed to only just clear the roof of the house.

'That's just taken off from Wadworth airfield,' said Ken, 'I didn't realise it was so close. It looks as though the Hall is in line with the main runway.'

'It'll be a big help if we have a dozen of those taking off on sale day!' said Rupert. 'No one will be able to hear a thing.'

He went on to say 'I suggest that my firm orders the marquee and deals with advertisements in the national newspapers, while you organise the local advertising. I will write to Lady George and set out our proposed timetable and estimated costs.'

Ken and I agreed and arranged to meet Charles in two days time to start cataloguing: we knew that we wouldn't see Rupert again until sale day.

I found the task of cataloguing to be an absolute joy, and realised that I must be a secret hoarder! We wrote down a careful description of every item of furniture, china, glass, silver, plate and sundries in each room. A provisional number was stuck on to each item – the first lot of furniture was F1, of glass G1, and so on. Ken and Charles agreed the descriptions for the catalogue and I wrote them down in a notebook beside the appropriate number.

The range of chattels in the Hall was staggering. It was a time capsule. Several generations had thrown little away and the contents of the late sister's house had added more to the total. In one drawer was a selection of ostrich feather fans, while in the cupboard beneath was a nineteenth century magic lantern with the original coloured glass slides. A stuffed owl in a glass case rested on a Georgian mahogany pedestal games table, while gloomy oil paintings of ancestors gazed disapprovingly over Chinese carpets. Porcelain figurines were arranged haphazardly in display cabinets, a rack of copper saucepans twinkled in the kitchen, and dusty dinner services were stored in even dustier cupboards.

Any jewellery of note had been kept by the family but in a house like this we couldn't assume anything was worthless, so I asked Peter Christopher to come and check what was left. After a careful inspection he said, 'the family know what they're doing: there's nothing left of any value.'

The bedroom wardrobes were full of clothing, so I spoke to Lady George.

'Yes,' she said, 'I quite agree. Apart from the two or three 1920s "flapper" dresses which could be worth a bit, give all the rest to the Red Cross.'

We worked hard and soon had a complete list of the contents of every room divided into categories, with each item labelled. We knew that space in the marquee would be limited and decided that the largest furniture and paintings should stay in the Hall to be viewed. The former carriage house behind the Hall was a substantial building, and we decided that about a hundred low-value lots could be set out there, together with the garden equipment, carpets and rugs; they would be sold there as the first lots in the auction.

The sale in the marquee would start with the copper, brass, treen and metalware, followed by the costume jewellery, glassware and sundry lots, such as the two dresses, fans, magic lantern, workboxes and writing cases. Then would come the china, silver plate, silver, clocks, paintings and furniture.

The catalogue was compiled and sent to the printers, the marquee ordered, advertisements drafted, and the sale day drew closer. The marquee was erected on the Friday before the sale, a matting floor laid and chairs stacked at one end. Alf and Bill brought our rostrum and a supply of trestle tables from the salerooms and spent several hours at the Hall taking the early lots out to the carriage house, and substituting lot numbers for the preliminary labels. When the marquee was in place, they and the porters from Bawtry began the task of transferring lots from the Hall. The entire marquee would be used for displaying lots on view day, and I had to ensure that the various items were put in the right place. On sale day the tables exhibiting the china, glass and other lots would be moved to one end of the marquee with the smaller furniture, so that chairs for the buyers could be set out in the remainder.

I had asked Lady George if she could suggest any local people to deal with night-time security and supervise car parking.

'Well, I suggest Simon Johnson as your security man,' she said, 'he's a retired army sergeant, and no one will get past him. For car park supervision I think Oliver Leivers will do a good job: he's a farmer' son from the other end of the village, and I'm sure he'll stand no nonsense.'

There was a handy field beside the Hall that we could use as the car park, and I had a talk with the local policeman who agreed to make an occasional appearance, as well as monitor traffic on the public road. The pay office would be in a convenient summer house that stood on the other side of the gravelled drive from the marquee. We brought an office table and chairs from Oak House, as I was determined not to repeat a mistake we had made some years ago at another auction.

This was a much smaller sale at a cottage, including a few hens, poultry huts, tools, farm equipment and furniture. We took a pine table and two kitchen chairs out of the sale to use in the office, and then sold them as the last lot. The purchaser paid his bill, loaded his other lots into a van and then stood in the office, waiting impatiently for the clerks to finish their work. He wanted to go home as soon as possible with his purchases, and moaned continually at the delay. The staff felt harassed, and finished as quickly as they could, after which the buyer put the two chairs in the van, tied the table to the roof rack and drove away. Half an hour passed before one clerk said to the other:

'Where did you put the cash?'

'Oh good gracious – it's in the drawer of that table!'

A car chase followed worthy of any film sequence, but the buyer was eventually overtaken and the cash recovered, to our great relief, and more moaning from him.

A marquee sale is quite an event in local society, and a constant stream of people arrived on view day. Some were interested in what we had for sale, some wanted to have a look round the house, some wanted to see who else was there and others had nothing better to do. The car park was soon full and the marquee heaved with people. I thought we had ordered too many catalogues but they almost ran out, and we had to hold some back for sale day. Our two firms had provided as many members of staff as possible to supervise the viewing, and every one was needed. The small pieces of china, silver and jewellery were shown in glass cabinets manned by Stan Rowan and a porter from Smythes, and could only be handled on request. More staff were needed to watch the tables on which other valuable lots were displayed, particularly the silver plate and porcelain. A well-known ploy among the light-fingered is for one person to stage an argument with the porter, while the other walks off with the lot he has asked to examine: guarding against this amid a crowd of chattering people is not easy.

We set up a table in the marquee to cater for people who were interested in buying, but couldn't attend the auction. George was in charge of this, helping prospective buyers to fill in commission slips, and then entering their bids onto the sale sheets. It is critical that an auctioneer buys a lot as cheaply as possible for an absentee bidder, as Oliver had found at William Hall's dispersal sale. Apart from the morality of the matter, failure to do so soon becomes general knowledge and does a lot of harm to an auctioneer's reputation. I was pleased to see that George was very busy. In my experience bids left by absentees are nearly always less than buyers attending the sale are prepared to pay, but it's good for an auctioneer's morale when he sees that there are several bids for the next lot.

We needed vigilant staff in the carriage house, and also in the Hall where the main paintings and large furniture were displayed. Several women were determined to have a good look round the Hall, and although those parts not in use were roped off, this was no deterrent.

'I'm sorry madam, but you can't go in there. There's a large sign saying "Private",' the porter had to say.

'Oh, I'm terribly sorry, I didn't realise,' was the stock reply.

Arthur and Oliver came to look round, and Oliver announced, 'I'll do some selling tomorrow.'

He had taken no interest in proceedings so far, but enjoyed selling by auction and realised that many of his farming and hunting friends would be there tomorrow. In view of this, we decided that I would sell the lots in the carriage house and Oliver would start in the marquee, followed by Charles, before Rupert provided his own inimitable finish. Stan Rowan and I would do the booking, and the porters from Smythes would hold up the smaller lots as they were being sold. The running of the sale office would be shared between the firms.

Oliver added 'I shall expect you to give me an estimate of the value of the lots I'll be selling.'

'There are catalogues on display around the marquee giving anticipated prices for everything,' I replied.

While I was in the carriage house a dealer came up to me...

'I and my colleagues,' he said (meaning the other members of the ring) 'are concerned that there's more furniture in the sale than is warranted by the size of the Hall. I suppose several lots have been entered by dealers.'

'No, they haven't,' I replied 'Lady George's aunt died some years ago and her furniture was brought here. No outside lots have been included.'

Another dealer followed soon afterwards...

'There's a print over there that you've catalogued as a watercolour, and you've described one of the rugs in the carriage house as "oriental", when I'm sure it was machine made in Birmingham.'

'I'm sorry about that. We've had a great many things to catalogue in a short time. I'll announce corrections when we sell them. By the way,' I added, 'would you have come to see me if the mistakes had been made the other way round.'

He smiled and agreed this was unlikely.

After Arthur had viewed the sale he said, 'Everything looks very well. It will do the firm's reputation a lot of good. I won't do any selling tomorrow, but I'll come to the sale to talk to clients, and have a chat with my old friend Rupert.'

As he was speaking another Vulcan bomber took off, the fifth of the day, and we had to stop talking as it passed over us with a shattering roar.

'I'm really concerned there might be a lot of those flying over tomorrow,' I said.

'Why don't you have a word with the commanding officer at RAF Wadworth?' said Arthur, 'The Air Force is usually very keen to maintain good relations with local people.'

'I'll do that,' I said, "and if he's co-operative we shall only have the weather to worry about. There hasn't been a spot of rain since we've been here: I hope it's not waiting for tomorrow.'

'Well, you know the old Lincolnshire saying?' said Arthur,

'No, what's that?'

'It never rains in a dry time.'

I laughed and wondered why our forebears had nothing better to do than make up stupid sayings like that, but as I thought about it, there is a grain of truth there. If a black cloud appears in the sky after two weeks of dry weather it seldom rains, but if it shows up after a week of wet weather you can be sure that another soaking is on the way.

The set of rope twist dining chairs

I duly rang RAF Wadworth, explained the situation and asked to speak to the CO. To my surprise I was put through, told him of our problem, and asked if it was possible for the Vulcan aircraft to fly less frequently tomorrow.

'When will you be selling in the marquee?' he asked.

'Between about 12 noon and 4.30.'

'I can't promise anything,' he replied, 'but I'll see what I can do. We may be able to leave a chink in the nation's defences for an hour or two!'

This was much better than I expected, and feeling reassured I went for a last walk round. The crowd was thinning out and it would soon be time to close down until tomorrow. As I was walking out of the marquee a third dealer sidled up to me, looking around furtively. He was a studious-looking man with horn-rimmed glasses, who only came to our sales occasionally.

'Have you got a minute?' he asked, looking over his shoulder again. No one was watching, and he continued, 'I'm interested in that jade pendant – Lot 218.'

'Yes.'

'It's Maori you know.'

I had to confess that I didn't know, and neither did the experts at Henry Smythe and Sons.

'I'm very interested,' he said, 'but I don't want the others to know that I'm bidding.'

I realised exactly what he meant. He was a member of the dealer's illegal 'ring', and would certainly expect his share of the profits when they re-auctioned their purchases after the sale. He was keen to get the benefit of his colleagues' specialist knowledge, but not prepared to share his expertise with them. If they saw him bidding for a lot that appeared commonplace, they would realise it was valuable, and make sure after the sale that he 'paid up' accordingly.

'So what I suggest,' he continued, 'is that I'll stand in a prominent place as you're selling that lot: when I take my spectacles off I'm bidding, and when I put them back on I've finished.'

'All right,' I said, 'I'll remember that, and make sure the other auctioneers know.'

He thanked me and walked away, still looking around to ensure that no one had overheard our conversation.

It was soon 5 o'clock, the time for viewing to finish. The security man arrived to take over for the evening, and agreed that his son would work for us tomorrow, taking the completed sale sheets from the auctioneer's clerk to the office.

We were ready.

Chapter 17

Sold to you Mr Couples

I was woken by thunder in the night, and watched anxiously as flashes of lightning lit up my bedroom and rain beat heavily on the windows. So much for Arthur's 'it never rains in a dry time' I thought, before drifting back to sleep. Mercifully the rain had stopped in the early morning when I fetched Alf and Bill from the cattle market, but I was concerned that the car park and the area around the marquee might get waterlogged. When we arrived, there were several puddles on the lawn and the sky was still black, so I rang a local farmer who agreed to have a tractor standing by, in case vehicles needed pulling out of the car park.

Simon Johnson was still in the marquee.

'How was your night?' I asked.

'The thunder certainly helped to keep me awake,' he replied. 'I thought the rain might get through the seams of the marquee, but as far as I can see it hasn't.'

'We'll have one more check before you go,' I said, 'the last thing we need is rainwater dripping onto the furniture.'

Thankfully all was well. Some water had run from the stable yard under the doors of the carriage house, but no harm had been done. I was concerned to see how gloomy it was, because I hadn't thought it necessary to install lighting in the marquee in the middle of summer. It was so dark that I wondered if we would be able to see bidders who were a long way from the rostrum, but it was too late to do anything now. Ken and I had a quick check through all the lots to ensure that nothing had 'gone missing' overnight, but everything was there.

Charles and the staff from Henry Smythe and Sons soon arrived, as did Ella and George who would help to run the office.

'When will Rupert be here?' I asked.

'About 12 o'clock I should think,' said Charles.

Some 'early birds' were also arriving. It was not worthwhile for people from the south of England to spend two days at a country house sale in Lincolnshire, so they came to view early on sale day.   The trickle became a rush and the car park was soon full, so we diverted the extra traffic to an overflow area.

Arthur arrived to circulate and talk to our clients.

'Oliver will be coming, but he's decided not to sell,' he said.

I suspected that Arthur had spoken quietly to him. This was a relief because his interest in furniture and fine arts was minimal and I was anxious that Weatherill and White should put on a good show, particularly as we were acting with the regional experts. I told Charles what had happened.

'I suggest we share the auctioning in the marquee until Rupert's ready,' he said.

Ken's health didn't permit him to auction, or to stand for a long period, so he stayed in the office to help the staff.

The marquee was very crowded now and our security staff were working hard answering all manner of questions. As I walked around behind the tables I saw Lady George come into the marquee with Mrs Cousins:

'Let me take you to your seats,' I said, and went with them to two chairs in the front row which had large 'Reserved' signs on them. Two farmers' wives were sitting there.

'Oh, I'm terribly sorry, we didn't realise,' replied one, as they moved grudgingly.

Surprise, surprise!

Jim Baker was the next person I saw, strolling round the marquee.

'I don't think I'll be staying long,' he said, 'the prices you'll make at this sale will be well above my level.'

I certainly hoped he was right.

William Hall came over for a chat.

'Haven't you had enough of sales this year?' I asked.

'I can relax and enjoy this one,' he said. 'I was a nervous wreck during my sale. By the way, I don't agree with your description of a lot over there. Come and have a look.'

He led me to a table and pointed to a set of six small cut glass tots.

'You've described those as whisky glasses.'

'Yes, that's right.'

'Well if you ever offer me a scotch in a tiny glass like that, I shan't come to your house again.'

We laughed, and I thought I would be happy if that was the harshest criticism I got during the day. Somehow I doubted it!

Anne was doing a good trade from her tea van, particularly with hot soup. It might be summer but the weather was cool, and I looked with foreboding at the dark clouds overhead. No Vulcans had flown over so far, so the CO at the airfield was doing what he could to help.

It would soon be time to start, but then I saw something – or rather somebody – that I didn't want to see. Swaggering down the drive in his brown suit, with a red cravat at his neck, was Frank Couples. He came to our sales occasionally and was always a nuisance because he needed to let everyone know he was there by being as ostentatious as possible. He was certainly a natural dealer, and told anyone who would listen that buying and selling were in his blood, because his forebears were of Romany stock. He had opened a shop in Grantham selling bric-a-brac, and anything else that he could buy cheaply and sell at a profit.

I had never forgiven him for pulling a shabby trick on me soon after I arrived at the firm. He came to a furniture sale at an isolated cottage and bought several lots, while strutting about and looking important. After the sale he took me to one side and said…

'I have to get back to the shop urgently. It would be a big help if you could take one of my lots back to Grantham: could you do that for me?'

'Yes, all right,' I said, eager to help – and stupid!

When I went to load the lot, I found that it was a night storage heater – a metal cabinet filled with bricks that were warmed by off-peak electricity at night, and released their heat during the day. It took four of us to lift it into the tiny office car and as Ken drove back to Grantham the headlights were pointing to the sky. There was much muttering from other members of staff about 'people who have just left college and know nothing'.

Frank thought it was very funny, but I didn't, and hoped we wouldn't have trouble with him today.

Stan rang the brass bell at 10.30 and I started the sale in the carriage house. As usual I told the company that 5% commission would be added to the sale price, that no purchases could be removed without a receipted bill, and reminded them where they could find the sale office. A large part of the crowd were not interested in this part of the sale and stayed in their seats in the marquee so they would be in a good position for the main auction.

To my mind, however, the lots in the carriage house gave a better picture of life in an English country house than the principal items displayed in the marquee and Hall. The stone statuary would have been admired by Lady George's ancestors during their promenades through the gardens, while the wooden wheelbarrow and ancient lawnmower gave a reminder of the generations of gardeners who had toiled there all their lives for little reward. The croquet set provided genteel entertainment on summer afternoons, watched from the garden seats by aged relatives. Old cricket bats, prams, fireguards, coal scuttles and boxes of dusty copies of the Illustrated London News had been brought down from the attics, where they had been kept because they 'might come in handy one day', or because no one had bothered to throw them away. Pine washstands, wardrobes and dressing tables, all painted in a sickly green, had come from dingy bedrooms once used by the servants.

There were boxes full of prints, inferior paintings and old photographs, mostly of family members, perhaps in uniform or ranged in a stately group at a christening or house party. The prints and paintings were mainly those hung by the family in the servants' rooms, and not chosen to inspire. Black and white prints of Highland cattle were a favourite, followed by small ugly oil paintings of Venice done by a member of the family, and not good enough to hang downstairs. Sepia prints of Victorian ladies in distress were also in evidence, together with ornate framed texts such as 'Thou Lord Seest Me', none of which would have added to the jollity of the servants' quarters. The dirty painted rocking horse with its threadbare mane had been ridden and loved by generations of children, but the abandoned pianola rolls, once prized by the family as the latest technology, had been discarded when they became commonplace. Sets of floral china toilet jugs and bowls recalled the days when maids trudged up the back stairs carrying hot water, so the family and guests could wash and shave before breakfast.

Selling at a country house auction is much easier than at a regular sale, because the general public long to own something, however humble, that has belonged to the aristocracy. The lots in the carriage house attracted keen interest and made excellent prices – particularly the garden statuary – and I was sorry when this part of the sale was over. It was time for Charles to start in the marquee, and Stan did the booking there while I had a quick cup of tea.

Charles had watched Rupert sell for many years and anyone in that privileged position should be a good auctioneer. He sold quickly and with a genial manner, not allowing prospective buyers to linger over their bids, but maintaining their interest and keeping the company in good spirits. All the lots being sold now were listed in the catalogue starting with the copper, brass and treen, and the bric-a-brac dealers competed against the general public but with little success, as most lots made a high price. The pewter and metal section came next including 'Mr Punch' cast iron door stops, tankards with the family crest, and bronze figures of Minerva and Diana the Huntress.

The order in which lots are catalogued takes a good deal of thought. Two or three expensive lots are listed consecutively and sold by the auctioneer -

'£400, £420, £450, £480... £500 – sold to you sir'.

'£600, £620, £650... £680 – and that's yours madam.'

'£300, £320, £350... £520 – sold to Harold Redmile.'

The next lot will be much less valuable, worth about £20.

'Who'll start me at £70 for this lot?'

A forest of hands shoot into the air from people thinking how cheap this must be compared with previous lots and frantic to buy something from this prestigious sale.

I took over the booking from Stan as the decorative lots were about to be sold – the stuffed owl, magic lantern, crocodile skin evening bag, and the ostrich feather fans which Alf displayed provocatively hand on hip, to the delight of the upper-class tricoteuses.

'Don't overdo it,' said Charles smiling, 'no one wants to see you do a strip tease!'

There were a few lots of costume jewellery, and then came the jade pendant. The dealer who had spoken to me yesterday stood at the side of the tent, not wearing his glasses but holding them in front of his chest. I had told

Charles of my conversation, but since our friend didn't even want the auctioneer to look in his direction in case it aroused his colleagues' suspicion, I bid on his behalf by tapping Charles on the knee. None of the other dealers showed any interest, the spectacles stayed by his chest, and he bought the lot for a modest price.

'Sold to your client Robert,' said Charles, and I entered the secretive dealer's name on the sales sheet. He put his glasses back on and strolled casually back to join his fellow dealers, with the suspicion of a smirk on his face.

The marquee was packed. The first few rows of seats were full of the female county set who had brought their Thermos flasks and sandwiches to ensure they missed nothing. This was a pity, because they are renowned for spending as little as possible, and the seats would have been better occupied by people who had come to buy. Their principal interest was in making loud comments to one another, such as 'Look at that pewter – not been cleaned for years!' and 'That stuffed owl looks miserable – but so would I, sitting in a glass case in the middle of that family!'

They knew that Lady George was sitting well within earshot in the front row, and tittered behind gloved hands at their own effrontery. If the lots had belonged to a Duke they would have been quiet and bid with vigour, but were not about to open their handbags to buy lots from a family they had always considered socially inferior.

The bidding came mainly from the bric-a-brac dealers, and from the middle classes of Grantham and district who were sitting behind the county set. This group was made up of shopkeepers' and farmers' wives, and the nouveaux riche from the district, such as garage proprietors, builders and factory owners. Having furniture or ornaments from Cardingford Hall in their houses would be a matter of great pride, to be pointed out frequently to visitors. At the back of the tent and spilling outside, stood small groups of men talking among themselves and seeming to take no interest in proceedings. These were the principal dealers whose hour had not yet come: they were waiting for the more important lots in the sale. I was concentrating on entering each auction price on the sale sheets, when suddenly an agitated Lady George appeared at my side.

'Do you remember cataloguing a lidded bronze vase decorated with carved lions?'

'Yes,' I said consulting my copy of the catalogue 'It was Lot 136.'

'You mean it's already been sold – who bought it?'

'Yes it has been sold, but the sale sheet's gone to the office, so I can't tell you the name of the buyer at the moment. I'll send them a note and ask someone to come out and tell you.'

'No, I must go and find out now,' she said and rushed out of the marquee. I could see her running across the lawn to the office and after a short time she came hurrying back with Ella.

'That vase – Lot 136,' said Ella 'it was bought by Mr Cummins of Barthorpe Road, Grantham. Lady George wants it back.'

'Why?' I asked.

'She'd forgotten that her late husband's ashes are in it!'

I had a quiet word with Charles and suggested that he asked the man in question to come to see us.

'We'd be very grateful if Mr Cummins would come to the rostrum and make himself known to us,' he announced.

A man in his sixties, with gold-rimmed glasses and an immaculately trimmed grey moustache, got up from his seat near the back of the marquee and came forward. I recognised him. He had run a successful car sales business in the south of England for many years and had recently retired, buying an expensive house on the edge of Grantham. I explained the situation to him as Lady George stood anxiously by, and asked if in the circumstances he would agree to cancel his purchase.

'Of course,' he said theatrically in his sincerest manner honed by years of car selling, and then, turning to Lady George and bowing slightly from the waist he added 'for you dear lady – anything.'

Visitors to his fine house would be even more impressed by this story of gallantry, than if he had shown them the actual purchase. We thanked him very much and I asked Ella to take the vase into the office to avoid any more trouble.

The Royal Air Force continued to help us by keeping their Vulcans grounded, but the sky was getting darker and it was becoming increasingly difficult to see the end of the marquee from the rostrum. Most of the glass had now been sold, with excellent prices realised for several sets of Waterford tumblers and wine glasses. The china came next, starting with various tea sets, followed by willow pattern meat dishes, sets of dinner ware, garnitures of Victorian vases, a few Wedgwood basalt urns and some nice figurines from the display cabinets.

We were about to start on the silver plate when Frank Couples staged his entrance into the marquee, and it was apparent that he had fortified himself at the local pub.

'How much may I say for this plated cruet,' said Charles, 'start me at £10'

'£20,' shouted Frank.

It was sold to him at that figure, whereupon he told everyone around how cheap it was. This pantomime was repeated for the next three lots until he was satisfied by the attention he had drawn to himself, and sauntered out of the marquee announcing that he would soon be back.

The sky became even darker and then a noise could be heard which grew louder and louder.

'A Vulcan,' I thought, but then realised that people standing outside were running into the tent. It was a hail storm, and the noise of the hail stones on the roof of the marquee became so loud that Charles could hardly be heard.

'I'm very sorry ladies and gentlemen,' he shouted 'but I shall have to stop selling until this storm passes.'

It was ironic that we had managed to keep the Vulcans away, but had been forced to stop by a midsummer storm. Mercifully it only lasted a few minutes, the sale resumed, and Rupert Smythe strolled into the marquee.

He was a broad shouldered man in his sixties, with a jolly red face and the air of a person leaving a pub after a good night out. This jovial, relaxed appearance concealed the ability of one of the top furniture experts in the country, who had built up a thriving and much-respected business. He walked around the groups of dealers at the back of the tent exchanging pleasantries and shaking hands, and it was part of his magic that they all seemed in a better mood after meeting him.

He walked slowly down the side of the marquee towards the rostrum nodding to the farmers and clients he knew, and when he got to the rostrum said to Charles:

'I've had a look at the sale sheets in the office. Things are going well.'

'Yes, we're very pleased,' said Charles, 'when would you like to take over?'

'You finish the plate and silver, and then I'll sell the clocks and curios to get the feel of the company before I auction the paintings.'

He then turned to me. 'After that young man, perhaps you'll sell the first few lots of furniture, before I finish the sale.'

I was delighted. He walked away after a brief word and handshake with Lady George in the front row, beaming at the ladies around her, while Charles finished selling the plated ware and started on the silver. The first lots were some odd mustard and pepper pots, then a few complete cruets, a christening tankard, some specimen vases, serving spoons and several sets of cutlery. Some of these sets were made up of individual pieces, which although solid silver and seemingly identical, were shown by the hallmarks to have been made in different years. They were catalogued as 'harlequin sets' – a lovely phrase. Then came the better lots of silver, including candlesticks, salvers, three ornate candelabra, two table centres and a fine Georgian peg top tankard. The main dealers had stopped chatting now and were paying attention to the sale, although they pretended not to in case they gave the impression that the lot being sold was valuable. They made an occasional languid bid, and Charles sold them a few lots before finishing this part of the sale.

Rupert was now standing by the side of the rostrum ready to take over and Charles changed seats with me so he could do the booking while I had a break, but I didn't intend to leave the marquee. I had heard so much from other auctioneers about Rupert's skills that I didn't want to miss any of his performance.

He gazed benignly around the company and told them how good it was to be in Lincolnshire and how fortunate his firm was to be instructed by Lady George and act in conjunction with Weatherill and White. The first lot he had to offer was a series of small brass bells attached to a leather strap, which was held up by Alf.

'Give them a shake Alf,' he said, 'marvellous,' and listened intently to their tinkling sound, before saying, 'Do you all remember the time when we opened the door into a sweet shop, and the bells rang out like that – those were the days. Ring them again Alf – wonderful!'

He had his audience. There was no chattering and no cynical comments. All eyes were fixed on Rupert, except for the dealers who had heard it all before, and Frank Couples, who had come back into the marquee and resented anyone else being the centre of attention. The few clocks, which were of modest value, the curios and miscellaneous items were sold quickly and then came the pictures.

After some framed etchings and pleasant watercolours, came six oil paintings which were the principal lots in the sale. Early in the nineteenth century a member of the family from the Hall, was riding through a nearby village when he saw some brightly decorated farm carts outside the smithy. He enquired who had done this work and was told it was the blacksmith's son. He promptly gave him an order to decorate carts at the Hall, and being well satisfied, asked him to paint a simple mural inside the summer house. This was noticed by a guest who was staying there during the hunting season, and he asked the young man to come to London and paint a portrait of his favourite horse. From these beginnings he progressed to family portraits, and in a few years the young man was one of the foremost society painters in the land. He never forgot the start he had been given at Cardingford Hall and agreed, at the height of his fame, to return and paint a series of family portraits.

It was this series that Rupert was about to sell as the principal attraction at our sale. The first portrait was of the lady of the house, gorgeously dressed, sitting beneath a tree in the Park with her young daughter and two spaniels. After a brief resume of the provenance of the paintings, which was in any case printed in the catalogue, Rupert offered it for sale.

'How much may I say for this first one - £8000?'

A voice rang out from the back – it was Frank Couples.

'I'll give you £800!'

Rupert ignored him, got an opening bid of £5000 and after spirited bidding sold the painting to a Bond Street dealer for £9250.

The second portrait showed the squire of the time, also in the Park, standing beside his favourite hunter, with a view of the Hall in the background.

'£9000 for this?' asked Rupert.

Frank shouted out again, 'I'll give you £900.'

He was ignored for a second time and after a similar opening bid, and keen competition, the portrait was sold for £9500.

The same pattern recurred during the sale of the next four paintings, with Rupert asking for a bid close to the final selling price, and Frank Couples shouting out a stupidly low offer, usually 10% of the suggested figure. He was not studying his catalogue because he was looking around the company to ensure that everyone appreciated his bravado. Rupert appeared unruffled, but missed very little, and noticed this.

After the sixth and last of the featured paintings had been sold – for £10,000, Rupert came to the next lot, which was an ugly amateur daub in oils of a horse looking out of its stable.

'How much for Lot 403 – start me at £9000' he said.

'I'll give you £900,' shouted Frank, right on cue.

The hammer fell instantly.

'Sold to you Mr Couples for £900.'

The lot was correctly described in the catalogue, he had bid loudly making quite sure that everyone could hear, and the hammer had fallen. He had paid £900 for a painting worth £50 at the most. The eyesore was his and there was nothing he could do about it. The company realised what had happened, and several turned round to look at him. He had his audience now that he didn't want it, and although he tried to appear unconcerned, his smile looked a little forced as he walked slowly out of the marquee. I hoped that he had been taught a lesson by a master auctioneer and would be less trouble in future, but somehow I doubted it.

It was soon time for me to sell the first 40 lots of furniture. I had to get the best prices I could, but my main task was to sell them quickly and keep the company in a good mood for Rupert's finale. The pine furniture and modern furnishings had already been sold in the carriage house, so the remaining lots, listed in the catalogue were mainly good-quality minor antiques. I sold a pair of oak coffin stools, followed by some Windsor chairs, three nests of tables and two china cabinets. Then came several pedestal tables, a music Canterbury, refectory table, Victorian mahogany chests of drawers, an oak bureau, carved oak chests and a set of rush-seated ladderback dining chairs. Although these lots were not very valuable they were of interest to the general public because they were small enough to fit into most houses, so the bidding was spirited and the dealers couldn't buy much.

Unfortunately the temporary grounding of the Vulcan aircraft came to an end mid-afternoon and I had to stop selling on two occasions as they passed over the marquee. This inconvenience was mitigated by the absence of Frank Couples, who had gone home, having endured enough humiliation for one day. My selling stint passed all too quickly, and I handed over to Rupert who finished the sale in style by selling the better furniture with his usual panache. A walnut bureau bookcase was followed by the Georgian mahogany three-pedestal dining table, a set of twelve Hepplewhite dining chairs with sheaf decoration, tallboys, an escritoire and the long case clocks.

Most people stayed until the end of the sale to see the better furniture being sold, but many went beforehand because they were only interested in earlier lots or had to fetch their children from school. They needed to pay their bills and collect their purchases before going, and we had to accommodate them without interrupting the auction, so the smaller lots that had been sold were taken to a secure area at the back of the marquee where buyers could collect them. This area was now very busy, so I went there to help, as many of the staff were still involved in running the auction, and I could watch Rupert as he sold.

At the end of the sale he walked around the marquee to talk to Lady George, the main dealers and other clients. After this he came over to shake my hand.

'I must go,' he said, 'it's been a pleasure working with you and thank you for all that you have done. I watched you selling – you'll make a good auctioneer.'

That was certainly a compliment, coming from him, but we both knew I had a lot to learn.

Chapter 18

He's with the Lord

Weatherill and White's principal business was the management of agricultural estates. In the first half of the twentieth century there were several in south Lincolnshire and Leicestershire, some with mansions and parks that had been enjoyed by generations of landowners. A number of these fine houses were requisitioned by the army during the Second World War, and a few were treated so badly they had to be demolished when they were returned to their owners.

This was the fate that befell Fairfield Hall, an impressive mansion standing in a glorious position on the edge of the village from which it took its name. The Hall had been the seat of the Earls of Liverscore for many generations, but the last of the line died childless before the war, and the surrounding estate passed to another branch of the family in the south of England.

Reg Weatherill was a charismatic man in his earlier years and popular among the hunting fraternity, although he didn't take part himself. One of his particular friends was a London solicitor who hunted extensively and had a large house in nearby Leicestershire, building up a substantial legal practice among his neighbouring landowners. Reg managed his friend's estate very efficiently, and he recommended Weatherill and White to any clients looking for a land agent.

From this introduction the firm became managing agents in the 1930s for the Fairfield Estate, an extensive landholding around Grantham including several villages. We were land agents for a number of other estates that were managed from Oak House, but the size of this one dictated that it should have a separate office, so a house in the village was extended and adapted for the purpose. Reg managed the estate very successfully for many years but his health was now failing, so he handed the duties over to Oliver, who went to live in the village and divided his working time between the estate office and Oak House.

There were three full-time staff at the Fairfield office. Henry was the chief clerk, and, since he was in charge in Oliver's absence, felt it necessary to speak in a slow, carefully cultivated drawl. The other clerk Herbert rolled his own cigarettes, and moaned constantly that he was underpaid with some justification, as Weatherill and White saw little point in encouraging staff to improve their station in life. The third member of staff was Doris, a woman from the village who acted as typist, receptionist and tea-maker.

Oliver performed his duties as land agent conscientiously and well, but since the estate belonged to absentee landlords he was in a position of power, which he enjoyed to the full – opening summer garden fetes in the various villages, and expecting to be treated as the squire.

Ironstone had been quarried extensively on the estate's land for many years. An agreement had been reached with an extraction company, whereby they were entitled to enter an area of farmland each year after paying appropriate compensation to the tenant. The seam of ironstone was close to the surface and, after the topsoil had been removed and stored, the ore was quarried by large mechanical diggers. The soil was then spread back over the field, and after a few years the only indication that quarrying had taken place was the drop of about three metres in the surface of the fields from the level of the surrounding hedges. The ironstone companies laid railway tracks over the land to take the stone to the main line, which was only a few miles away, and all this activity provided considerable employment in the area. Unfortunately however, ironstone could now be bought more cheaply overseas, and these activities were coming to an end.

During one of my days out with Oliver, we talked about the duties of a land agent.

'Managing a rural estate needs many skills,' he said. 'You've got to have a wide knowledge of agriculture, because many estates have home farms that must be run profitably. The Fairfield Estate doesn't have one, but I still need to know whether tenants are farming well or badly, and appreciate the pressures under which they work. An agent must also know a lot about agricultural law, which is complicated. Formal notices for an increase of rent, requiring a tenant to carry out work, or quit a holding, are subject to rigorous statutory time limits, and if I miss a deadline I'm in deep trouble.'

I relayed this to Ken knowing his mischievous views on the subject.

'He's very lucky there isn't a home farm on the Estate,' he said. 'Nothing gives tenant farmers more malicious glee than seeing bad crops on the owner's farm.'

Most of the estates around Grantham were managed by resident agents who acted for that one landowner, and Ken also had forthright views about them.

'The main quality they need is diplomacy,' he said. 'It's important for his relationship with the owner, but critical for dealings with the owner's wife. Most owners are considerate, but still possess that sense of effortless superiority peculiar to their kind. An occasional agent will discover that his client has not forgotten the humiliation he suffered as a fag at public school, and resolves to rectify matters in later life at his expense. However, providing their wishes are carried out immediately and without question, the agent can expect a reasonably tranquil life.

'It's when these wishes can't be carried out, because they are against the law, or will cause local turmoil, that he needs to be a diplomat. He must gently steer his principal in the right direction, and gradually convince him that his instructions were actually different from those he thought he'd given.

'Dealings with an owner's wife require more guile,' he continued. 'She will probably have been brought up in a house full of servants who had to carry out mother's quirky instructions immediately, or face the consequences. During her formative years at Roedean and finishing school the Second World War will only have been a marginal inconvenience, so she won't have noticed the staff leaving mummy's house in droves.

'After finally "hooking" her landowning husband, she is shocked to discover after the wedding that she has to run the ancestral home on her own, apart from a woman from the village who comes in to dust on Tuesday and Thursday mornings. She realises that having struggled for so long to get her husband to the altar, it would not be wise to moan to him, so it's the land agent that bears her full displeasure. Old-fashioned charm and a little firmness may sometimes prevail, but otherwise he has to steer an uneasy course between the besotted but indecisive husband and his demanding spouse.'

Mercifully Weatherill and White didn't have this problem, since the owners of the Fairfield Estate lived a hundred miles away.

A rural estate mainly consists of agricultural land, but there are usually considerable areas of woodland that also need careful management. To help prepare me for one of my forestry exams, Oliver arranged for me to have a day with Fred Ward, the head woodman, who took me on a tour of the estate woods.

'This is a new one,' he said at our first stop. 'It was planted only five years ago and you can see that the young trees have been placed close together so they'll compete with each other and grow quickly to get their share of sunlight. After about ten years each one will need more space, so the plantation must be thinned by taking out alternate trees and any defective ones. This is repeated every few years.

'A wood must have internal tracks, known as "rides", to let vehicles in for management work, and to extract timber when the trees are mature: they can soon get overgrown or waterlogged and need constant maintenance. Individual trees standing by public roads or in field boundaries, also need to be inspected regularly to make sure they're not dangerous.'

'That's a tremendous lot of work,' I said, 'how many woodmen do you have?'

'There are three under me,' replied Fred, 'and I report to Oliver.'

We stopped at a pub for a welcome sandwich lunch, and I said, 'The woods we've seen so far have been mainly conifers - don't you plant any broadleaved trees? It's wonderful to walk in a wood of mature oak or beech trees, but a plantation of conifers is dark and forbidding: it makes me feel that wolves will rush out of the gloom at any moment! Pine and fir trees in straight lines seem foreign in this gentle countryside.'

'I agree,' replied Fred, 'but unfortunately the only way an estate can get an economic return from its woodlands is by planting conifers. They mature in about 60 years, while oak and other broadleaved trees take much longer than that.'

The valuation and marketing of mature standing trees is an interesting exercise. Timber merchants travel the country looking for good hardwood trees, and a land agent is never short of offers to buy his best specimens. Walnut trees are the most valuable as the timber has an attractive figure, and is used to make veneer for furniture. This is done by placing the trunk of the felled walnut on a giant lathe with a sharp blade pressed against it: the trunk is rotated and the blade 'peels' it in thin layers, like an onion. This thin sheet is then used as a decorative surface for new furniture. A good walnut tree is not felled, but dug out of the ground so no part is wasted.

The sycamore is regarded as a weed among timber-producing trees, but is sometimes used to make veneer. It's valuable when the tree has an affliction that causes the timber to be 'ribbled' – or corrugated – and to find out whether a given tree has this characteristic, a small square is cut out of the bark with an axe. If the surface beneath is smooth the tree is normal and of little consequence, but if it is ribbled the timber will provide an attractive veneer. The square of bark is replaced so the tree is not damaged.

The principal hardwood timber trees are oak, ash and elm, while the corresponding conifers are pine, fir, larch and spruce. To value a standing tree the circumference is measured and the height estimated. A special tape measure with a hook at one end is used to measure the girth at waist level, and the height of the trunk is estimated to the point where the lowest branch projects. A set of tables gives the volume of the trunk from these two measurements, and the tree is then priced per cubic foot at the prevailing market rate. The branches are treated as worthless, and carted away for firewood or burnt on site.

I had a fascinating day with Oliver valuing a number of trees that had to be felled due to the widening of a main road near Grantham.

'Stand well back from the tree,' he said, 'and estimate the height by imagining a man, six feet tall, standing by the trunk. Then imagine another man of similar height standing on his shoulders, and so on till you get to the level of the lowest branch.'

I suspect that the woodland on the Fairfield Estate was managed more for its shooting benefits than as a source of timber. Weatherill and White rented the shooting rights over most of the Estate and the partners shot there, or as guests on other shoots, about twice a week in the season. They employed three gamekeepers to organise matters, kill vermin, rear pheasants and maintain their habitat. They had constant clashes with the forestry staff about the management of the woods, and more disputes with the tenant farmers about the crops growing nearby. The gamekeepers always won these arguments, because the woodmen had their jobs to think of, and the tenants had to consider how they might fare at the next rent review. The Fairfield shoot was widely thought to be excellent, and daily bags of 300-400 pheasants and partridge were expected.

I always thought shooting to be more of a ritual than a pastime, but I couldn't afford it anyway, and played hockey instead. It is the aim of every participant to be considered 'a good shot', which involves the successful pursuit of what must be the stupidest creature in Britain – the pheasant. When this large bird hears a line of people walking towards it, beating the undergrowth with sticks and shouting loudly, it could save itself and do them some damage if it only had the sense to fly directly at them. However it has no sense, and flies away from them over the waiting guns where the cock bird, being brightly coloured as well as large and stupid, presents a target that's difficult to miss. In case the guns, having enjoyed their morning glass of port, still don't realise that this plump and gaudy bird is lumbering towards them, it advertises its presence by squawking loudly as it breaks cover.

Their intelligence scarcely extends to fending for themselves in cold weather, so part of a gamekeeper's job is to feed them with corn, and they devour such quantities that they have great difficulty in lifting themselves off the ground. Stories of shooting exploits told in pubs should be treated with suspicion, because if accepted as gospel it would seem routine for a sportsman to see pheasants performing high-speed aerobatics at a height of two hundred feet before shooting one with each barrel. My sympathies were closer to those of George in our reception office, who watched the partners march out of the door in their shooting kit for the third time that week and observed loudly…

'It only needs one pheasant to fire back and they'd all pack it in!'

Although I didn't hunt or shoot, I soon realised that much of the beauty of the local countryside is due to these pursuits. When a shoot is being held and pheasants or partridge are flushed out of a wood by the beaters, their instinct is to fly to another one nearby, so it's important to have several small woods close to one another. Hunting obviously needs foxes, and their favourite habitat is an area of gorse and bushes known as a covert. Most landowners either hunt themselves or are sympathetic to it, so many of these were established over the years and eventually grew into spinneys. It doesn't make economic sense to plant small areas of woodland, and they wouldn't exist if it weren't for hunting and shooting.

As I discovered at the tenantright valuation between Fred Coke and David Tims, gamekeepers like high hedges on farms so that game birds present a challenging target. Tenants are therefore encouraged to keep their hedges in good order rather than rip them out and amalgamate fields into ever-larger units. Scattered woods and well-kept hedges are a crucial part of the attractive countryside in this area, but if landowners didn't enjoy their hunting and shooting, the Lincolnshire/Leicestershire borders would be an arable prairie.

Fairfield is an idyllic village with a handsome medieval church and a delightful cricket ground, which was well maintained by the local club, for which Oliver had been an enthusiastic wicket-keeper until shooting, golf and business took over most of his time. Arthur was not as good a cricketer, but each August Bank Holiday Monday he selected and captained an eleven to take on the village side, and I was asked to play several times. I had more enthusiasm than skill, but was a useful opening batsman and a 'military medium' bowler. The game started at 11am followed by lunch at 1 o'clock with plenty of beer, then tea at 4.30pm, before close of play at 7pm. The village side was usually stronger than our scratch XI, but were sensible enough not to flaunt it, and occasionally Arthur's team won a glorious victory.

In the centre of the village stood the Liverscore Arms, a stone-built pub with little external charm, but a place of much merriment, particularly after cricket matches. Villagers still spoke of a wager that was placed there in the 1930s when Bernard, a successful local businessman bought a new and expensive car and was bragging about its performance. Christian, a gentleman farmer from the next village, who played cricket most of the summer and hunted all winter, told him that the car couldn't possibly be as fast as he claimed. Bernard became more and more exercised, and eventually a £50 wager was agreed between them that he couldn't complete the 22-mile trip down the Great North Road from the George Hotel in Stamford to the George Hotel in Grantham in half an hour.

The appointed day arrived and news of the wager had spread, so a crowd of farmers waited expectantly in the George bar in Grantham. A telephone call came from Stamford at 11.30am to confirm that Bernard had left, but at mid-day there was no sign of him. Ten minutes later he rushed into the hotel red-faced with fury, and slammed ten £5 notes down on the bar counter.

'Infuriating!' he said, 'my car was going like a dream and I was well ahead of schedule until I reached Great Napton, just three miles from here, only to find a flock of sheep blocking the road. It took 15 minutes to get them out of the way.'

'Oh dear,' said Christian, pocketing the money 'it sounds as though I'm a very lucky man. Let me buy you all a drink.'

Bernard left early, but the others enjoyed a very liquid lunchtime before the winner of the wager decided he had drunk enough, and after congratulations all round, left the bar with a friend who had volunteered to drive him home.

'Christian', said the friend as they drove home, 'you keep sheep don't you?'

141

'Yes.'

'Don't you have some grass fields by the Great North Road at Great Napton?'

'Yes,' he replied, 'but you're surely not suggesting anything!'

The friend said no more. He didn't need to. The broad wink was enough.

The Trustees of the Fairfield Estate had their formal meetings at the Estate Office twice a year. Oliver would present a financial statement, together with his management report for the preceding period, after which Reg would join them for a convivial lunch followed by a tour round parts of the Estate. Reg would drive some of the Trustees in his Jaguar and, passing a pair of cottages, announce with a wave of his hand, 'We've just done those up.'

After a further mile there would be another wave of the hand and he would say, 'The tenant of that farm retired last month. We've re-let it to James Entwhistle, the son of another tenant. Good family!'

After an hour or so, fortified by this information and a good lunch, the Trustees would be put back on the London train at Grantham and not seen again for another six months.

The Fairfield Estate was the largest managed by Weatherill and White, but there were several others. One of these lay in north Lincolnshire, the remaining fragment of a once substantial estate. The titled owner possessed a large area of land around his stately home in East Anglia, and had decided to sell off his outlying properties as they became vacant. Two tenanted farms and some cottages still remained, together with a few properties in a small and sleepy town. The clerical work for this estate and several others was done at Oak House by Herbert Sandsome, a kindly but dour Methodist local preacher. Every six months he arranged a rent audit, and the estate tenants were notified that they should go to the Bull Hotel in the local town on a certain date and pay their dues. I wondered why he collected the rents in this way when there were so few tenants: it would seem simpler to send the demands by post. During my articled years he once took me with him, and I found out.

Weatherill and White had a Ford Popular that was used by the staff as an office car: a trip in this vehicle was like travelling in a telephone kiosk, and about as comfortable. We set off in it to the rent audit, with Herbert driving at a maximum speed of 30 mph – slowing down for any bends in the road. The 45-mile trip took us almost two hours, but when we eventually arrived at the Bull Hotel an upstairs room was ready for us, and cups of coffee appeared. To encourage the tenants to attend the audit they were given a token after paying their rent that could be 'cashed' in the bar downstairs. The first tenant, who rented one of the farms, came around noon and paid his rent. After Herbert had handed over the token the farmer gave him a small carton.

'Just a few eggs for you, Mr Sandsome.'

'Many thanks,' said Herbert 'by the way I've ordered that new fireplace: has the builder told you when he'll put it in?'

'Not yet,' said the tenant.

'I'll see what I can do.'

The next person to appear was a short man wearing a red and white striped apron, who rented his butcher's shop from the Estate. He paid his dues, and was about to leave with his token when Herbert said:

'We did enjoy that pork pie last year.'

'Bless my soul Mr Sandsome, I forgot to bring you one. I'll be right back.'

And so he was a few minutes later, with the pie, which was graciously accepted. I noticed then that Herbert had not brought his cash book and paperwork in the small brief case that he usually carried, but in a holdall big enough to take his clothing for a week's holiday. The eggs and pie vanished into its ample depths. The audit continued, with a joint of ham, a basin of brawn, a fruit cake, more eggs and other goodies finding their way into the capacious bag. Herbert was teetotal, as a good Methodist should be, so we didn't join the tenants gathered in the bar, but snatched a quick lunchtime sandwich and set off back to the office. The return journey was no quicker and just as uncomfortable.

Another estate managed by the firm lay in the heart of the finest fox hunting country in Leicestershire, and included a magnificent Tudor stately home surrounded by a park. The owner was an elderly titled gentleman who had hunted all his life but was now very frail. Another clerk, Roger Fellowes, did the bookwork for three of the larger estates, including this one. He was much younger than Herbert, and certainly not a Methodist, as he enjoyed his beer and had introduced me as a member of the Grantham Golf Club. The partners of the firm valued his services highly, because he dressed well and knew how to converse with our up-market clients. This appreciation, however, did not extend as far as paying him an adequate wage.

On one occasion Roger was ill and couldn't make the weekly journey to deliver the wages to this Leicestershire estate. I went instead, and drove down the imposing approach to the front entrance of the Hall following my instructions by continuing to the tradesmen's entrance at the back. The door was opened by the butler, and I had to satisfy him that I was the genuine representative from Weatherill and White, before asking for the owner's secretary, who would distribute the weekly wage packets to the staff.

'He's with the Lord,' replied the butler loftily.

I feared for a moment that the secretary had met an untimely end, but then realised he must be in a meeting with his lordship.

'Can I wait for him?' I asked.

The butler said no more, but turned and glided away from me into the recesses of the mansion. I gathered that I was to follow and we walked down several corridors to arrive at the main entrance hall.

'Wait there,' he said, indicating a hard chair on the other side of the hall and I started to walk across the floor. It was like walking over a ploughed field and I was concerned that I might twist my ankle. Square white marble slabs had been laid in diagonal rows, and at the corner of each of these was a much smaller square of black marble. Over the centuries the larger slabs had worn to a depth of around three inches in the centre, but the small black ones, being much harder, had remained at their original level. I negotiated my way with difficulty to the appointed chair and, after a few minutes, the secretary appeared with our client behind him, who looked very frail, but walked across this dangerous floor as if it were a bowling green. I marvelled at this as he greeted me warmly, and I delivered the wage packets. I left the Hall, but this time through the main doors at the invitation of our noble client – much to the dismay of his butler!

Chapter 19

The Family Bible and the Scrapbook

I courted Sarah for several years and despite two intervals when the romance was definitely 'off', she finally said, 'Yes' on New Years Day 1964, and we fixed the wedding date for March of the following year. We looked at several houses before deciding that asking prices had reached ridiculous levels – three-bedroomed detached houses on estates were making £4000 for heavens sake! We decided that since prices had got so high (!) we would build our own, and I made several approaches to local landowners asking if they had any building plots available. I had no success, but then remembered a farm that we managed at Great Somerton, and Arthur agreed to contact the owner to see if he would sell a plot from a field near the church. He was delighted at the prospect of some ready money, and we negotiated a price of £500 subject to planning consent.

I made an appointment to see the local Planning Officer, showed him a plan of the site, and asked if I would get permission to build a house there.

'Well,' he said, 'it's up to the Committee of course, but there's a bungalow next door, and a house immediately opposite, so I think they'll agree.'

Howard, a good friend of mine from the Round Table, was sales manager for a local firm that was building houses in Grantham and several other towns, and my next appointment was with him.

'I can show you lots of designs: what sort of property are you thinking of?' he said.

'We want a three-bedroomed detached house,' I replied cautiously, 'if we can afford it!'

He reached into the cupboard behind him and pulled out several leaflets showing the elevations, floor plans and specifications of houses they were building.

'Have a look through these,' he said, 'then come and have another word with me.'

'Can we ask for modifications to your designs?' I asked.

'Yes, we're very flexible, in fact some clients need a couple of pages to list all the alterations they want,' he replied.

Sarah and I went through the designs very carefully and eventually chose the one we wanted – with several alterations.

'Good grief,' said Howard, 'this is a new record! Your list's three pages long.'

He agreed to the amendments, a price was settled, planning consent given, and building began. The house was finished well before our wedding day, and we were very pleased with our new home, which was only four miles from the office, had the village church across the road, and views over open fields at the back.

We met the local vicar to discuss the wedding.

'We'd like to get married in this church at Great Somerton,' said Sarah.

'Do you have any relatives living in the village?' asked the vicar.

'No.'

'Well, according to Church of England regulations I can only use the church to marry people who are resident in the village, or have a significant connection to it.'

'We're building a house across the road from the church,' I said, 'surely that's a "significant connection". It seems silly for us to be married anywhere else.'

Fortunately the vicar agreed.

Sarah's parents organised a wedding reception for us at the George Hotel, guests were invited and all arrangements made, but I did have one major worry. I had been to several weddings of my cricket and hockey friends and the celebrations often got a bit out of hand! On one occasion the couple's 'going away' car was decorated so enthusiastically that it needed a complete respray, and after another wedding the bride and groom's car was chased by fifteen or twenty vehicles for many miles at high speed through narrow country lanes, before they finally made their escape. The day came when the ringleader of these exploits was married, and having subjected many friends to various humiliations, they were waiting for him. As he left the reception he was seized and his arms fastened to his sides by a chain, which was then padlocked and the key thrown away. Although his treatment was richly deserved, I did feel sorry for him and his new wife as she drove away in their car – mercifully a nearby garage came to their rescue with a pair of bolt croppers.

I could see difficulties of this kind looming for me, so before our wedding we left our car in Frank Branscome's isolated stackyard six miles away from the hotel, and the best man drove us there after the reception. We also arranged for one of the ushers to use his vehicle to block the entrance to the hotel car park, so that no one could set off in pursuit. We thought all the wedding arrangements had worked perfectly, until we discovered that the friend who had offered to film the ceremony forgot to take the lens cap off his camera! We drove to the Norfolk coast for a brief and blissful honeymoon before returning to our new home.

We were now residents of Great Somerton, where Dan Robinson was the unofficial squire, and the Stumblers Cricket Club had their ground. On the other side of the churchyard stood the Old Rectory, home of Major Glass, chairman of the local Hunt. He was nearly eighty, but walked and rode with his back as straight as a ramrod, and although he must have been horrified to see our new house being built within sight of his windows, he welcomed us warmly into the village.

We had only been in the house for a week, and I was working in the garden when he rode by on his horse.

'Will you both come and have a glass of sherry with me tomorrow?' he asked.

'We shall be delighted,' I replied.

When we arrived the next day we were given our sherry and then invited to walk round the garden.

'There are some rather nice petunias in that bed,' he said, 'I'll dig some up for you', and we continued on our tour while he pointed out interesting plants – complete with their Latin names. Two days later his gardener delivered a barrow load of wonderful specimens, which formed the basis of our new garden.

Many stories were told of his gentlemanly conduct in the hunting field, and one described an occasion when the Hunt was in full cry over open country to the east of Grantham. They were about to jump a hedge with Major Glass and a retired Colonel in the lead, only to find their way barred by an irate farmer who was shouting, threatening them with a shotgun and making it very clear that the Hunt was not to cross his land. The riders stopped, and Major Glass trotted forward, leaning down from his horse to speak to the farmer for a few minutes. He then straightened up and waved the others forward.

'We may proceed,' he said.

'How did you change his mind?' asked the Colonel.

'I find that he was a member of my regiment.'

'Ah,' said the Colonel 'that would account for his abominable language!'

Another of the Major's Army friends lived in a lovely house enclosed by a park in the Vale of Belvoir. His family owned a substantial business that manufactured a well-known food product, but his intelligence was such that they paid him handsomely to keep out of the way, and he spent most of his time hunting and shooting. One day he was sitting in his parlour after luncheon when he noticed some activity inside the boundary of his park.

'Wright – fetch my binoculars,' he shouted to his butler, and having focussed on the offending area, he continued:

'Would you believe it? An Austin Seven car has come in through my gates and – it's stopped – a family's getting out – they're spreading a rug on the grass – good heavens, they're having a picnic. Wright – note down the registration number of that car.'

On a Sunday afternoon three weeks later a gleaming Bentley drew up outside a terraced house in Nottingham. The butler got out, opened the boot, set up a table with a white cloth in the tiny front garden, placed a chair beside it and a military-looking man sat down.

'Will you have Indian or China tea sir?' asked the butler, but before his employer could answer, the man of the house stormed out and enquired in fundamental language what was going on, only to be told...

'You had a picnic in my grounds – now I'm having one in yours!'

The village where we now lived had once been two settlements – High Somerton and Low Somerton – but recent housing had connected them to form a single community. Our house would once have been in the former, which was a cluster of houses around the Church and Rectory, while Low Somerton comprised the properties by the main road, including the Coach and Horses.

Across the road from the public house was a low stone cottage with a pantiled roof, and attached to this was the former village smithy. Bertha Farr, the village postmistress, was a spinster well into her seventies and lived there using one room as the post office: going in there was to enter a time warp. The outer door opened into a small lobby enclosed by a heavy curtain, which had to be pulled aside to enter the parlour where a fire burned in the iron range and Bertha waited behind a pine table to serve her customers. She not only ran the post office but delivered letters and parcels around the village winter and summer, striding through the lanes and fields despite her age and frailty, wearing an old brown coat, woollen hat and Wellington boots.

Bertha was born in this cottage, and brought up there with four older brothers. Her father was a martinet, ruling them all with a rod of iron, and probably due to his overbearing influence none of the five children married. He was the blacksmith and wheelwright for the village but none of his sons followed him and the smithy closed when he died in the 1930s. Sometimes we could get Bertha to reminisce about the 'best room' on the ground floor of the cottage:

'As children we were only allowed to go in there on Sundays, and then we could either read the Bible, or the family scrapbook. This had been assembled over the years by sticking in extracts from books and magazines, poetry, selected passages from the classics that were supposed to be uplifting, pictures of animals and foreign countries, and religious texts.'

One brother lived with Bertha for many years but had recently died, and she now lived alone refusing to spend any money on the cottage or herself, so her brown coat became more and more threadbare as the months passed. The few people that managed to get through the front parlour into the rest of the cottage said that the only fitting in the kitchen was a sink with a plank beside it serving as a draining board. There was no mains water inside the cottage, so she fetched it from a tap outside the back door.

Great Somerton was a small village with few facilities, probably because it was so close to Grantham. The primary school had recently closed and there was no shop, although mobile vans called daily selling bread, groceries, meat and fish. There was no village hall or playing field, so the Coach and Horses was the social centre, and Dan Robinson encouraged local children to play on the outfield of the cricket ground. Democracy had not yet reached the village – there was no elected Parish Council, but an annual Parish Meeting was held in one of Dan's barns.

He had inherited the farm from his father Gerald, and after he took over, the standard of farming improved dramatically. Dan was a true 'character' who enjoyed hunting and shooting, served on the District Council, played cricket and had a wide circle of friends, but never allowed himself to be diverted from managing his farm. His father had many of the same characteristics, a great sense of humour, and enjoyed visiting local hostelries. One lunchtime he was with friends in the George Hotel when an anxious young man came into the bar asking for Mr Robinson. He was directed to Gerald, and said:

'Mr Robinson I'm terribly sorry but I was driving out of Great Somerton towards Grantham about an hour ago, skidded on that bad bend and my car went through the fence on the left-hand side of the road and into the field.'

'You mean that three-rail wooden fence just before the spinney?' asked Gerald.

'Yes.'

'Well, that'll cost you a whisky!'

The unfortunate man bought the drink, and Gerald downed it in one.

'Thank you young man: that's paid for the bottom rail.'

Second and third whiskies followed in quick succession in payment for the middle and top rails. The young man, now much poorer, turned to leave the bar, 'Goodbye Mr Robinson, and I'm sorry I damaged the fence.'

'Think nothing of it lad, I'm delighted you came. That field isn't mine. It belongs to Philip Ford, so you'd better go and see him next!'

The annual Parish Meeting took place soon after we moved in, and we went along to see what happened and meet other villagers. We weren't surprised when there was no opposition to the election of Dan as chairman, as the Meeting was held in his barn and many of those present worked for him. He conducted most of the proceedings with avuncular charm, but this affability lapsed when another newcomer, who had moved to the village from Grantham, asked a question:

'Why isn't there any electric lighting on the tarmac footpath that runs through the playing field in the middle of the village?'

This path was known in the village as 'the thirst after righteousness' because it ran from the church, through the cricket ground, to the pub. There was no lighting and it was hazardous on dark evenings, but after the question had been asked by the new resident, the chairman's face darkened.

'Firstly, it isn't a playing field. It's my paddock and I allow people to use it. Secondly, anyone who moves into the countryside and expects the same standard of street lighting they had in the town, would be well advised to go back as quickly as possible.'

This outburst discouraged any further business and the Meeting soon finished, after which we adjourned to the Coach and Horses without the disgruntled newcomer, who was left to stumble home along the unlit path. Dan and I talked about farming, and the sheep trade in particular, before he asked how we liked living in Great Somerton. We told him that we liked it very much, and Sarah said how remarkable Bertha was at her age to deliver the mail so promptly and in all weathers.

'Yes,' said Dan, 'she is remarkable, but she can't go on for ever.'

He started to chuckle, and warmed to his theme when he noticed that others in the bar were listening.

'She's got to go sometime,' he continued, 'I must have second sight, because I can see her gravestone in St Mary's churchyard now. It'll read:

"Here lies
Bertha Farr
Spinster of this Parish
Aged 74
Village postmistress
1932 – 1965
Returned unopened".'

We joined in the general hilarity at Dan's prophecy but unfortunately it soon came true, when Bertha's frail body wore out and she died in her sleep. James Trimm, senior partner of a legal practice in Grantham, lived opposite us in the village and acted for her executors. Although our new house must have affected their view, he and his wife did not object to our planning application, and we became good friends. He was a man of few words, and I soon learnt that any business telephone conversation with him was long, if it lasted more than three sentences. He rang me some weeks after her death.

'Bertha Farr,' he said.

'Yes.'

'Will you act for the estate?'

'We'll be pleased to.'

'Letter in the post.'

This duly arrived, instructing us to deal with the sale of the cottage and its contents on behalf of the beneficiaries, who were distant relatives living in Birmingham. The keys to the property were held by a neighbour who had been one of Bertha's few close friends, and very helpful in her last months. When

Ken and I called at her house she asked us to come in and gave us a cardboard box.

'I cleaned some of the rubbish out of the house, and found this on top of the wardrobe in her bedroom.'

In the box was a pile of old white £5 notes, that had been withdrawn from circulation about 10 years ago and were no longer legal tender. I remembered handling one of these as a boy when I helped behind the counter in my father's shop, but they were now collectors' items. We agreed with the neighbour how sad it was that Bertha had hoarded her money, when spending just a few of the notes would have taken some of the drudgery from her life.

It seemed strange to push aside the heavy curtain inside the front door, knowing there would be no fire burning in the range beyond, and no Bertha to welcome us. The pine table still stood in the parlour, but the Post Office authorities had taken away their booklets, rubber stamps, ink pads and parcel scales with the official brass weights. The kitchen Windsor chair in which her brother had sat for so long, stood forlornly beside the range, with a Victorian settee and two button-backed chairs on the other side of the room. I started to take measurements, while Ken listed the contents, which would be taken to our salerooms.

Unfortunately the reports about her kitchen fittings proved to be true. The shallow stoneware sink had a plank beside it and shelves beneath housing a few chipped cups, saucers and plates, while two dusty saucepans stood on the old electric cooker. We had expected this, but not the sight that greeted us when we opened the door into her 'best room'. A Victorian red mahogany sideboard stood by one wall, with a china cabinet facing it across the floor. Beside the cabinet was a small mahogany kneehole desk with strange fitted pigeonhole compartments in the cupboards beneath. We learnt later that a member of the family had once been the local collector of tithes and taxes, and these small compartments housed the payment records of everyone in the parish.

It was the circular pedestal dining table in the centre of the room that made us pause in astonishment, for on it lay the family Bible and the scrapbook, which had remained there since Bertha and her brothers were required to read them as children. Had she made a solitary pilgrimage to this lonely room every Sunday, to remember the lost days of her childhood?

There was another surprise to come. After taking details of the accommodation in the cottage, and listing the furniture, we went outside to look in the former blacksmith's shop. The two-part door was secured by a rusty padlock, which we opened with difficulty. It was obvious that we were the first people to go in for a long time, but as we lifted the door latch, we didn't appreciate for just how long. The light was poor inside the smithy because the windows were festooned with cobwebs, but as our eyes adjusted to the gloom we could see that nothing had been moved since Bertha's father had died thirty years ago. The iron water trough, now dry and full of rust, stood beside the forge and the hand bellows remained on top of the coal where they had been laid down. The large barrel-sized bellows, which had been worked by the blacksmith's foot, stood on the other side of the forge beside the anvil. Before he closed the door for the last time he had taken off his leather apron, and laid it down on an old tree stump in the middle of the shop, where it stayed... rotten now and hanging in shreds. The pincers, hammers and other tools of his trade, all covered in dust, hung on the wall or lay on the workbench beside the heavy vice, while horseshoes, wheel rims, nails and iron bars were scattered ankle deep around the floor.

Blacksmith's 'barrel' bellows

There seemed no point in trying to list all the tools and equipment: they needed to be kept together and displayed in a museum. We closed the door gently, humbled by this glimpse into the past. It didn't seem right to move the contents of the cottage or smithy which had remained undisturbed for so long, but it had to be done. The furniture was taken to our salerooms and the better items kept back for an antique auction. The beneficiaries of the estate agreed that the contents of the smithy should be preserved intact, so they were sold to a local stately home where a crafts museum was to be opened. The cottage and buildings were offered for sale by private treaty, and attracted considerable interest. If ever a property could be advertised as 'having many original features' and 'suitable for modernisation', this was the one. It was bought by a young couple who spent a lot on improvements, and opened a tea room in the old smithy.

Chapter 20

A Stooge and a Public House

Auctions are usually interesting and sometimes dramatic. The role of an auctioneer has been compared to that of the chairman in an old time music hall, but it's more central than that because he can't escape the limelight by introducing other acts. I mentioned earlier that his role has been compared to a parson conducting a service, but auctions don't take place in an atmosphere of reverence. My friend Jim thought that an auction sale was like a Catherine wheel, with the auctioneer acting as the central nail that keeps it steady. It's certainly true that bidding revolves around an auctioneer and provides the excitement; if he's too inflexible the "wheel" doesn't get going, and if he's too relaxed it spins away out of control.

To continue the theatrical comparison, when an auctioneer sells in his own cattle market or saleroom, the backdrop and cast are familiar, and he knows the stagehands are experienced. The situation is very different when he is 'on tour', and conducts an auction in unfamiliar surroundings.

Soon after I came to Weatherill and White we were instructed by a large industrial company to sell their factory in Grantham in conjunction with a national firm of commercial estate agents. Arthur went to the factory to meet one of their partners, and found that he was extremely arrogant.

'I have told our clients,' he said, 'that we sell commercial properties all over the country, and it's quite unnecessary to appoint local agents, but since they've insisted we've had to agree. We generally sell properties by auction: is there a decent hotel in the town?'

'We can use the George Hotel,' said Arthur, keeping his temper with difficulty.

We booked a room there, brochures were prepared and printed, and an advertising programme agreed with the client. The auction was fixed for 3pm on a Wednesday afternoon, and on the morning of that day the same partner of the national firm arrived by rail from London, but this time with a colleague. I met them at the station and took them to see Arthur at Oak House, and after a brief discussion they adjourned to the George Hotel for lunch, where the Londoner told Arthur:

'I shall, of course, conduct the auction'.

I went to the hotel to set out chairs for the expected company, with a brochure on each one. I put a small table at the end of the room with three chairs behind it, and at around 2.30pm Arthur came into the room with the joint agent, but not his colleague. The London auctioneer asked Arthur if he could have a quiet word with him in the corner of the room.

153

'I'll bring Robert with me,' said Arthur, 'he's "learning the job".'

'I've brought my colleague,' said the agent, 'to help me with the auction. He'll sit with the rest of the company and bid as though he's a genuine buyer.'

'You mean he'll act as a stooge,' said Arthur, 'it's not the way we do business.'

'I doubt if you have many commercial auctions,' came the reply. 'We have them all the time, and that's what we do.'

The ploy was designed to demonstrate to any potential buyers that there was other interest in the property, and hopefully keep them bidding until the reserve price was reached.

'By the way,' he added, 'our client has agreed our recommended reserve price of £100,000.'

I went to the back of the room so I could watch proceedings, and a few minutes before 3 o'clock saw the colleague saunter into the room with an air of studied nonchalance, and take his appointed place. He was in his early twenties and obviously considered himself to be on the brink of a glittering career, which was conceivable, as ignorance and arrogance have proved no hindrance to many successful people. There were about twelve people in the room when the auctioneer stood up to introduce the solicitor and Arthur, and give a short description of the factory. He asked if there were any questions, but there were none and he asked for an opening bid.

'May I start the bidding at £150,000?'

Then came the bombshell!

'Yes!' said his colleague loudly.

The auctioneer's complexion changed instantly from rosy to ashen. He had 'flown a kite' by asking for a high price, so that when bidding actually started – probably at around £50,000 – prospective buyers would have this initial figure in their minds. He knew there was very little chance that the bidding would ever get that high, so he thought hard – and desperately!

'I must suspend the auction for a few moments,' he announced, 'while I discuss that bid with the gentleman in the centre of the room.'

He walked towards the door, indicating with a jerk of his head that his associate should join him outside. After a short time he came back alone.

'As I suspected, that bid was a mistake,' he announced, 'so can I start the bidding at £100,000?' – but there was silence – '£70,000 then,' followed by an even longer pause – 'start me at £50,000.'

But the damage was done. The market for commercial property was weak at the time, and this ridiculous episode had snuffed out any interest there might have been. The factory was withdrawn from the auction, although Weatherill and White – not the London agents – did sell it later for just under £100,000. I never found out what had caused the young man to have this aberration – indeed I never heard of him again, but I would like to have heard the conversation between the two of them as they travelled back to London.

We booked the same room at the George Hotel some months later, when we were instructed by the Ministry of Defence to sell a block of four hangars by auction. These vast buildings were part of Radstone airfield, about six miles east of Grantham, but on the other side of a public road from the rest of the property. They had housed bombers during the Second World War, but the aerodrome was now used solely as a satellite landing strip for a major Air Force training base nearby. Pilots used the runway for take-off and landing practice, or 'circuits and bumps' as they called it.

The four hangars were now surplus to requirements, and the Ministry got planning consent from the local Council for change of use to warehousing. When a statutory body is disposing of property the sale is usually by auction, because if it is well advertised and held in full public view, the Government can't be criticised for underhand dealing or selling too cheaply. We advertised the sale widely, and circulated our brochures to property companies all over the country, but there seemed to be little interest. The Ministry fixed a reserve price of £90,000, which appeared very reasonable, but the buildings still had the original corrugated iron cladding, which would need to be replaced. Arthur asked me to be his clerk at the auction and on the afternoon of the sale I sat with him and the solicitor behind the usual small table at the end of the room. Five minutes before the auction was due to start there were only two other men sitting in front of us, and we knew they were hotel regulars who had just come out of the bar to see what was happening.

Three minutes later, two strangers came in together and sat at the back of the room deep in conversation. We thought they might be interested, but more bidders were needed for us to have a successful auction. No one else came.

Arthur whispered to me just before 3'o clock:

'I don't like the look of this: it's going to be a wasted afternoon.'

He then stood up and went through the usual preliminaries, before asking for bids from the four people in front of him.

'Start me at £100,000.'

No response.

'£80,000 then.'

Still nothing.

'£60,000 to start. It doesn't matter where we begin. It's where we finish that matters.'

No one spoke.

He was on the point of announcing that he was withdrawing the property from the market since there was no interest, when one of the strangers spoke:

'£50,000,' he said.

We had a start. But where was the next bid to come from? It isn't easy for an auctioneer to produce an imaginary bid when there are only four people in the room. But then:

'£60,000,' said the person sitting next to him.

So they were not colleagues.

'£70,000,' replied the first bidder.

The two continued until the price had reached £110,000, when the second bidder shook his head and the hangars were sold to his neighbour. The contract was signed, the deposit paid, and the two men left together. We were able to report a satisfactory result to the Ministry, but they had no idea how unusual the auction had been. We could only think that the men represented two property companies specialising in warehouses, and toured the country seeking similar opportunities. Since they met frequently at auction sales, they realised it was better to enjoy each other's company and see who was authorised to bid highest on a given day, than operate in an atmosphere of continual confrontation.

Radstone airfield was one of many that had been built around Grantham during the Second World War. Much of Lincolnshire is relatively flat and within easy reach of Germany across the North Sea, so bomber squadrons were concentrated in this area. In 1939 there were only 10 military aerodromes in the county, but by 1945 the number had grown to 46 employing 80,000 people, and Lincolnshire was known as 'Bomber County'. Many airfields were built in a hurry in the early 1940s, and became redundant soon after the war. They were gradually decommissioned, and Weatherill and White were instructed to hold several auction sales of surplus Nissen huts, furniture, fencing and equipment.

Nissen huts are simple structures, semi circular in cross-section, and clad in corrugated iron. During the war they were built quickly in various sizes, with the ends either bricked up or left open so they could be used as dormitories, mess rooms, stores or garages. The dormitory huts were dispersed well away from the runways to minimise casualties if there was an attack by enemy aircraft.

Most of these closures and subsequent auctions took place in the early 1950s, before I came to the firm, but one airfield to the south of the town beside the Great North Road had lingered on. It was built for RAF bombers, and then transferred to the United States Air Force during the second half of the war, before finishing its days as a training centre. The airfield was sufficiently important as an American base for Glenn Miller to bring his famous band and hold a concert in one of the hangars, only a few weeks before his tragic death. The American servicemen bonded enthusiastically with the local community, giving bananas to the local children, who had never seen them before, in the hope of getting fresh eggs in return. They gave nylons to local girls with different expectations.

In the early 1960s the airfield closed and we were instructed to hold an auction sale of the equipment and Nissen huts, which had to be removed from the site after the sale. Building materials were scarce in those days so although very basic, the huts were in demand, usually to start or expand a small workshop, storage or agricultural business. Mike, who became a good friend of ours, started work in a Vale of Belvoir village after leaving school with very little to his name, and saved enough to buy a three-acre worked-out quarry with a derelict cottage. He and his wife made the cottage habitable, and then went around local airfield dispersal sales, buying an occasional large Nissen hut that was going cheap. He dismantled each one, reassembled it in the old quarry, and filled it with laying hens. Before long he had a flock of several thousand birds and a substantial egg production business.

He was the first person I saw as I drove into the airfield on sale day.

'Are you looking for another one?' I asked.

'Yes,' he said, 'but I shall be pleased when I've no room for any more.'

'Why's that?'

'Well I've taken down several Nissen huts, and each one seems trickier than the last.'

'It's a mystery to me how you do it' I said.

'It's easy to strip off the corrugated iron cladding' he replied ' although the screws are usually very rusty – this exposes the framework of semi-circular iron hoops connected by metal purlins, which have to be taken away.'

'Is that when the trouble starts?' I asked.

'It certainly is,' said Mike. 'We start at one end and take out each hoop in turn, but at the halfway stage the rest of the skeleton can lose its stability and fall like a pack of cards. We've got a bit better at it now, but some years ago we were taking a big hut down and I ran for my life when it started to collapse. When the last hoop crashed to the floor behind me it was so close it ripped the heel off my shoe. A very narrow escape!'

He did buy a hut from the sale, but mercifully dismantled it without any problems.

The number of wartime airfields concentrated around Grantham made it necessary to have a regional command centre. A large Victorian stone house in the town with grounds of three acres was requisitioned by the RAF, and a reinforced concrete control room added. It had no windows because if an enemy bomb had dropped nearby, the flying glass could have caused severe injuries. The room contained a vast table on which was a map showing local airfields, the North Sea and target areas in Europe: women moved models over it to indicate the position of bombers taking part in raids, or fighter aircraft intercepting incoming planes. The famous Dam Busters raid was controlled from here.

After the war, the Ministry of Defence was granted planning permission for residential development of the grounds, which were then sold to a builder. The house continued to be used as offices, but in the mid-1960s the civil servants left and we were instructed to sell it by auction. The house had been built at the end of the nineteenth century by an eminent industrialist, who developed and manufactured engines and agricultural machinery, providing work for thousands of local people. It stood on a hill on the edge of the town, and the architects may well have had Scottish connections, because it seemed to have been designed for a Highland laird. It was built of stone with the front door opening into an imposing hall, with a polychrome tiled floor, an arched ceiling supported by columns and a wide staircase with stone banisters leading to the upper floors. A circular tower stood at the corner of the house, with a conical roof and a room on the second floor overlooking Grantham. I could imagine the industrialist looking out early each morning to ensure that work had begun and his factory chimneys in the town below were belching smoke.

The control room had been added to the south side of the house, with access from the main hall and when we went round the property it was a dark, empty, echoing space, the only reminder of its original purpose being a wooden box with a gauze front, mounted high on the end wall. This was the loudspeaker that had once relayed news from the radio room, perhaps of a mission successfully completed – or a distress call from a damaged aircraft about to crash into the sea.

The sale of this historic house attracted considerable interest from the press, local radio and television. It was the only time I conducted an auction in front of a television camera, although my performance was not sufficiently dramatic to grace the nation's screens. The property was sold to a local firm of engineers who had decided, in their wisdom, to set up a separate company to sell their own products. This piece of empire building was not destined to last, and unfortunately the same applied to the control room, which was demolished, albeit with great difficulty.

This control room had been an integral part of the nation's defences, but the onward march of science soon rendered it, the Lancaster bomber and the Spitfire as obsolete as the Zeppelin. Only a few years after this sale we were instructed to hold auctions at two other RAF installations, once critical to our defence but now redundant in their turn.

Twenty Thor rocket sites were set up in 1958/59 on disused airfields in eastern England, and two of these were within 15 miles of Grantham. These rockets were fearsome weapons, operated under joint American/British control, and capable of delivering a nuclear warhead 1700 miles, at a speed of 10,000 mph. They were 65 feet long, stored horizontally in a simple hangar, and it took 15 minutes to raise them to a vertical firing position. This exercise was practised frequently and the rocket could then be seen for miles around; local people came to realise that if a war came they would be in the front line.

Not only did it take several vital minutes to get the rocket into its firing position, but the nuclear warheads were stored separately at a central depot at least an hour's delivery time from the sites, so the effectiveness of the weapon in response to a surprise attack was questionable, to say the least. This was soon realised, the sites closed in 1963 and our defensive strategy moved to mobile rockets carried by ships and planes.

We were instructed to sell by auction the removable fixed equipment on the two sites, and decided to hold one sale in the morning followed by the other in the afternoon. This involved selling the concrete post and wire netting perimeter fencing in sections, about seventy concrete lamp standards, underground cabling, metal doors to the buildings and sectional concrete surface ducting covered by paving slabs.

The lamp standards had to be numbered individually, which I did with a 'Magic Marker' – a small bottle of red colouring fluid with a felt marker sticking out of the top. It was certainly magic, because after I had trudged round the site on a scorching hot day numbering each standard, I arrived back at the first one only to find that every number had already soaked into the concrete and disappeared. I had to repeat the exercise with a brush and pot of paint.

We were lotting the surface ducting in lengths, when there was a commotion under the paving slabs and a fox ran out. We didn't find any holes under the perimeter fence, and could only assume it had lived there – under conditions of maximum security – since the base was built.

Although I was a failure as an auctioneer/television star when the control room was sold, I had more success later as an auctioneer/bartender. Leroy Moss owned and ran a public house known as the Blue Cow in Killingthorpe, a village south of Grantham. The strange name was due to the hostelry having once belonged to a local landowner, whose ancestor in the nineteenth century decreed that all his public houses must be renamed to incorporate the word 'blue', the colour of his political party – and so the Cow Inn became the Blue Cow. Leroy lived at the pub and was an innkeeper in the evening, but during the day he was a butcher, with a slaughterhouse and shop in the outbuildings, and a sales van travelling around the villages. He bought his livestock from our market.

His sons were keen to follow him into the butchery trade but didn't want the pub, so he reluctantly decided to sell it and buy a retirement bungalow for himself and a shop for one son, while the other would take over the mobile business. We recommended a sale by auction, and what better place to hold it than in the pub itself. On sale day we set up a table in one of the bars as usual, but the interest was so great from Killingthorpe and nearby villages, that the two public rooms were jammed with people. We took the table away and I conducted the auction from behind the bar. The bidding was spirited, and the Blue Cow was sold at a good price to a publican from an adjoining village.

When I visit the pub I always say to successive licensees:
'I sold this pub by auction from behind the bar a few years ago.'
Unfortunately none of them have shown any interest, and certainly no inclination to offer me a free drink!

Chapter 21

A Family Feud and Coarse Cricket

Weatherill and White was widely regarded as an old-fashioned firm, but 'sound' and trustworthy which didn't help our estate agency business, but did bring in a variety of other work. To illustrate this Arthur had a telephone call from a firm of solicitors in another town:

'Do you remember George Fuller of Great Barwith?'

'Yes,' said Arthur, 'we did some work for him at one time, but I heard that he died several months ago.'

'Yes, and two of our partners are executors of his Will. As you probably know he had three sons who all farm, and hate each other with a passion, so he wisely divided most of his land between the family in his lifetime. However, he still owned four areas when he died, and each son is quite determined to stop his brothers having them. We've been trying to resolve this for a long time, and they have eventually agreed that the land should be sold by auction, and that Weatherill and White should be the auctioneers. We're sending formal instructions and full details in the post.'

The family stipulated that the auction should take place in the village hall next to their late father's house, on the last Saturday morning in September. The hatred within the family was well known in the area and a main topic of conversation in local pubs, so the hall was packed. One brother, Francis, who was the mildest of the three, came early and sat at the front. The other two, John who was slightly built with a yellowish complexion, and Howard – stocky and red-faced – arrived separately and stood in the back corners. Arthur conducted the auction, with me as his clerk, and gave the usual preamble before introducing the solicitor, and asking for any questions. There were none, so he offered the first lot, which was a seven-acre arable field close to Howard's house. He asked for an opening bid of £2000.

'£3000,' said Howard from one back corner.

The company gasped.

John said nothing, but moved his little finger slightly.

'£3100 I'm bid,' said Arthur.

'£3500!' said Howard, becoming redder in the face.

The finger moved again.

'£3600'

And so the auction continued, with those seated in the body of the hall turning round to watch the two brothers bidding, but never looking at each other. Eventually John stopped moving his finger and smiled sardonically as the field was sold to Howard for the unheard of price of £1000 per acre.

The second lot was a ten-acre field close to the village hall and farmed by Francis. Howard and John seemed to be channelling their hatred towards one another, and each of them only bid against him once, so he was able to buy at a relatively reasonable price.

The pause in hostilities was short lived! Lot three was a block of fifty acres of good arable land, out of the village on the edge of the fens. Howard again opened the bidding at a high figure, and John kept moving his finger, before treating himself to the same dry smile as the land was sold for £1200 an acre to his brother, whose face was now scarlet. The last lot was a twenty-acre field very close to John's house, and Howard again gave an opening bid well above the figure suggested by Arthur. John had ensured that his brother paid a big price for two lots, but he needed to buy this field, and Howard knew it. John started to bid by moving his finger as usual, but as the price rose he changed to making abrupt movements with his clenched fist, and when he eventually bought it for £1500 per acre, he had the red face, and Howard was smiling. The brothers signed their contracts and paid their deposits as quickly as possible, before leaving the hall. The sale had certainly done nothing to mend the family rift, and I reflected that compared to them Granville Hart and his brother were bosom pals.

After the sale Arthur said, 'I need a drink now,' and asked the solicitor and me to join him in the local pub.

'I'm sorry,' I replied, 'but I'm playing for the Stumblers this afternoon, and I need to get home for a quick sandwich. It's our last Saturday afternoon match of the season and we have to start half an hour earlier than usual so we can finish before it's dark.'

Our ground lay in the middle of Great Somerton and the only vehicular access was through Dan Robinson's stackyard. He charged the club a nominal rent for using the field, and his men mowed the outfield and prepared the pitches under his supervision.

Preparing a good cricket pitch is a skilful job. One Sunday Dan opened the batting and faced a very hostile left-handed bowler. The pitch was hard, so the ball was lifting dangerously, and since Dan was also left-handed the natural path of each delivery was towards his body. He was nearly sixty at the time and found it difficult to get out of the way, taking several painful blows on the chest. A few days later I was walking down the village street when I saw Fred, who worked for Dan and had the job of maintaining the pitch.

'Whatever happened to the boss last Saturday?' he said.

'Why do you ask?' I replied, eager to know more.

'Well,' said Fred, 'I got into the farmyard early on Monday morning to start work, and he was waiting for me. He lifted up his shirt to show me his chest, and all I could see was one big bruise – I've never seen so many shades of blue, yellow and purple outside an aviary! He shouted, "Call yourself a f......

groundsman", limped out of the yard and I haven't seen him since. I've taken the hint though, and used the heavy roller on the square every day this week.'

'Very wise,' I said, but Fred hadn't finished.

'The boss is very sensitive about his cricket,' he continued, 'I remember some years ago his father came to watch one of our home matches. The Stumblers fielded first and Dan bowled several overs, took no wickets and was hit all over the field by two tail-end batsmen. When it came to our innings, he opened the batting and was clean bowled by the first ball he faced which kept a bit low. This was too much. He strode off the field with a face like thunder, threw his bat into the pavilion when he was still five yards from the door and declared loudly, "I'll plough this b….. field up and plant it with tates (potatoes)".'

'That's a good idea Dan,' said his father, 'if the pitch was in a furrow between two rows of tates they'd be a good guide for you and your bowling would be a lot straighter'.

The square in the centre of the ground was reasonably level, but the outfield sloped down towards the pavilion, which was not a half-timbered and thatched vision of loveliness enclosed by a low white fence, as expected by readers of 'This England', but a small brick and pantiled former calf shed. It had been 'improved' by whitewashing the walls, adding some coat hooks and installing a wash basin and urinal in one corner, but was only big enough for one team to enjoy such luxury, so the visiting team changed in a wooden shed.

Between the cricket field and Dan's farm buildings was a pit from which limestone had been quarried years ago to build many of the houses in the village, but it was now overgrown with nettles and elder bushes. Part of this intruded into the cricket ground, so the edge had been graded and seeded to form a steep grass slope rather than a vertical rock face, but it was still a feature of our ground, and provided a constant source of amusement. A fielder could stand on the boundary of the cricket field in the pit and not be seen by the batsman, who was understandably not pleased when he was caught out by a player whose presence he hadn't detected. When a fielder was stationed near the pit, and the batsman hit a lofty shot that was due to land a few yards away from him, there was always a murmur of appreciation when the hapless player ran round the boundary in an attempt to make the catch, only to disappear from view.

Dan insisted on traditional cricket, so the Stumblers didn't join any leagues, but played friendly matches at weekends, and an occasional twenty-over cup match in the evening. We had some useful players, but were better known for our hospitality in the pub after the match, than our cricketing skill. This brought problems, because we weren't as good as the first elevens of the local town clubs, so our fixtures were against their second teams. When the better players from these clubs saw the list of matches however, they often chose to come to our ground, because they knew they would have a 'good night out'. Our social reputation was no help on the field, and we suffered some heavy defeats, but now and then we brought better teams down to our level and appreciated a victory all the more for its rarity.

The social prowess of the Stumblers once cost them dearly. The Club usually entered three evening Cup competitions, but was rarely successful and often knocked out in the first round. The Final of one of these competitions was held over two evenings, with a complete match of 20 overs a side played each time, and the scores aggregated to establish the winner. One year – wonder of wonders – we got through to the Final; not only that, but on the first evening we trounced the opposition, scoring 40 runs more than they did.

Great were the celebrations that night! After several hours in the pavilion bar, the team returned to the Coach and Horses at Great Somerton where festivities continued until early next morning. The second evening had a certain inevitability about it, as the Stumblers took the field listless and with sore heads. The other team scored 50 runs more than us, and one of our few chances of glory had gone.

The Club also entered the National Village Competition, the Final of which was held at the cricketing Mecca – Lords Cricket Ground in London. This was an afternoon competition with each side bowling 40 overs, and since this longer form of the game suited us better, we often won our match in the first round and were sometimes victorious in the second. Needless to say we never got close to Lords, but one year we did get through to the Regional Final, the winners of which would go through to the last eight in the competition.

In our previous match we had played an XI from a Nottinghamshire colliery village, whose standard of cricket was much higher than ours. They realised this and during our innings we could hear their players saying, 'Who do we play in the next round?' and 'When we've won this match, is the next one home or away?'

In this first innings we were all out for 150. They then cruised to 120 for three wickets after only 20 overs, before Gordon, our Club Secretary, came on to bowl. Gordon was a man of similar age to Dan, and it was quite impossible for anyone to bowl slower than he did, as he launched the ball skywards after only two steps to the wicket. We expected this bowling change to bring a quick end to proceedings – and not in our favour! However, our opponents were bemused by this bowling, which dropped so slowly from the heavens, and within quarter of an hour they were all out for 135. It was the Stumblers that made it through to the next round, and the shocked opposition did not stay to help us celebrate!

In the Regional Final we faced another team from Nottinghamshire, who played at an even higher level than the colliery XI, in fact three years previously they had got through to the National Final. We played on our ground again, but this time the afternoon was cold and damp, and they batted first, reaching only 160 from their 40 overs so we thought we had a chance. As their innings began, a few spectators arrived in their cars to watch the game, then more vehicles came, first ten, then twenty, thirty and forty. We weren't used to this. An occasional villager would lean on his fence and watch us for a few minutes as a break from his gardening, but the only cars parked around the ground belonged to the players.

Since the Stumblers were now in the big time, Dan searched his buildings during the tea interval, found a small wooden box, put a slot in the top, and said to the attractive girlfriend of one of our players, 'Will you go round the ground with this and take a collection for Club funds? I don't think we'll see as many spectators as this again.' She was very successful and our bank balance had a welcome fillip.

Unfortunately the opposition's bowlers used the damp conditions better, and we were all out for little over 100. Any faint dreams of appearing at Lords had gone, but we each received a glass tankard from the sponsoring brewery, and felt obliged to help our opponents with their celebrations.

Although our players had limited ability, the Club was of international standard in the art of 'coarse cricket', and I learnt a lot from the older players about this crucial aspect of the village game. During one match against a local side, one of its later batsmen came to the wicket without batting gloves – a sure sign of a 'hitter', and Dan, standing at first slip, said quietly as the newcomer walked towards the wicket:

'We'll "old man" this chap out.'

I didn't know what he meant, but I soon found out. He waited until the new batsman was about twenty yards from the pitch and then called out to the bowler...

'This lad can hit the ball a long way: put your fielders further back.'

He then added in a 'stage whisper', which the batsman was intended to hear:

'I've never seen anyone clear that ash tree by the farmyard, but I reckon this chap could do it.'

The fielders duly retreated towards the boundary and the batsman arrived at the wicket congratulating himself on the reputation he had acquired, while sizing up the ash tree which seemed well within his reach. Gordon was bowling, and the first ball dropped slowly out of the sky towards the newcomer. His bat made two complete revolutions before it landed, but there was no contact and unfortunately the ball missed the wicket. The process was repeated with the second delivery, as he tried again to clear the ash tree, but his wicket still remained intact. His efforts were brought to a merciful end by the third ball, which again evaded the frenetic whirling of his bat, but this time hit the middle stump.

'Ha ha,' chuckled Dan, 'we've "old manned" him out: another triumph for guile over vigour.'

Since the Stumblers did not play league cricket, we didn't have specialist umpires for our matches. A former player was sometimes prepared to spend an afternoon with us and officiate at one end, but the other umpire was usually a member of the batting side. Gordon enjoyed taking a turn, but the Coach and Horses across the road opened at 7pm, and every Stumbler knew that if he was batting after that time and the ball hit his pads, Gordon's finger would shoot up like a rocket as he was given out 'Leg before Wicket'. He was not interested in watching tailenders bat when the pub door was open and he could be drinking Ruddles Bitter.

This Saturday we were playing our last match of the season, against the Nottingham Caribbeans who had agreed an earlier start at 2pm – but at 1.45 there was no sign of them. With only a few minutes to go, an aged mini-bus made its way through the stackyard and eleven men of West Indian origin, all looking very fit, hurried into the wooden shed to change. Our captain won the toss, decided that they should bowl first and told me that I was to open the batting. My partner and I made our way to the wicket, passing several of their players doing 'limbering up' exercises, any of which would have put a Stumbler in hospital! Having noted this, my opening partner walked smartly to the non striker's end and left me to face the first ball. When I arrived at the far end I met their wicket keeper and captain, a massive man with a black beard, who positioned his fielders, then clapped his gloves together and said in a deep bass voice:

'Right, let's go.'

I looked ahead for the bowler, and could just see his head as he started his run from the boundary line near the pavilion. He was a short man, with a look of Sammy Davis Junior about him, and as he ran up the slope towards me I wondered if he could sing and dance like that famous member of the Rat Pack. I never found out, but a few seconds later I was doing both as the ball crashed into my thigh. The ball was so fast I hadn't seen it coming, but I did get a very good view of him because he finished his follow-through a yard away from me with his eyes staring into mine. The second ball somehow evaded my immaculate forward defensive stroke and thudded into the wicket keeper's gloves, but when I made a similar attempt at his third delivery, the ball flashed off the edge of my bat and between the slip fielders to the boundary. I could tell the bowler wasn't pleased from the expression on his face, which was now only an inch from mine, and the next two balls passed my nose at great speed to be taken head high by the wicket keeper. I somehow survived this first over, and having controlled my shaking legs, strolled down the pitch with a show of nonchalance to discuss matters with my partner. He didn't help my morale when he observed:

'Good grief he's quick!' and returned promptly to the other end.

The second bowler was medium paced and my partner kept him out with no difficulty, in fact on the last ball he played a lovely shot, square of the wicket, which almost reached the boundary. I called him for a run but he declined, and after the umpire said 'Over', came down the wicket and explained

'Wonderful fielders these chaps; daren't risk a single.'

We both knew the reason for his reluctance to move, and I faced the speed merchant again with considerable apprehension, which was fully justified as he ripped my middle stump out of the ground with his third delivery. He took three wickets in his first six overs, but then started to tire and we managed to accumulate around 100 in our innings, before adjourning for tea.

This was prepared by a lady from the village, and we walked through the stackyard to enjoy it in one of Dan's farm buildings. Eighteen horses had been stabled there when he was a boy, and he could still recite their names in the order they used to stand:

'Buttercup, Clover, Ginger, Jenny, Robin,' he would say, and so on until the line of horses, dredged from his memory, reached the end of the building.

Cups of tea were poured from large pots, and we helped ourselves from plates of sandwiches, cakes, scones and biscuits before returning to the field.

The captain of the Caribbeans opened the batting and showed he had no intention of just hanging about, by hoisting a massive six into the pit in the first over. Our second bowler, Geoff Cumberland, was a shrewd old boy, and after the other batsman had taken a single, he was up against this impressive bearded figure. He announced that he knew how to get him out, and asked me to stand in a certain position on the boundary, where I could expect a catch. He was nearly right: the ball was hit in my direction, but unfortunately it cleared me by two yards – six runs to the batsman. Geoff was confident he could tempt him into a similar shot with the next ball and was right again, but this time it cleared me by five yards for another six. However, he was consistent, and held his nerve. On the third occasion the ball was hit towards me again, but this time it was still going up as it passed overhead.

The captain was soon out, but the Caribbeans reached our score in little over an hour, losing only three wickets. Unfortunately they decided not to join us in the Coach and Horses, but shoehorned themselves back into their mini bus to return to Nottingham. We adjourned there however, and the usual jollities erased all memories of a heavy defeat.

Chapter 22

Corby Fair

A hundred years ago most large villages held at least one fair every year which were major events for country people who weren't able to travel far, and looked forward to a day of local entertainment. There were special sales of cattle and sheep, everybody ate and drank too much, listened to strolling players, and spent their hard-earned money on simple amusements and useless merchandise.

When the railways and then motorised transport arrived, most of these annual festivities petered out, but Corby Glen still held its Fair every year on the weekend prior to October 10th. The village was simply known as Corby until its namesake in Northamptonshire was massively increased in size and importance, when it was 'rechristened' by adding the name of the little river that runs through it – but the annual celebration stubbornly retained its title – Corby Fair.

A travelling funfair opened on the Friday, with a roundabout, coconut shy, shooting gallery and other amusements for young people, and for older inhabitants when they left the pubs. The festivities continued throughout the weekend, and finished with the Sheep Fair on Monday. Weatherill and White owned a field close to the village green where they sold up to 5000 sheep every year, while another firm of auctioneers put up their pens on the green itself and the roadside verges.

There were three pubs in the village, and they got a special licence to stay open all day. Sheets of cardboard were laid on the floor to protect carpets from boots caked in mud (and worse), extra staff were employed, and vast quantities of alcohol consumed. This was before the breathalyser, there was little traffic on the roads, and the village policeman had enough sense to realise that if he was too officious on Fair day his social life would be ruined for the rest of the year.

The story is told of a visiting cricket team that were carousing with the home side in a pub in another village until well after the statutory closing time, when they heard a knock on the door. The bar became very quiet as the landlord went to see who it was, and his worst fears were confirmed when he found the village policeman standing there. Mine host was expecting him to produce his notebook and start taking details prior to a prosecution for staying open too long, but the policeman asked:

'Is Herbert there?'

'I'll have a look,' said the landlord, knowing full well that he, the secretary of the local Cricket Club, was sitting at the bar.

'Don't bother,' said the policeman who knew quite well where he was, 'I'm sure he wouldn't be drinking after hours! If you happen to see him, just tell him the gate to the cricket ground isn't locked. We don't want stuff stolen from the pavilion do we?'

Having delivered his message he walked away.

It could have been the same officer in his police car on patrol late one evening, when he spotted a carload of local cricketers returning from an away match and their usual après-cricket session. He switched on his flashing light, overtook them, and stopped their car. He knew that the players who drove were usually careful not to drink more than they should because, living in the countryside, they couldn't afford to lose their licence. He needed an excuse to make the younger ones realise he was watching them and if they did take silly chances they'd be caught. He walked over to them.

'Let's have a look in your car boot.'

'What for?' they asked, 'It's full of cricket gear.'

'We have orders from the magistrates to look out for poachers at this time of year.'

These instructions had indeed been given to the constabulary by the landowning magistrates: burglary might possibly be overlooked prior to the shooting season, but certainly not poaching.

He had a good look round in the boot, and finding nothing as he expected, gave them a lecture on not drinking and driving and told them to get off home.

The driver continued on his way, pleased to have escaped with a caution as he wasn't completely sure he was under the limit but within a few minutes saw the flashing light again as the police car went by and stopped them for a second time. This time he was really worried, convinced that the officer had changed his mind, so he wound down his window expecting the worst but the policeman said: 'Sorry to trouble you lads again, but when I stopped you before I left my helmet in your boot.'

After he had retrieved his headgear, the relieved cricketers drove back to their local pub, where they could resume their celebrations within walking distance of home.

The nearest pub to our field in Corby Glen had a central archway through which stage coaches once ran, and we rented a room off this to use as an office on Fair Day. It was cramped and far from ideal but then an opportunity presented itself. A nearby Parish Council instructed us to sell their old wooden village hall, which had to be dismantled and removed from site, as they were building a new one in brick. We tried to sell it by auction but no one turned up, so Arthur agreed a price with the Council and had it rebuilt near the top of our field, as an office and store for our trays. The field sloped steeply upwards from the road and no attempt was made to level the floor, so it followed the same gradient as the land. Working there felt like being on board ship in a rough sea – but we put up with it for one day in the year.

Our preparations for the annual sheep sale started about two weeks beforehand, when Stan Rowan, Alf and Bill took the sheep trays out that were kept at the cattle market. A tractor with front-end loader was hired from a local farmer and these trays, plus those stored in the old hall, were assembled into rows of pens just as they were at farm dispersal sales, but on a larger scale. Stakes were hammered into the ground at frequent intervals and fastened to the trays to keep the pens steady when they were under pressure from sheep. Each pen held about 12 breeding sheep or 20 lambs and was individually numbered.

Entry forms were sent out from the office at least six weeks prior to the sale, for vendors to return telling us how many rams, theaves, ewes or store lambs they wanted to send. Theaves are females that are about 18 months old and have usually borne no lambs, although one crop is permissible. Several local farmers and dealers bought six-month-old sheders from the north of England each autumn, and kept them for a year to sell on as theaves. Ewes are older females that have borne several crops of lambs and, as at William Hall's sale, a warranty is given as to their condition at the time of sale. Store lambs are young sheep, born in the spring but not fat enough to be sold for slaughter: many farmers prefer to sell at this stage, and let someone else do the fattening.

Rams entered for sale are mainly pedigree and belong to specialist breeders, the predominant local breed being the black-headed Suffolk. Most lambs are born in March or April, but ram breeders ensure that the ewes in their pedigree flock give birth much earlier – in December or January. They then select the best male lambs and give them special attention so they are in peak condition when ready for sale in the autumn. Farmers like to buy their rams from a breeder whose stock has performed well for them in the past, and Peter Surtees had a particularly good reputation, usually entering ten Suffolk rams in our sale. Corby Fair was one of the last sales of breeding sheep in the year, and many farmers had already bought their rams by then so we only had buyers for 70 or 80. Sometimes 150 were entered and many went home, but Peter's always sold.

When all the entries were in, Oliver decided on the order of sale of the various categories of sheep and allocated pens to the vendors, which was tricky because as we knew from the cattle market, no vendor wants his sheep sold first. The principal theave sellers would enter 200 to 300 animals, and stipulate on the entry form that their sheep must be in the second or third rows, and preferably near the top of the sloping field where they would look bigger. The main ram breeders, like Peter Surtees, would insist on being the fourth or fifth vendor – certainly not the first, when latecomers wouldn't have arrived, and they would also try to stipulate that their rams would be sold before those of their principal competitors. We couldn't satisfy everyone and there were always complaints, particularly if trade was bad. After the allocations had been made, a simple catalogue was printed listing all the vendors, the number and breed of their sheep, and the pens they would occupy.

Selling cattle in Grantham Market by Joe Flauto

We prayed for fine weather on the few days beforehand, and on the Monday itself. There was an apron of stone inside the entrance gate, but occasionally when the field was wet a heavily laden lorry would get bogged down between there and the collecting pens, and as the driver tried harder and harder to get out of the mess he had made, his wheels would sink deeper and deeper into the mud. Meanwhile, a line of lorries would be waiting on the road outside, and the policeman on traffic duty got more and more exercised. After this happened in two successive years we hired a tractor and driver from a local farmer, so that vehicles in trouble could be towed out, but once we had done this the problem never seemed to recur.

We needed to start early on Fair day morning. Stan, Alf and Bill were there at 6am to open the gates, and sometimes a flock would be waiting on the road as vendors living close by preferred to drive their sheep to the Fair, rather than pay for a lorry. Anne would be there soon afterwards with her tea van, and the rest of us arrived at around 7am, as did the first of the lorries. These reversed up to the collecting areas beside the pens and the drivers would let us know whose sheep they had brought. We checked the catalogue to find out their position in the field, and one person went to the allocated pens to open the gates. The sheep were unloaded and driven to these pens, the gate was tied up, and the animals left in their random order until the owner came to draw them.

This part of the day should be straightforward, but a sheep's reputation for stupidity is well deserved, and when a number are gathered together the most stupid always seems to take the lead and the rest follow. If one thinks it's a good idea to jump over the trays around the collecting pen, there will soon be twenty having a go. If a person is driving a group of two dozen lambs down an alleyway and one decides to turn round and jump over his shoulder, he will soon be surrounded by 12 aerial sheep.

Not all the problems relate to animals. Lorry drivers are impatient people, which is understandable because those working for large haulage firms, like Hameys, often had three loads to bring into the Fair before 11am, each of which could include sheep from several different farms. They were in a hurry, and anxious to drop them in the first available collecting pen, so a load of theaves would be unloaded beside the lamb pens, and 200 lambs left by the ewes. This meant that unless we were careful, flocks of different sheep would be driven into each other and get mixed up on the way to their pens. More trouble started when the owners arrived and began to draw their animals, because they needed to pull a tray across the alleyway at each end of their pens and work within this enclosed area. When this process was well advanced they would be asked:

'Will you put your sheep back in the pens? These lambs need to go higher up the alleyway and we've got to drive them past you.'

'You can wait until we're done.'

'We can't: there are two more lots coming behind these.'

After much fruity language, agreement was usually reached.

The rams were treated as 'monarchs of the pasture', being unloaded and displayed in a much more stately manner. The fleece of each pedigree animal was meticulously trimmed to emphasise the broadness of its back, their hooves polished, and every part of its anatomy displayed in spotless order. They were taken out of their trailers individually and led by halter into the large pen reserved for that breeder's sheep. Straw was scattered on the floor lest their feet should be soiled, and cabbages hung from the sides of the pen to ward off any pangs of hunger. The ram section was set up outside the office, and comprised two rows of spacious pens on each side of a central alleyway leading to the sale ring, which was dominated by the rostrum we used at farm dispersal sales.

A local firm of agricultural merchants had a stand just inside the gates near Anne's tea van, selling a variety of products mainly relating to sheep. We didn't charge them for this space, but they gave a harness to the buyer of the most expensive ram, an ingenious apparatus consisting of a block of colouring matter fastened to its breast by leather straps buckled over the shoulders. When the ram joins his harem of ewes and begins to mount them, the coloured block marks the back of each ewe that he serves. If a lot of ewes in that field don't have coloured backs the ram hasn't been doing his job, and will be quickly replaced!

The sale started at 9.30am with the rams. Stan strode around the field ringing his hand bell and shouting 'Ram buyers!' before taking his place on the rostrum with Arthur. Both of them stood, as the seated comfort of a furniture sale was not to be enjoyed at Corby Glen. The first owner listed in the catalogue brought his ram into the ring and paraded it around for appraisal by the discerning company. Bidding was conducted in guineas (£1.05), a relic of the sales at the Lincolnshire Horse Repository, with the auctioneers keeping a shilling (5p) in every guinea as commission. The bidding was often desultory at the start – matching the quality of the first entries into the ring – but as rams belonging to the main breeders came in, competition was fierce for the best animals, with prices realised of up to 400 guineas. If bidding became particularly spirited the owner would offer a further inducement by putting a £10 note on the animal's back.

Some vendors brought six or eight rams into the ring and announced, 'The highest bidder can take his pick,' and the buyer would then choose the one he wanted.

'Fancy picking that,' the others would say 'the one on the left's in a different class.'

This was a feature of the sale. As the animals were being sold, the farmers around the ring talked animatedly about their qualities.

'Look at the length of that one'.
'That's got a good head.'
'It's back's far too narrow.'
'I don't like the way he's walking.'

However, as is often the case in farming circles, only a few of them knew what they were talking about. Any auctioneer will tell you that those who point at the animals most during a sale, and talk the loudest, are the ones that rarely bid and know the least. They simply come to show off their 'knowledge' to anyone gullible enough to listen.

It was easy work for Arthur to auction the rams belonging to the main breeders, but hard after that when the older and inferior animals came into the ring. We allowed an hour to sell the rams because we had a full day in front of us, but it often took longer, so at 10.30am Oliver would stand impatiently by the first pen of theaves waiting to start.

After I had helped to pen the sheep I went to 'book in' the theaves, while others did the same for the ewes and lambs. This involved counting the sheep in each pen, recording the breed and agreeing the total number with the owner. We also had to note down anything that he wanted the auctioneer to announce before selling his first pen.

'Tell them they're bred in North Yorkshire, and all right and straight.' Or…

'They've all been injected with "Co-ortho-vexin"' (or something similar guaranteed to ward off every disease).

Counting theaves and ewes was easy because there were usually only 12 in a pen, but lambs were a nightmare. There could be 24 in a pen, they never stayed still while being counted, and one or two often lay down under the others. We usually tackled this job in pairs, but often got it wrong.

We also had big problems with children and cameras. The Fair was a major event in the calendar of the village Primary School, and pupils were despatched class by class to walk round the field and inspect the sheep. We groaned inwardly when we saw the next crocodile of children coming through the gate, because they had been looking forward to this for weeks, and their excitement peaked in our field as they jumped up and down beside the pens, squealing and shouting.

'Look Miss, it's having a wee.'

'Haven't they got big ears?'

'That one's got horns.'

'If I pull its wool hard, will it come off?'

'If I put my face close to theirs, and stare at them they don't like it.'

All this unnerved the sheep, so they panicked and tried to jump over the trays, sometimes successfully. However, a quiet word with their teacher, and a suggestion to the children that they must behave calmly when close to sheep, were usually effective and hopefully added to their education.

Similar comments can't be made about the photographers. It seemed that every person in Corby Glen owned a camera, which they brought into our field on Fair day, intent on pushing it within inches of a sheep's face. There must have been more portraits of sheep on the mantelpieces of this village than any other in Britain. No doubt some animals relished their role as photographic models, but most didn't, and there was more panic in the pens.

Oliver was a good sheep auctioneer and needed all his skill when selling the first few pens of theaves, as most buyers were waiting for the better animals in the next rows. Sheep farmers need to refresh their flocks each year by bringing in young breeding animals from a different lineage, and as with the rams they prefer to buy from a breeder whose stock they have bought before and know to be good.

When Oliver had finished selling the first row and turned into the second, prospective buyers were waiting, which is what any auctioneer wants to see, but he now had a different challenge: he had to satisfy one of our main vendors – Magnus Oldfield, a dealer from Leicestershire. He was a tall, imposing man, who lived and breathed sheep, handling tens of thousands every year, and notoriously hard to please. This year he had entered 300 theaves, which he had bought in Yorkshire twelve months ago as lambs, and kept in local fields, shepherding them daily. He always bought the best quality and never tired of telling us he had incurred a lot of expense during the year and needed to sell at a high price to make a profit. He told me when I was booking his sheep that the minimum price he would take for the first few pens was £70 a head.

'Now Magnus,' said Oliver as he reached his first pen, 'what have you got to tell us?'

'I think they're the best sheep I've ever handled,' said Magnus (he thought that every year), 'they were bred in the north of England and they've had all their injections.'

Fortunately trade was good and the first pen made £82 a head, but Magnus looked glum.

'It's a poor price Oliver,' he said, 'but it's late in the season. I shall have to let them go.'

Magnus had agreed, like most vendors, that the purchaser of one pen could have the option of taking the next at the same price. The buyer exercised this option and Magnus said gloomily...

'I've made a mistake in giving that option. That second pen's much better than the first'.

His sheep all sold wonderfully well, but Magnus shook his head after every sale, looking more and more disappointed. After they'd all been sold I thought I detected a glimmer of a smile as he talked to another dealer, but I was probably mistaken! Oliver had a better reception from other vendors, who appreciated the excellent trade and smiled broadly as they wrote down their prices.

After the theaves came ewes, and Arthur took over as auctioneer. These older sheep were either entered by farmers who had decided to reduce the size of their flocks, or by dealers who had bought them elsewhere and hoped to sell at a profit. The trade was still good and the first few pens sold very well as they had been entered by a respected local farmer who was selling his entire flock. The next vendor, who had entered five pens, was Henry Singer, a heavily built, dealer with a ruddy complexion from North Lincolnshire, who stood in his first pen smoking a cigar. Arthur got a decent opening bid from a thin-faced individual wearing a tweed cap, but there was little interest from anyone else and the pen was sold to him.

'Can I have your name sir?' I asked.

'Fred Williams from Horncastle,' he replied.

Henry's expression didn't change during the bidding, and the cigar didn't leave his mouth. A farmer from Leicestershire was interested in the second pen, outbidding Fred, and as I took down his name I noticed that Henry wasn't smoking his cigar, but holding it in his hand. The farmer exercised his option to buy the third pen at the same price but then walked away. Henry's cigar was firmly back in his mouth while pens four and five were offered, both of which were knocked down to Fred Williams. As we moved on, Henry sidled up to me and said: 'only the second and third pens were sold'.

The penny dropped. I realised that he'd used his cigar as a signal. When he had it in his mouth he wasn't satisfied with the price and his friend Fred kept on bidding: when he was holding it, the price was acceptable, and his stooge could stop. We earned no commission from three of his five pens.

When Arthur had finished the ewes Oliver began to sell the lambs, which was easy. When the theaves and ewes were being sold we were lucky to have four people bidding for a pen, and often there were only one or two. Competition was keen for the lambs, and he was able to sell quickly as there were ten or twelve potential buyers for every pen, all of whom were anxious to have a look at the animals being sold, and be in a good position to attract the auctioneer's attention. Some made their bids surreptitiously, as they did in the market, some called out, others gestured, and some thumped Oliver in the back. In this melee it was easy to miss a bid, and if this happened the usual protests could be expected concerning the auctioneer's eyesight and parentage.

Many farmers bid themselves, but others who needed hundreds of lambs to graze through the winter didn't have the time to go to lots of sales. They instructed a dealer to buy for them, and some had orders for thousands of lambs: they had their own fraternity and at the start of a sale would bid against farmers, but not each other. This understanding would break down when they came to a pen of good animals that they all wanted, and sharp words would follow.

'So that's how you want to play it John.'

'You buy your sheep and I'll buy mine!'

'Right! Let's see how you like this.'

The trade improved temporarily while they quarrelled and bid angrily against each other, but the status quo soon returned.

The sale finished at around 3pm and I was ready for a drink and something to eat: it had been a long time since we arrived, and the sloping field seemed steeper now than at 7 o'clock. We each brought our own flask of coffee and sandwiches, but it was a tradition that Arthur and Oliver stocked their cars with pork pies, ham, beer and whisky for the vendors, buyers and us. This was very welcome but our day's work was far from over, because all receipted bills had to be checked before sheep were released from the field.

For many years Weatherill and White had been very relaxed about security procedures at their sales. Their inclination was to trust people, but an event took place at Corby Fair soon after I joined the firm that changed their outlook. A man arrived in our field dressed as he should be in a Barbour coat and green Wellington boots (a country gentleman never wears black ones), gave his name and Yorkshire address to the auctioneer's clerk, and then bought sixty of the best theaves. Shortly after the sale had finished we realised that these sheep had gone, but hadn't been paid for. We found that he had instructed Hameys Transport to take them out of the field, which was another smart move because they were well known to us and above suspicion. The police made enquiries and established that the Yorkshire name and address were genuine, but the person in question had been at home all day! The 'buyer' had paid Hamey's driver in advance and arranged to meet him at a roundabout on the A1, where he would lead him to the farm where the sheep were needed.

That was all we could find out on the evening of the sale. Later that night Hameys were able to contact the driver and learnt that he had been paid more cash at the roundabout and told there was a change of plan – he was to take the sheep to Banbury cattle market, the biggest in England. There was nobody manning the telephone there during the night, so at 6am I drove down to recover the sheep. When I arrived I went to see the market foreman and told him the story.

'Did you have a load of sheep delivered here last evening by Hameys Transport of Lincolnshire?' I asked.

'I'll check my Movement Book' he said – and then after a short pause, 'Yes – here we are – they came in at 9.30pm. I've got a note of the pen numbers: I'll go and check them.'

I waited in his office for what seemed a long time, before he came back and consulted his records again.

'I'm very sorry,' he said, 'but my staff say that another lorry came in about an hour later and took them out. There's no record of that in my book.'

That was the last that was seen of them, and since Weatherill and White had to pay the vendors the full auction prices, there was no profit from Corby Fair that year. The partners realised that if they had taken basic security precautions this couldn't have happened, and took steps to ensure it wouldn't occur again.

Many lorries belonging to the big transport firms brought in sheep from several different vendors, and took out loads belonging to a number of buyers. Each transport firm had a foreman, and it was his job to make up these loads and allocate them to the individual drivers. Most lorries were 'double deckers' and if the driver had to deliver sheep to four different farmers, the foreman had to work out his route and which farm he should go to first: the sheep for this farm had to be loaded last. Having worked all this out, the foreman gave us several receipted bills.

'I want 30 theaves bought by Joe Carr of Blankney on first, because that'll be the driver's last call. Then I need the 60 lambs bought by Mike Wardell of Timberland, and lastly those 40 ewes from Henry White of Rauceby that didn't sell.'

We checked the first receipt, took the theaves out of their pens and down to the collecting area where they were driven up the ramp of the lorry into the upper deck of the vehicle, and an internal gate fastened behind them. The next lot would be penned behind these, and the remainder driven into the lower deck. We found this was the best way to help the drivers, who worked a very long day and whose patience hadn't improved since the early morning. They were anxious to get away as soon as possible, and if their clients' sheep weren't immediately available, they would rip out stakes and trays to provide the shortest route to their lorry, regardless of the havoc created for everyone else.

The number of full sheep pens diminished rapidly as vehicles left the field with their loads, and as twilight came we walked up and down the rows with a torch to check what was left: a few lorries had two journeys to make and hadn't yet returned for their second loads. Sometimes we were told that sheep wouldn't be collected until the morning, and made a large pen for them with a trough of water and room to graze. Arthur, Oliver and the office staff had long since gone home, and at last we could leave the field, and visit the nearest pub.

This was jammed with people. Many of the buyers, had brought drivers with them and were still there, although the sale had finished four hours ago. Henry Singer was in excellent form, standing at the bar and regaling the company with his latest exploits.

'Do you know, I bought 200 sheep down from Scotland last week, and sold them for £30 a head profit before they were even unloaded!'

Many lamb buyers were complaining about the extortionate prices they'd been forced to pay, but several vendors were still there trying to 'soften the blow' by making sure the dealers' drinks were topped up.

'Now David let me get you another – Henry can I get you one?'

They hoped their generosity would be remembered when they had sheep to sell next year, but this looked increasingly unlikely as the memories of the recipients were fading rapidly. Other vendors had gone home after the sale but came back to join the festivities, and many village residents were there to enjoy the most important night of the year.

As we walked into the bar there were a few cheers, and cries of 'Here comes the night shift!'

'Let me get you a pint, Robert,' said one vendor.

This went down very well – and quickly. The dealers were discussing which pub they should go on to for their supper, and a decision was near when Henry made an announcement.

'I'll bet anyone a fiver I can drink a half pint of bitter with a teaspoon quicker than they can eat three cream crackers.'

The bet was promptly accepted by David and, having obtained the teaspoon and biscuits from mine host, the two sat at a bar table surrounded by friends and curious onlookers, all with a lot to say. Henry started proceedings by taking a teaspoonful of beer from his half pint pot, while his opponent started confidently on the first cream cracker. However, part of the bet was that the biscuit eater couldn't drink anything, and his mouth became drier and drier and his swallowing more and more difficult. He had barely finished the second one when Henry drank his last teaspoonful, turned the empty tankard upside down on his head as tradition demanded, and claimed his fiver, to general hilarity.

It had been a long day and after a second pint we decided it was time for home and a bath. Corby Glen would celebrate their big day for many hours to come, then look forward to next year's Fair – one more thread in the rich rural tapestry of South Lincolnshire.